FROM MAINSTREAM TO MYSTICAL

EMBRACING THE POWER OF
INTUITION AND SYNCHRONICITY
IN A NEW PARADIGM OF LEADERSHIP

ANN W. ELLIOTT

From Mainstream to Mystical:
Embracing the Power of the Intuition and Synchronicity
in a New Paradigm of Leadership

Copyright © 2023 by Ann W. Elliott.
Published by: AWEthenticity Press

All rights reserved.
No part of this book may be used or reproduced in any form without written permission of the author.

This book is a recollection of actual events in the author's life. Names and identifying characteristics of individuals and places have been changed where appropriate to maintain anonymity and protect privacy.

eBook ISBN: 979-8-9873398-4-8
Library of Congress Control Number: 2022921596

Every attempt has been made to properly source all quotes.

Printed in the United States of America
Second Edition

2 4 6 8 10 12

This book is dedicated to you and
all the brave leaders embracing the unknown
and allowing synchronicities to guide them.

May your journey be filled with awe
and may you inspire others to venture
from mainstream to mystical.

CONTENTS

Introduction	7
Chapter 1: Humanness and Beyond	9
Chapter 2: Trust Your Experience and Be Open to More	15
Chapter 3: A Professional Psychic and a Premonition	21
Chapter 4: Perceptions and (Mis)Interpretations	27
Chapter 5: From Rocks to Boulder and Seattle	37
Chapter 6: Blurred Lines and a Silver Lining	43
Chapter 7: As Above, So Below	49
Chapter 8: Satisfaction and Suffering	55
Chapter 9: Integrating Spirituality and Business	61
Chapter 10: Egypt: Surrendering to Sekhmet	67
Chapter 11: Brazil: "Surgery," and a New Normal	79
Chapter 12: Rebirth in Berkeley	89
Chapter 13: The Power of Intuition and Emotions to Heal	95
Chapter 14: Check Oil	101
Chapter 15: The Liberating Quality of Truth	109
Chapter 16: Lessons Learned	117
Chapter 17: Morocco: Tea in the Sahara	123
Chapter 18: The Physics of Miracles	135
Chapter 19: Waaaay Past the Edge	141
Chapter 20: Art and Tom	147
Chapter 21: Odd Sense of Foreboding	153
Chapter 22: Simply Spooky	159
Chapter 23: Stretching in New Directions	167
Chapter 24: Extrasensory Perception at Work	173
Chapter 25: Manatees and Metaphors	179

Chapter 26: Finding the Path Inward	185
Chapter 27: Jungle Love	191
Chapter 28: The Art and Paradox of Non-Striving	197
Chapter 29: Big, Big Cats	203
Chapter 30: France: Luminous Light	209
Chapter 31: In the Roundabout	219
Chapter 32: Surrender	225
Chapter 33: The Full Litany	231
Chapter 34: Going Solo	237
Chapter 35: Premiering	243
Chapter 36: Turning Toward the Light	249
Chapter 37: AWE & Co, LLC	255
Chapter 38: The Fixer	261
Chapter 39: Business as an Expression of Consciousness	267
Chapter 40: This or Better	273
Chapter 41: The Hero's Journey	279
Chapter 42: Quantum Alignment	285
Chapter 43: Intuition and Multiplying Money with Ma'at	291
Chapter 44: Seeding a New Paradigm of Leadership	297
Chapter 45: Maximizing the Human Spirit at Work	303
Chapter 46: Mainstream Meets Mystical	309
Chapter 47: Full Circle	315
Epilogue	319
Afterword: Full of Grace	325
About the Author	331

INTRODUCTION

For many years, I've known I have access to information I did not learn from the news, the internet or from any traditional sources. These curious insights often arrive unbidden and their origin is undefined. With time and validation, I have learned this information is very reliable and mostly accurate, and I have grown to trust it and to treat it with great reverence.

During the past two decades, I chronicled hundreds of instances of unexplained knowingness and crazy serendipities in a Word document titled, *Stories of Intuition and Guidance*. Ten years ago, in all caps at the bottom of the page, I typed the words:

THIS WILL BECOME A BOOK

And, now it has.

I knew I had unusual and perhaps unbelievable stories to share, but I had no idea writing them would lead me on a journey of even deeper self-discovery and awareness, as if honoring my past provided an opportunity to gain more wisdom, clarity and direction.

In recent years, I have helped others who are interested in learning how to utilize their own intuitive gifts and cultivate metaphysical awareness. Having overcome my own hesitancy, I smile when skeptics experience an undeniable flash of insight, leading to some amazing and useful revelation along with a new, more enlightened way of life. I love to witness disbelief melting, allowing trust and space for more divine insights to arrive.

Along with the mystical, I am fascinated by our one common denominator, our humanness.

I have always been curious about who a person really is behind their position, title, accomplishments and external appearance. When I know something about a person intuitively, that precious insight allows me to join them in their humanity.

As I have chosen to seek the unconventional and welcome the unexpected, the Universe has choreographed an unbelievable series of synchronicities, propelling me along an evolutionary trajectory through a series of winks and nudges. My path has definitely included some stumbles and mishaps, but eventually silver linings were revealed, allowing me to step into something even more enriching. Ultimately, these challenges enabled me to discover and embody a deeper truth and have always strengthened the foundation of my life and professional work.

In reading my experiences, I hope you delight in discovering the richness of your own and the interconnectedness of all life.

CHAPTER 1
Humanness and Beyond

As I sat in the lobby of the Buckhead Club, I fidgeted nervously, waiting for someone I knew only from a photograph in the *Atlanta Business Chronicle*. Two weeks earlier, I had been charmed by Martha's face smiling back at me as I read a profile piece called "Sixty Second Strategist." Martha coached executives using a variety of unconventional techniques from her background in acting and theater, and to Martha, a business presentation was a performance.

I underlined a quote that resonated with me, "Some speakers have such issues with perfectionism that they fail to exhibit the one thing that has been winning audiences over for centuries: Humanness."

Maybe that's what my presentations needed — Humanness.

In the 1990s, I had worked sixteen-hour days managing big distribution centers for global companies. Still in my twenties, I ran warehouses bigger than football fields stacked to the rafters with pallets of consumer products moved by dozens of forklifts whizzing back and forth across loading docks and in and out of eighteen wheelers 24/7. I soon tired of working in someone else's system where my long hours and commitment to operational excellence were not rewarded. With naive optimism and a few ideas hatched in collaboration with a colleague, I founded my own company.

While working to get the first idea for a truckload transportation network off the ground, I fielded calls from executives I knew from past jobs in big corporations, and unexpectedly those calls turned into consulting projects.

A former colleague, Scott, sent a broadcast email to his network looking for support with an operational turnaround at a $4 billion subsidiary of a $20 billion company. Scott was staffed on a huge strategy project at one of the largest, most prestigious management consulting firms. During that project, his client's distribution network had massive operational failures, so strategy was put on hold while the crisis was addressed. The management consulting firm did not do tactical, boots-on-the-ground work, but it had a vested interest in solving the problem quickly so it could continue generating stratospheric fees.

Two days after Scott's email, I sat in the client's headquarters being interviewed by the CEO and the following week, I started what grew to become a grueling, yearlong operational turnaround. I hired staff, lived at a Hampton Inn for weeks at a time, and figured out how to stay warm while working in a sub-freezing warehouse filled with hot dogs and pepperoni pizza toppings. That operational turnaround grew to include a pink hard hat and collaboration on construction of a new, state-of-the-art, multi-million dollar distribution center.

My company, Solertis, went on to complete high-profile projects for several multi-billion-dollar behemoths, and we won industry attention for our work. I wrote a white paper called "The Distribution Death Spiral," showcasing our expertise in operations and logistics, and was invited to speak at conferences. While the case studies were compelling and my PowerPoint was filled with relevant metrics, I felt something was missing.

Conference surveys showed I was a top-ranked presenter, and my presentations were often standing-room-only, but I discounted these external reference points because I really craved something more. No matter how much applause I received, my sense of satisfaction and fulfillment waned quickly.

Reading Martha's profile piece and that word, *humanness*, I had felt a spark and a yearning. I sensed the pull of some odd inner-knowing. Now I felt nervous as I waited to meet her.

Ten minutes past our planned appointment time, a four-foot-ten redhead flew into the lobby of the Buckhead Club. Despite her small physical stature, Martha could command a room. She walked right over to me and apologized for her tardiness. We moved to a conference room with a long table, a dozen chairs and the smell of new carpet. Despite the privacy of frosted glass walls, I felt uncomfortably exposed and vulnerable.

I began by providing a summary of the last few years of my business life and what I wanted to get from working with her, or at least I explained what I thought I wanted. As I told my story of starting Solertis and achieving recent success, I felt Martha looking through me and listening beyond my words as if she had superpowers of perception. From behind her bright eyes and engaging smile, she quietly studied me.

I told her I felt something was missing in my presentations. I craved connection with an audience beyond just case studies, metrics, and factual information neatly packaged and presented in PowerPoint slides. The word "humanness" in the *Business Chronicle* interview had grabbed me like an expletive. Perhaps I needed to acknowledge my own humanness and use it to meaningfully connect with my audiences. I knew my desire for excellence often crossed into perfectionism. It also occurred to me this feeling of connection was something I was seeking in more than just presentations.

Perhaps sensing this desire, Martha casually asked, "Would you be open to coaching on other things besides business presentations?"

I paused and asked, "Like what?" And with that, Martha began to delicately scrape away layers of glossy veneer to help me discover what I wanted to feel and who I really was.

Martha set me on a path to acknowledging my humanity and weaving more of my unvarnished truth into my presentations and into my life. As a coach, she gave me insight into parts and pieces of myself I did not know existed. A seemingly innocent question from Martha sent ripples through my world as I explored my feelings and beliefs and discovered deeper levels of inner wisdom and new truths.

As I worked with Martha over several months, I also became more aware of subtle energies and how to better manage and direct my own energy. All my life I had convinced myself I could power through anything, and I took pride in demonstrating this capability. I would work until I was so exhausted I collapsed.

I once gave a presentation at a supply chain conference while having excruciating pain in my lower right torso and back. At that time, I lifted weights with a fury, so I figured I had just overworked a lower back muscle. Upon finishing the presentation and leaving the stage, I discovered I was running a fever. I had mistaken a severe kidney infection for a sports injury. My white blood cell count was high enough to require a short hospital stay.

I built my professional reputation on responsiveness and determination, and I was crazy busy traveling six days a week fueled by adrenaline and intensity. I hired a personal assistant, Wendy, who handled almost everything except my stress. Martha encouraged me to take time for myself. She herself participated in several unorthodox practices, including short periods of isolation without any other people or electronics.

I viewed white space on my calendar as a sign of a serious deficiency. If I were not accomplishing something, I was worthless. I was not good at sitting still, but with practice and patience, I turned off the electronic flow of information and temporarily reduced human interactions to experience a new kind of rest. Allowing my central nervous system a respite slowly led me to deeper peace and a new kind of self-assuredness.

One week, Martha was flying to Florida for an appointment with a "medical intuitive" and invited me to join her. I had never heard those two words in the same sentence, but I love sunshine, the beach, and the ocean, so I decided to join her. After the short flight, we picked up a rental car and drove to the medical intuitive's office. Martha introduced me to Rebecca, who ushered us into separate treatment rooms. As I reclined on a table, Rebecca spoke with me while tapping acupuncture needles into my hands, feet, arms, and legs, and one directly into the center of my forehead. With the prick of each needle, I felt energy zooming around like electrical connections being made.

Rebecca paced back and forth in the room and asked me questions about my work, family, physical ailments, and life experiences. I could tell she sensed more than my verbal responses as I lay on a massage table, careful not to disrupt the acupuncture needles. I mentioned I still had chronic pain from a freak accident many years prior. After forty-five minutes of cardio at the gym, I had gone to a mat to stretch as I had done hundreds of times before. As I did my usual wide leg forward fold, I had heard an audible popping sound in the area deep inside my groin at the right hamstring attachment.

Immediately, I had felt excruciating pain and had needed to be helped to my car. I knew I had torn something, and once at home, I sat on an ice pack and took an anti-inflammatory. I did not seek medical treatment, figuring it was minor.

For several years after that event, I had ongoing, unexplained pain in my inner groin and hamstring. It would come and go without any direct correlation to physical activity. I saw a renowned chiropractor and would leave my appointments feeling great, but within forty-eight hours, I was back in the same pain. When I accepted a girlfriend's invitation to be a bridesmaid in her wedding, I prayed it would be a small church so I could walk the full length of the aisle without any obvious sign of agony.

Upon hearing about my injury, visits to the chiropractor, and recurring discomfort, Rebecca asked what I was doing to address the emotional, mental, and spiritual aspects of the injury. With that question, I began to explore metaphysics and the interconnectedness of my physical body with my energy field.

I thrived on being invincible and was so disconnected from parts of myself that my body's best means of communication was pain, and it took a lot of pain to get my attention. I began to examine random little accidents and injuries for deeper meaning rather than writing them off as inconsequential. As part of a new phase of self-discovery, I began to see these as messages that I should decipher.

My desire for presentation coaching serendipitously led me to energy work and started my exploration of metaphysical reality. That powerful pull of inner knowing sent me on a trajectory I never expected. I felt empowered to make shifts in areas of my life where I had been on autopilot chasing someone else's idea of success.

Martha was more than presentation coach; she was a conduit to many expansive experiences and a bridge to other practitioners and traditions. I traveled to Florida regularly for acupuncture and intuitive sessions with Rebecca. Both women offered wider perspectives on reality and launched me on my path to study with dozens of practitioners.

I had often heard the adage, "When the student is ready, the teacher appears." In my case, it wasn't just one teacher. It was a pair.

CHAPTER 2
Trust Your Experience and Be Open to More

As I waded deeply into the inner realms of self-discovery, my life got even busier, with more consulting opportunities, more travel, and more invitations. I joined the board of a private company in New Jersey and other philanthropic and advisory boards. I hired staff and moved to a bigger, nicer office in The Biltmore, a stately historic building I had coveted for office space for many years.

A pivot of one of my first business ideas became a program for optimizing truckload freight. By pairing companies that shipped truckloads of Pop Tarts, Froot Loops, and SpaghettiOs with a carpet manufacturer and a snack food company, each of which owned fleets of eighteen-wheelers, we pocketed some of the savings and helped the environment by reducing the number of trucks running empty across the country. I called this our *Collaborative Transportation Network*. Once the shipping lanes were set, the carriers and shippers ran the day-to-day operations and we were paid a percentage.

In one instance, someone on my staff agreed to partner with a company called MHI. We each brought something to the table and agreed to split the commissions. MHI received the total commission and then passed along half to my company.

After two years, this arrangement was generating substantial revenue, and I asked Ed, my resident "spreadsheet jockey," to audit the payments. A week later, Ed came to me and said there might be a problem. MHI had paid us accurately the first year, but the second year, our percentage of the total commission had dropped by half and the payments were coming more slowly.

I called Mike, the CEO of MHI, and in his slow Southern drawl, he told me an employee of my company had agreed to "sunset" our portion of the commissions so that by the fourth year of the deal we would get nothing. Zero. Mike was at least twenty years my senior and spoke to me like I was a school girl as he explained that our deal was done on a handshake and no contract was ever signed.

Mike knew that employee who negotiated this deal was no longer with my company but what he didn't know was that we had turned down other deals with "sunset" clauses. I started sifting through emails and found several to corroborate my assertion. Despite having no written contract, my attorney thought enough money was at stake to warrant legal action, so we filed a complaint and began the process.

In the meantime, consulting opportunities continued to expand and I crisscrossed the country visiting client sites. Tampa was a short hop from Atlanta making it possible for me to continue sessions with Rebecca. I left every session feeling stronger with greater clarity and certainty. As I questioned beliefs, dropped expectations and discovered new aspects of myself, I became more and more my own person and more in touch with my own humanness.

Rebecca thought I might enjoy learning meditation from two teachers of Ascension she had studied with. Their weekend-long introductory course, "First Sphere," was being offered in Tampa. I bought the book, Ascension, read it, and showed up for the course Friday evening where I met my next two teachers, Gomati and Vasistha Ishaya.

I thought meditation would be serious and solitary, but the camaraderie and light-heartedness were a welcome surprise. Two dozen people were packed into a small, garden style apartment and I spent much of the weekend sitting on the plush carpet under the host's baby grand piano, befriended by two more experienced students.

First Sphere consisted of both instruction and practice, so Gomati and Vasistha would talk about the *Ascension Attitudes* of *Praise, Gratitude, and Love,* and then we *ascended* together as a group in silence. This meant getting comfortable, closing your eyes, and focusing your attention inward. Compared with other types of meditation I knew of, one key distinction was to be as physically relaxed as possible. The Ishayas said when the physical body feels comfortable, the mind is more likely to get quiet. Sitting stiffly upright and forcing your legs into lotus position was not required. I smiled thinking anyone observing us would assume 25 people were just taking naps.

Occasionally, I heard muffled snoring and expected someone would be reprimanded. I discovered the Ishayas philosophy was if you needed sleep more than meditation, there was no shame in that. On the other hand, there was also no shame in admitting you were completely distracted by thoughts and mind chatter. Every experience was accepted, and every sensation was embraced without being labeled as wrong or bad. At mealtime, the group assembled a huge potluck lunch covering every available inch of the kitchen countertop and table. I piled my plate with kale salad, quinoa with Bragg's Amino Acids, delicious raw veggies and sprouted grain bread.

Beyond learning to meditate, making new friends, and consuming copious quantities of delicious food, I felt something profound; I felt deeply accepted and valued just by being there. Acceptance was not based on performance, achievement, wealth, or status. Everyone was valued and loved regardless of circumstances, challenges, or successes.

I wondered if this was unconditional love I had read about.

I left this warm cocoon of *Ascension* and went straight into a courtroom in Georgia. Following months of depositions, court filings, and a pathetic settlement offer from MHI, our lawsuit finally went to trial. My testimony as the plaintiff in the lawsuit required two long days of answering questions in front of a jury.

In depositions taken months prior to the trial, MHI's attorney had been personally confrontational and disrespectful. My attorney once stopped a deposition when opposing counsel hurled a pad of Post-It Notes at me in frustration.

Now in the courtroom in front of the judge and the jury, MHI's attorney continued his barrage of personal attacks. I used the *Ascension Attitudes* to pace my responses to questions and to avoid reacting to his provocations. The defense attorney for MHI would say something intentionally inflammatory, thinly veiled in the form of a question, and I would pause and choose an *Ascension Attitude* as my attorney shouted, "*Objection, your honor!*" This pattern went on for hours, and the opposing attorney's attacks finally got so ridiculous the judge had him removed from the courtroom and another was brought in to finish the trial.

Despite the plot twists and antics, I was always certain we would prevail. This process, from discovering the fraud through depositions and jury selection, witness testimony and courtroom theatrics, lasted two years. After six days in the courtroom, the jury found in our favor, and we were awarded the money we were owed. Along the way, I learned much about the judicial system, and most importantly, I learned how to incorporate my new spiritual practices into tense situations.

After the First Sphere course, I continued to develop my friendship with Gomati and Vasistha and often visited their Tampa home. The Intracoastal Waterway was right out their back door and the beach just a few blocks away. Staying with them for several days at a time, I basked in their love as they imparted their wisdom on organic food, energy work, physical movement to assist in releasing emotion, and how to hold compassion for anyone suffering without jumping into quicksand to try to save them.

I was still traveling extensively for work, and during some months, I spent more days at their home than in my own apartment in Atlanta. I relished their warmth, support, laughs, and long walks on the beach. I advanced my daily practice of *Ascension* and learned the *Attitudes of Second, Third, Fourth, and Fifth Sphere*s over many months. I also traveled with Gomati and Vasistha to visit other *Ascension* teachers at centers in New Mexico and North Carolina. These experiences brought welcome reassurance during a time of intense self-questioning.

One afternoon, I was sitting on the dock in the Ishayas' backyard when I got a call from the chairman of the board of a $300 million company where I was a director. I had voiced concerns over the misconduct of the company's top salesperson; he was having an affair with a female employee in marketing who was married to a man who worked in finance. Some had filed complaints with Human Resources as they overheard sexually explicit conversations and believed the woman had been given an unmerited promotion. The situation had come to the attention of the Board.

Rather than address it directly, they simply hired a law firm to provide perfunctory sexual harassment training. Executives were afraid any direct disciplinary action would send their top salesperson and his book of business to another firm. When I was asked to destroy my notes from a meeting related to this situation, I knew this director position was no longer a fit.

I was grateful for four years of seeing the inner workings of a company from the perspective of a director, for interacting with very bright people, for one incredibly lavish party in Manhattan, and generous director fees. I loved the experience until it was no longer consistent with my values, ethics, and consciousness.

As I sat on the Ishayas' dock speaking to the chairman by phone, he and I mutually agreed I would step down. We parted amicably, and just as I disconnected the call, a dolphin surfaced off the end of the dock and exhaled audibly. It felt as if the dolphin echoed my own sigh of relief. Minutes later, Vasistha was sitting beside me on the dock, ready to practice *Ascension*.

Gomati and Vasistha imparted much wisdom, and their most empowering advice was "*Trust your experience and be open to more.*" As spiritual teachers, they never allowed me to see them as gurus or to become reliant on them for direction. They were always smiling and supportive as they lovingly reminded me, "*Trust your experience and be open to more.*"

While learning to quiet my mind through *Ascension*, I began to recognize my ego's chatter. I caught voices in my head telling me how things should look, feel, or be. As I made more space for self-inquiry, I began to question my definitions of success. I realized those definitions were built on beliefs, expectations and values imparted by those around me. Simply questioning expanded my capacity to include new perspectives and possibilities.

It seemed an odd juxtaposition, but opening myself up to allow new ideas in required deepening my self-trust. To optimize one, I simultaneously needed the other. When this awareness registered viscerally inside me beyond just a mental thought, I had an "aha moment." I knew something inside me was stirring as I kinesthetically felt what it meant to "*Trust your experience and be open to more.*"

CHAPTER 3
A Professional Psychic and a Premonition

I often joked that Martha had a knack for picking up strays—both human and animal. She had a big personality and an ability to connect with strangers quickly. While vacationing in Santa Fe, New Mexico, Martha befriended Susana, whom she described as a professional psychic. Martha invited Susana to Atlanta to offer readings. I was skeptical, but I decided to take another leap and book a session.

Susana was absolutely gorgeous, with blonde hair, big brown eyes, and a smile that lit up the room. She knew things about me I had never disclosed to anyone. I found her talents utterly mystical and admired her unwavering confidence in her unusual abilities.

After a week in Atlanta, Susana went back to Santa Fe. We stayed in touch through email. In one exchange she wrote:

> *You're such an extraordinary person, Ann! You function so well in the "linear" world. Then your interest in psychic and soul worlds. I haven't put a "bottom line" to you yet! I'm normally able to summarize people...perhaps I have to wait because YOU are "happening"!*
>
> *Anyhow, you are such a weird and wonderful creature.*
>
> *Much love...Susana*

Susana saw me for who I was becoming and cared little about my past. I felt great freedom in that. From her stories, I knew Susana was nomadic by design, preferring it that way. She was often invited to visit friends in lovely places and did readings for those friends and their friends. I was intrigued by her unconventional lifestyle and her capabilities.

For my birthday, Susana created my astrological chart and offered me surprising insights. She could explain how the position of planets had influenced decisions I had made throughout the years. I began to sense how my life had been guided by forces and influences bigger than my logical mind. I had always loved numbers and geometry, and Susana encouraged me to pay attention to repetitive numerical patterns and synchronicities.

Susana returned to Atlanta, and with Martha's introductions and a network of referrals, she built quite a following. She planned to stay for a week, so I offered to reserve the guest suite at my apartment building for her. The logistics of the guest suite were perfect for Susana's clients. They could park in guest parking, check in with the concierge, and walk up a few steps to the guest suite.

Susana was seeing as many as ten clients a day and the front desk was definitely not accustomed to this much traffic coming and going from the guest suite. Eventually, the manager called thinking something unsavory was going on. When I explained Susana was a professional psychic, the manager stuttered a bit and then politely hung up.

The next call was from Susana herself. It seemed the front desk staff and the manager herself now wanted readings. I laughed, feeling grateful she was not being kicked out.

After a busy and lucrative week in Atlanta, Susana went back to New Mexico. She had been invited to housesit again for her friends Jeff and Katherine who had a beautiful home in Taos. We spoke regularly, and after Susana described her friends' place near the Sangre de Cristo Mountains, I made plans for a detour to New Mexico to visit.

Susana picked me up at the airport in Albuquerque, and as we drove north to Taos in her gray Pontiac, she told wonderful stories. She eloquently recounted the details of two near-death experiences (NDEs) she had had decades earlier. After being badly injured in a car accident and losing consciousness, she spoke of being in a long tunnel toward a white light behind which she could see people who seemed familiar. At the moment she was about to join them, she was pulled back into her badly bruised body at the scene of the accident. Despite being unconsciousness in one dimension, she had full recall of another. Her life experiences were unique and so different from mine.

Our time in Taos was magical. Jeff and Katherine's ranch-style home was beautifully decorated and had stunning views of the mountains and green pastures bursting with wildflowers. I did yoga on the roof as the sun rose over the mountains. We took long walks accompanied by the neighbor's dog, met friends, ate great meals, and visited art galleries. Susana taught me about astrology, tarot, and other mystical traditions. We would often sip tea in the morning as she prodded me to explore my gifts and talents. Inevitably, our lessons ended with laughter.

One afternoon we took a drive north out of Taos into the dry, desolate desert. With the windows down, the warm breeze blowing through our hair and no particular destination, Susana told stories of her younger years as the sun beat down on the car and tumbleweed blew across the deserted two-lane highway.

Her stories turned to her decades-earlier run-ins with authority and a general distrust of law enforcement. Just as she spoke these words, a car appeared on the horizon traveling toward us. We had not seen another car in hours but as it got closer, we could see it had a band of red lights on the top.

As the vehicle passed, we could see a uniformed officer inside a marked police car. I watched Susana look in her rearview mirror and nervously tighten her grip on the steering wheel as the officer did a U-turn and proceeded to follow us. The lights atop the squad car began to flash and get closer.

I thought this was no big deal but Susana instructed me to stay calm. I smiled assuming she was really advising herself. Apparently cops smelled her distrust and although I didn't know of any reason Susana had to fear arrest, whatever fear she harbored acted like a magnet for attention. The cop issued her a warning for speeding and we continued our drive.

Of all the things I learned in Taos, this was one of the most valuable. A simple traffic stop showed me the power of energy trapped in beliefs, thoughts and karma.

Back at Jeff and Katherine's, I noticed I often felt unsettled and out of sorts particularly inside the house. I loved Taos and being with Susana, but I felt a sense of foreboding, like something ominous was looming. I was also aware I was intentionally cultivating esoteric skills and inviting unseen, mystical energies. I wondered if my uncomfortable feelings were a byproduct of new sensitivities.

Over several days, I came to realize what I felt was death. It was a direct knowingness without a sense of origin or explanation. Susana and I analyzed this from many angles. Perhaps it was a metaphor because I was stepping into new aspects of myself while other aspects were dying. Jeff was a hunter, and animal heads were stuffed and mounted on the walls in several rooms. While I thought taxidermy was creepy, I was certain I sensed human death.

Susana was teaching me to trust my intuitive capabilities and often confirming my instincts, but in this case, she could not sense or explain what I was picking up. In the context of the teacher-student aspect of our friendship, it was an interesting dynamic.

I enjoyed four glorious days in sunny Taos before I flew home. Susana planned to spend Thanksgiving with her friends, including

CHAPTER 3: A PROFESSIONAL PSYCHIC AND A PREMONITION

a neighbor, Kelly, whom I had met during my visit. My family was headed to Clearwater Beach, Florida, where we had rented a cottage for the holiday week. Susana and I had established a rhythm of talking every day. I would often ask her to help me read a situation or give input on a decision. I had become reliant on her insights.

Our rental cottage in Clearwater had limited cell phone service, and one day I could not hear Susana at all. I said I would call her back in a few minutes, put on a jacket and headed to the beach. A few minutes later, I hit redial and after a few rings, I got her voicemail. This seemed odd since she was expecting my call. I waited and then tried again, but my call went to voicemail. By evening, her voicemail was full and Susana had not called me back. This was very uncharacteristic of her.

The following morning when my cell phone rang, I was delighted to see Susana's name on the caller ID. When I answered, I heard Kelly's voice. Kelly said he could see I had been trying to call Susana. He had expected her to come over for dinner, but she did not show up and did not answer her phone. Kelly had gone over to Jeff and Katherine's house and had seen Susana's car parked outside, but she did not answer the doorbell. Kelly and a friend broke a garage window and went in.

My heart sank as Kelly described the scene they found when they walked into the den. Susana's lifeless body was on the terra cotta floor in a pool of blood. Somehow, she had fallen, hit her head, and died.

I was speechless and devastated as Kelly's words sank in. Susana was the only one I had talked to about feeling human death in Jeff and Katherine's house. I questioned everything. Should I have done something different? Should I have told Susana to leave? Should I have said something to Kelly?

Sitting in shock and disbelief at the news, I realized I had no one to confide in about this experience. My family did not understand how I could be devastated over the death of someone I barely knew, so I cried privately. I was already in Florida for Thanksgiving, and I sought support from Rebecca, the medical intuitive, who helped me process my sense of loss and responsibility.

Twenty years later, I'm surprised to find I still occasionally cry recalling all of this. I cherish wonderful memories of Susana's wild laugh and of her warm smile and bright eyes. I also have several keepsakes from my time in Taos. One is a dream catcher Susana had bought for me. She seemed surprised I had never seen one and delighted in explaining its symbolism.

The second keepsake is a book titled *Instant Horoscope Predictor—Find Your Future Fast*. The front and back covers are missing, the binding is broken, and the pages are yellow. I love it most because I clearly recall when she gave it to me. I was rushing to pack before she drove me back to the airport in Albuquerque. She encouraged me to keep studying esoteric arts despite my business commitments. She spontaneously grabbed the book and tossed it into my luggage just as I was zipping the bag to leave. She said I could give it back to her next time I saw her.

Sadly, there was no next time.

Even in death, Susana was mystical. What caused her to fall? Why had she survived two NDEs but not this accident? I learned as much from Susana in death as I did from time we spent together in this life. Despite my intense sadness, I understood this as a nudge into trusting my own unconventional capabilities.

When the feathers on the dream catcher blow in the breeze, I smile in gratitude for the brief and profound intersection of our journeys.

CHAPTER 4
Perceptions and (Mis)Interpretations

Among the activities I used to distract myself after Susana's death were several tied to the Duke University Alumni Association. Because I had been a volunteer leader since graduation, I was plugged into an endless flow of opportunities to engage. George was an alum I had worked closely with. He was also a paid staffer who had helped me organize dozens of events. One year, the Duke men's basketball team played some exhibition games in London, and George helped arrange my travel on short notice and graciously included me in special events.

On the trip, I met dozens of European alumni, including Jim, who lived in Amsterdam and worked in sports marketing for Adidas. Later that spring, I saw Jim again at a tennis tournament in Key Biscayne, Florida. Two friends from Atlanta were also there working for the Women's Tennis Association (WTA). The four of us bonded at the decadent poolside breakfast buffet at the Sonesta Hotel in Coconut Grove before driving across the Rickenbacker Causeway to the tennis venue.

Over dinner and several bottles of wine on our last night, the four of us made a pact to meet at Roland-Garros (the French Open) in Paris. Given my weekly commute to a consulting project in El Paso, Texas, I knew Paris was a long shot, but I raised my glass of Barolo and pledged my intention anyway. Weeks later, the stars aligned—I finished the project and flew to France. When I arrived, I was quite jet-lagged, but Jim had made plans for us to meet several of his colleagues and one of the top players signed to Adidas, Martina Hingis.

Seared into my memory was a scene from the finals of a previous French Open when Hingis ran crying to her mother after being walloped by Steffi Graf. Hingis had grown up under the media's watchful eyes and was just sixteen when she attained her number-one ranking. I knew I had an unfair perception of her based largely on a single incident. Jim noticed me rolling my eyes, smiled, and said, "If you two aren't best friends by the end of dinner, I will be surprised."

Jim's prediction turned out to be accurate. Martina had a feisty, competitive spirit and the life experience of someone decades older. She was not competing because of an ankle injury but was in Paris doing celebrity appearances. Adidas had hired a car and driver but had no staff to accompany her. We were all staying at the same hotel, and it sounded fun, so the following day I joined Martina at the Adidas store as she signed autographs and posed for photos.

From there, we had the driver drop us at Sacré-Cœur, the iconic basilica and highest point in Paris. Once inside, I observed Martina quietly kneel and take a private moment for prayer. I learned she made this pilgrimage every year during the French Open.

After lunch, the driver dropped us at the Arc de Triomphe. In the first of many windows into her competitive spirit off court, Martina challenged me to race up the stairs to the roof. I lost but the view at the top was just as breathtaking as the race to get there.

From there, we walked down the Champs-Élysées, and while browsing inside the huge Sephora store, I noticed two people quietly shadowing us. The woman wore a big floppy hat and stylish sunglasses, and the man looked imposing in a black jacket. The hair on my arms went up as I watched them seeming to follow Martina. I stood beside her, pretending to look at lipstick, and whispered I thought she was being followed.

At that moment, the woman said, "Hello, Martina," as she removed her disguise. I had mistaken Monica Seles and her security detail for kidnappers. We all had a laugh, and I took a couple of photos of the two of them in front of a cosmetics display.

The French Open was an Adidas signature event, so the company had a three-story suite overlooking Court Chatrier. I enjoyed the champagne and canapés while watching great matches, but the highlight of the trip was a new friendship.

Two months later, I met Martina and the Adidas gang at their charitable event on Cape Cod. Between exhibition matches, a Pro-Am, and an elegant dinner under a huge tent filled with celebrity athletes, we took bike rides and made plans to meet in Switzerland two weeks later.

I was attending a conference in Geneva with Duke's Global Capital Markets Center, a collaboration between the Fuqua School of Business and the law school. After a day of seminars, we were treated to a sunset sail on Lake Geneva and a beautiful gala evening at an estate with spectacular gardens, outdoor terraces, and acres of vineyards.

At dinner, I was seated next to J. B. Fuqua himself, the philanthropist who endowed the business school in the 1970s. When Mr. Fuqua realized I lived in Atlanta, he graciously offered me a ride home in his Gulfstream jet. I thanked him, but I was headed to the Montreux Jazz Festival and then Zurich.

Zurich provided another window into the challenges of celebrity life. I quickly tired of running to avoid a mob of fans at shops like Confiserie Sprüngli and was happy to go out into the countryside. As an athlete, Martina could pack a week's worth of physical activity into one day. From horse jumping to swimming races across a remote section of the Rhine River to jogging after dinner at a restaurant on the Bodensee, I felt both invigorated and exhausted.

We made plans to meet in Los Angeles for the WTA year-end championships. Days before the event, I was in a taxi in Manhattan when Martina called to ask if I would go with her to a birthday party in LA. I agreed, only to learn the party was black-tie optional. While clarifying I did not need a full-length gown, she mentioned this was Billie Jean King's birthday hosted by Elton John at the Beverly Hills Hotel. My next frantic call was to Wendy, my assistant, who knew my closet and had several options ready and waiting when I arrived.

The party's highlights included sitting next to Pete Sampras at dinner and hearing Elton John sing and play "Happy Birthday" before dozens of celebratory toasts honoring Billie Jean King.

Something else remarkable happened in LA. Pam Shriver was covering the WTA's thirtieth anniversary for ESPN, and as we passed one another in a corridor at the Staples Center, I felt something. As if some part of her were broadcasting a signal picked up by my subconscious, I knew she was pregnant. This spontaneous awareness opened me to new possibilities for intuitive insights. Shriver's son was born eight months later.

Martina and I met up in London during Wimbledon and again on Cape Cod. By 2006, she was back playing professionally, and I was focused on my romantic partner, Daniel, and living aboard our sailboat for weeks at a time between consulting projects. I managed to get to the Key Biscayne tournament for half a day only because we were already in Florida for a sea trial aboard a new sailboat.

Although my visit was short, I met Martina's mother briefly and learned Martina was dating Czech tennis player Radek Stepanek, whom she had known since childhood. She smiled and said, "This might be something."

A year later, I flew to Miami again for the tournament, thinking I would surprise Martina. I drove to Key Biscayne only to find her favorite hotel closed for renovation. I had a reservation at the Ritz-Carlton a half mile down the road where I was welcomed by Carla, a guest relations associate. When I told Carla my dilemma, she asked my friend's name. I whispered "Martina Hingis," and Carla simply winked.

CHAPTER 4: PERCEPTIONS AND (MIS)INTERPRETATIONS

The front desk would not confirm Martina was a guest, so I gave up on my surprise and resorted to texting her. I had to try three international cell numbers, but she was indeed at the hotel, and within minutes, we were catching up over espresso. By this time, Martina was engaged to Stepanek, who was also playing in the tournament. That night, we all went to dinner at the local sushi place. Radek was witty and funny while trying to teach me off-color Czech words. Despite his charm, I felt uneasy for no obvious reason.

I was toggling between several worlds at the time. Because of the project-oriented nature of consulting, I could work for several months at a client site and then go sailing with Daniel or travel internationally. My aspirations for building Solertis into a huge enterprise had dwindled as adventures beckoned.

I planned to see Martina again at the US Open in New York, and in the interim, I spent two months working, sailing, and traveling through Europe with Daniel. Several weeks after we returned from Europe, our relationship became tenuous, and by late summer, Daniel and I had broken up. I sought solace with Gomati and Vasistha at an *Ascension* gathering in Atlanta. During meditation, I was unusually distracted by a sense of something being off. I could have easily attributed my unsettledness to my breakup with Daniel, but when my mind was empty of thoughts, I felt Martina.

I was eager for distraction, so after the Ascension gathering ended, I decided to fly to Los Angeles where Martina was playing a tournament. I kept checking ESPN to see if she was injured or in some kind of accident, but I found nothing.

I arrived at LAX, got a rental car, and headed for the Marriott. I knew the hotel based on a combination of intuition and logic. The players usually stayed in a hotel near the tournament venue, and in meditation, I saw a flash of the red Marriott logo in my mind's eye. I called, effectively tricked someone at the front desk into confirming it was indeed the hotel the WTA was using, and made a reservation.

I sent Martina a text from the parking lot and found she was there having lunch. Normally stoic, I was surprised when she got up from the table and crossed the entire span of the patio to hug me. As we waited for a hotel elevator, I inspected a fresh patch of acne on her cheek and could feel her stress.

Once alone in the elevator, she asked, "How did you know?"

I replied, "How did I know what?"

Unbeknownst to me, Radek Stepanek was planning to call off their engagement publicly within hours. He was competing well in Canada and planned to announce their split on EuroSport. Now I understood at least one of the reasons I had been so restless at the *Ascension* retreat. I was reluctant to tell my friends and family Daniel and I had split, but having a breakup announced on international television was unfathomable.

After dinner, Martina and I went to the tennis venue to watch Maria Sharapova play Elena Dementieva under the lights. We flashed credentials and quietly slipped in, hoping to remain unnoticed as we sat courtside on a long, metal bench. Between sets, I saw Pam Shriver approaching us with her ESPN microphone and realized she intended to do a live interview. Once Shriver got the cue from her producer, she asked Martina several routine questions before noting Stepanek's win streak. Shriver asked Martina, "What's it like to see your fiancé playing so well this summer?"

In slow motion, I watched Shriver's smile shrivel and her shoulders droop as the news came through her earpiece. She apologized, saying she had just heard from the ESPN booth the engagement was called off. I was mortified but Martina did not flinch. The interview ended and we slipped out quietly and went back to the hotel.

I chose a trendy spot in Manhattan Beach for our last dinner in LA. As we shared stories, I realized how much of normal adolescence she had missed during her meteoric rise to success. Martina had never experienced the give and take of friendships the way most people do. The closest relationships in her life were with people serving in a paid capacity or those whose interest was predicated on her winning.

I was touched but not surprised when she said she considered me one of her closest friends at the time. I knew our friendship continued because I showed up, paid my own way and and offered a kind of support she was not finding elsewhere. I did this realizing she was never going to reciprocate in the same way. As a wink at the imbalance, I once joked I was going to put her to work on a Supply Chain project.

Despite the one-sidedness, I was getting enough in return in other ways to accept the unspoken parameters of our friendship. The humanness behind her fame and athletic accomplishments fascinated me.

Martina changed her schedule to include two weeks of training near Tampa, where she owned a home. She invited me to come to Saddlebrook in Florida and then onto New York for the US Open. I was in the throes of pitching a turnaround for a private equity firm and also going to Kansas City for my cousin's wedding, but I found myself committing nonetheless.

The next morning, Martina flew to Tampa and I drove to the Agape International Spiritual Center in Beverly Hills to see Michael Bernard Beckwith, a renowned New Thought minister who was very popular in spiritual circles. I had heard him on podcasts with Oprah and Deepak Chopra but attending his trans-denominational Sunday service in person was beyond anything I had imagined.

The choir itself was larger than some congregations and blessed with amazing talent, perhaps because of proximity to Hollywood. The building shook with energy as we raised our voices in song.

The moment the service ended, I was back in the rental car hurrying to LAX, grateful for the opportunity to meet another spiritual leader.

After two days in Atlanta, I flew to Tampa. Martina met me at the airport, and we drove north to Saddlebrook, a gated community with homes, a golf course, and world-class training facilities. Martina gave me a tour of her house and offered me a spacious guest room with a huge desk; it overlooked a lush green fairway where a magnificent blue heron stood watch over the swimming pool just outside my window.

We walked by a ping-pong table covered with stacks of colorful envelopes piled eight inches high. When I pointed, she said, "Fan mail." I nearly fainted. I had imagined a team of assistants politely replying to every letter and sending some autographed swag but the letters remained unopened.

Martina worked with a trainer at Saddlebrook doing intense drills in a sand volleyball court. Then she hit balls for several hours in the hot Florida sun. Later, I found her pedaling an exercise bike while watching TV. After dinner, she liked to take a short jog. I could not keep up, so I followed her in the golf cart. Our days ended with laughter and ice cream.

I flew home to Atlanta, then to Kansas City before heading to New York. Martina did not have a coach, so I booked the practice court times, hired a hitting partner, and coordinated our daily transportation from the hotel in Manhattan to Flushing Meadows. While Martina hit balls, I sat in the players' restaurant overlooking the practice courts writing consulting proposals, responding to email, and making calls.

I also enjoyed anonymously observing players. Novak Djokovic was a young, rising star, and I figured if he did not make it in tennis, he had a future in gaming. He and a redheaded kid who looked like a leprechaun played video games in the players' lounge several hours a day and were not exactly quiet about their victories.

When Martina finished practice and started to head for the locker room, I felt the buzz and looked down from my perch as security staff monitored adoring fans thrusting mega-sized tennis balls in her direction, hoping for an autograph. That was my cue to pack up my laptop and trade supply chain consulting for another kind of logistics.

Martina won her first two singles matches. Her third was against Victoria Azarenka, a youngster whose professional ranking was around 100. The day before the match, I did one of the dumbest, most regrettable things ever. I told Martina she would win her match based on an image I saw while looking at her career win-loss record on my laptop. Much like seeing the red Marriott logo in my mind's eye, I saw Martina's number of career wins increase. I leapt to a conclusion without considering timing or my bias toward believing what I wanted to see.

After winning the first set, Martina lost the second set badly. I was sitting courtside along the baseline with her agent, and every time she was on my side of the court, she would make eye contact as if looking to me for an answer. She did not win a single game in the third set.

After the match, I met her in the corridor outside the player locker room and was profusely apologetic. Those nearby likely thought I was simply expressing regret at the match's outcome. She knew my deeper apology. I had misused my gift and let my friend down. This felt like a smack from the Universe and a reminder of the responsibility to use intuitive insights wisely.

With competitive pressure off, we shopped in Manhattan, relaxed, and watched matches on Center Court from the suite of her sports management company. Martina invited me to stay for New York Fashion Week, but my company had been awarded a consulting project with a seafood distributor, and I was headed to work in a smelly, stadium-sized freezer of fish.

Martina arranged a car and rode with me to LaGuardia for my flight home. As we hugged goodbye, I thought back to how I had perceived her based on one highly publicized, adolescent response to defeat. Now I knew the humanness behind the celebrity sports persona, trophies, and accolades.

I had also learned a valuable yet embarrassing lesson about my intuition; perceiving an image is one thing and interpreting it is another. My regrettable interpretation would come to serve as a powerful reminder to consider the nuances and possible meanings of intuitive imagery before leaping to conclusions.

As I waited in line at LaGuardia security, about to fly back to my normal life, I realized what had kept my interest was the newness and unfettered access available with this level of credentials. I loved having a backstage pass to events occurring on the grandest scale and a peek into the humanness of a celebrated athlete. Intrigue in the hidden aspects and unseen challenges of those competing on a global stage and living in the public eye continued to pique my curiosity.

As the wheels of the plane left the runway, I closed my eyes in gratitude for incredible experiences I'd been afforded as a result of allowing enough wiggle room to change my (mis)perceptions.

CHAPTER 5
From Rocks to Boulder and Seattle

During the first week of Spring semester of my sophomore year of college, I entered a crowded auditorium, and sighed knowing my GPA was about to be compromised by an arbitrary science requirement. I had already dropped Physics after just one class and was now enrolled in Geology 101, fondly referred to as "Rocks for Jocks," and recommended by my roommate and her boyfriend, who were both varsity athletes.

The noisy lecture hall was packed and as I descended steep steps toward the front, I spotted David, who I had met a few times at Wednesday night kegs hosted by his fraternity. David and I found two seats together in the front row just as class started.

The professor quieted the group, presented the syllabus and announced quizzes and a final exam would be graded on a bell curve. I glanced over at David who seemed to be stifling a smile. We made eye contact and I instantly knew we were going to work to set the curve. After class, David and I half joked about our ambitions as we made plans to share notes and study together.

We quickly discovered we enjoyed hanging out and channeled our chemistry into our academic goals. David had an amazing voice and sang in The Pitchforks, a men's a cappella group I loved. In addition to sharing laughs and music, we did indeed set the curve for Geology 101. David scored 99 percent, and I scored 98.5.

David studied abroad the following semester and we lost touch, finally reconnecting during our senior year. Although we shared a lovely connection, affection, and admiration, we never dated because one of us was always in a relationship when the other was available. We often laughed and said the Universe must have some grand design because even if the chemistry was there, the timing was definitely not.

After graduation, I moved back to my hometown of Kansas City and started a job. David, an aspiring writer, stayed in Durham to apprentice with Duke professor and bestselling author Reynolds Price, and we lost touch again. Years after graduation, I attended a Duke Alumni event featuring Reynolds Price. When I spoke with him, I learned David was living in Boulder, Colorado. My mind must have filed this away because when I was headed to Boulder for a conference, I immediately recalled Reynolds' low-pitched Southern drawl and the exact words he had said about David.

I found David's number in the alumni directory and called. I heard a familiar voice on the voicemail and smiled as I left a message. A few hours later, David called me back and after a great conversation, we made plans to meet for tea in Boulder the following week. Twenty years had flown by since we had last seen one another and that meant catching up on marriages, divorces, moves, job changes, and other adventures. I discovered David had been on his own path of personal and spiritual growth. Tea lasted for hours, and when I had to get back to the supply chain conference, we agreed to meet again.

The next day, we met and hung out just as we had 20 years earlier. Rather than a tiny college dorm room with our geology textbooks and piles of notes, we were in David's charming bungalow with his vast collection of books, Tibetan bowls and a sunny backyard. Despite very different career paths, we shared common interests around consciousness and transformation.

CHAPTER 5: FROM ROCKS TO BOULDER AND SEATTLE

David's friend Rebecca joined us for tea that afternoon, and tea eventually led to dinner where I felt I was sitting with two of my dearest friends. I had skipped twenty years with one friend and was just meeting the other for the first time, but in another dimension, it seemed like we had all known one another for lifetimes.

Rebecca worked as a coach and had created some decks of small cards meant to help her clients challenge their thoughts and change their perspectives. She called them "Flash Cards for the Soul." She designed and manufactured the cards and was selling them to retailers as gift items. I liked the positive messages, the packaging, and Rebecca's creativity. I offered to help informally with supply chain, logistics, and general business advice.

Six months later, I traveled to Boulder again. I had offered to help Rebecca promote her business by staffing her booth at a trade show. While I had attended dozens of supply chain conferences and expos showcasing the latest forklifts, racks, and warehouse management systems, the International New Age Trade Show (INATS) was quite a contrast.

INATS catered to retailers who sold metaphysical and spiritual books, music, and gifts. Inside the convention center, I wandered through aisles lined with booths featuring aromatherapy essences and oils, candles, crystals, divination tools, and indigenous gifts. Rebecca had also recruited a female technology executive to work the booth. I giggled as two confident businesswomen enthusiastically explained metaphysical flash cards.

Being at the expo and in the booth accelerated my interest in merging aspects of spirituality and metaphysics with my love of mainstream business. I observed many forms of engagement and found inspiration in how each person had their own unique, personalized way to be spiritual in material world.

While I was in Boulder, David and I drove to Fort Collins to attend a program featuring the author of dozens of spiritual books. As we sat together in an auditorium with 1,100 people, I smiled recalling sitting next to David in the front row of Geology 101 listening to a lecture about shifts in the layers of the Earth's crust and the evolution of our planet. Both independently and together, our studies and interests had expanded from the terrestrial to the most mystical and multidimensional. The Universe must have a sense of humor.

After I left Boulder, Rebecca and I spoke frequently, and I learned she had used many different healers and healing modalities. One day, she called to say she couldn't make an appointment that week with someone named Isabelle who did energy work and had a months-long waiting list for new clients. She asked if I would I like to take her place? I knew nothing about Isabelle or what to expect, but I was intrigued and knew to trust synchronicity. Isabelle was in Seattle, so our first session was by phone. Little did I know this one serendipitous session would lead to hundreds more over many years, along with workshops and several international adventures.

Rebecca relocated from Boulder to Seattle and continued to market her flash cards. I assisted her while traveling and working for my other consulting clients. Eventually, I structured my schedule so I could spend three weeks in Seattle to assess a potential role in her business. I mentioned my intentions to a colleague who lived in Seattle, and within a week, I was connected to a couple who offered me the use of the guest house on their property near Green Lake. The location was perfect and I felt it was a nudge to commit, so I spent much of September in Seattle.

While my primary focus was Rebecca and her business, my extended stay included so much more. Seattle created separation from my Atlanta responsibilities and identity. The lush green climate, downshift in speed, and lessening of expectations were a reset I didn't know I needed.

I did Iyengar yoga several times a week and discovered a fondness for Macrina's zucchini bread and Top Pot coffee. I journeyed to Port Hadlock to see a crystal dealer from whom I had previously

CHAPTER 5: FROM ROCKS TO BOULDER AND SEATTLE

purchased a magnificent four-pound citrine. On her property, I sat in a twenty-foot matrix of crystals she and her husband arranged, and I marveled at the flow of energy. Something spectacularly powerful was created by the sophisticated geometry and I could feel the vibration in every cell of my body.

The Seattle weather in September was spectacular. I went hiking at Mount Rainier on a sunny mountainside where patches of ice glistened in the warmth of late summer. I loved the majestic beauty and felt deep gratitude for the opportunity to spend several weeks away from my normal routine. I came down a dirt trail with expansive views to my left and a hillside filled with grass and wildflowers on my right. Ahead in the distance, I heard a sound and noticed something tumbling down the side of the hill above the trail. The grass was too tall to tell what it was until it rolled to a stop twenty yards in front of me.

I realized I was staring at the backside of a bear cub. I quietly gasped in glee at its yellow fuzz and cuteness. I knew better than to get too close, but I also needed to continue walking down that trail to get back to my rental car. I waited until it popped its head up out of the grass long enough for me to get a single photo and then quickly tiptoed by. When I was a good distance past it, I looked back. Thankfully, the cub was still busy foraging in the grass.

I took the ferry to Bainbridge Island to see a supply chain colleague named Peter. Six years earlier, he and I had been introduced by a mutual friend who then brought us together in several cities for group dinners. Although I barely knew Peter, I observed he was always the life of the party with endless jokes around the dinner table. While he kept everyone laughing, I sensed his humor was masking something just beneath the surface. Peter was among the first people I called when I arrived in Seattle, and he invited me to dinner at his home with his wife and sons.

I loved watching the deer quietly roaming Peter's backyard and the delicious, freshly caught salmon. In a familiar environment among people he loved, I saw another side of Peter. I discovered his capacity for depth, honesty, and meaningful conversation. His mother had passed away just months before one of those group dinners. Perhaps humor had been necessary to deflect pain, but I discovered a new level of rapport and emotional honesty. Bainbridge itself was full of natural beauty and the ferry offered a picturesque view of downtown, but the real highlight was our conversation—the first of several with a raw realism I cherished.

I attended several programs at East West Bookshop, and I was also invited to a workshop called "Harmonizing with Spirit" where I met Jeni and several other members of Rebecca's cadre of healers and friends. I also met Isabelle in person for the first time, another adventure that would later prove to be significant for many years into the future.

The Emerald City definitely lived up to its name, and while I thoroughly enjoyed my time in Seattle, it became clear the juice with Rebecca was in our friendship, not her business. I was accustomed to running million-square-foot distribution centers for billion-dollar companies; she was shipping small orders out of her living room. While I loved the spiritual aspects of Rebecca's product, I left Seattle knowing this was not my next career move.

Professionally, I was yearning for something that utilized my range of capabilities and integrated more of my spiritual and metaphysical interests into my business life. And vice versa. I asked the Universe to show me how and then tried to find patience as I waited for synchronicities to lead me to next steps.

CHAPTER 6
Blurred Lines and a Silver Lining

While back in Atlanta long enough to do laundry, water the plants and repack for another trip, I went to an Iyengar yoga class and stayed after to work on an inversion pose called Pincha Mayurasana. With my forearms and palms firmly planted on the floor, I kicked up against the wall into an inverted vertical position. For the first time, I held the inversion without help.

I was elated but after a few seconds with my feet in the air and heels to the wall, I lost my balance and crashed, missing my yoga mat and jamming my left big toe into the hardwood floor. The instructor gasped at the sound of breaking bone. I thought it was no big deal and went home to shower and pack for my flight.

Within an hour, my toe was so swollen I could not put my shoe on. I figured I should get an X-ray, and since it was my left foot, I drove myself to an urgent care clinic. A technician took X-rays as the pain and swelling in my toe worsened. The doctor showed me where the bone was broken in several places near the joint and declared I would need surgery on my toe. He wrote me a prescription for some whopper pain medication along with a referral to an orthopedic surgeon.

I reluctantly canceled my flight and drove to the surgeon's office where he fitted me with crutches and a gray plastic boot with an inflatable support to stabilize my foot. The boot and crutches made moving through the airport untenable, so I decided to slow down for a few weeks and work from my sofa with my foot propped on a pile of pillows. I refused to schedule surgery until I had explored other options.

Thankfully, the accident was only inconvenient, not life-threatening, but it was definitely enough to get me to reconsider my pace and priorities. My ego loved the thrill of speed but if accidents were meant as messages, my body was clearly signaling it needed rest.

While I was home healing, Rebecca recommended a holistic treatment called Network Spinal Analysis. NSA is a type of care delivered by licensed chiropractors, but this version does not involve twisting or cracking of the spine. Instead, NSA relies on generating a wave of energy in the spine to release tension in the spinal cord while increasing coherence in the central nervous system.

I found a practitioner, Dr. Patrick, online, and as Rebecca predicted, I loved NSA and signed up for a package of sessions. I went to the Center several times each week for entrainments and attended a workshop on Somato-Respiratory Integration where I learned techniques to synchronize breath, energy, and movement. Long after my big toe healed and I was traveling again, I continued my sessions with Dr. Patrick.

Over two years, I also attended several international programs called Transformational Gates where dozens of practitioners and hundreds of participants from across the world came together for three days. Transformational Gates offered a way to experience many different practitioners in one location, and the group energy created at those weekends was incredibly unifying, supportive, and healing.

Dr. Patrick himself fostered a sense of closeness, warmth, and intimacy. During my first few months of entrainments, we developed a personal relationship. I resigned as a client and we began dating in spite of ethical boundaries.

While still working in supply chain consulting, I spent more and more time with him and at the Center. I quickly saw how the

CHAPTER 6: BLURRED LINES AND A SILVER LINING

Center would benefit from basic improvements in business processes, technology, and administration. With Dr. Patrick's support, I got involved in the Center's operations in an unpaid capacity. I installed scheduling software, managed finances, and worked on marketing.

Dr. Patrick also encouraged me to offer coaching to a handful of the Center's clients. NSA entrainments did not allow a lot of time for dialogue, and I found clients liked having a sounding board. I had become a familiar face, having worked the front desk for weeks, and I had completed nearly a decade of my own personal growth work. I set up a desk and chairs in an empty room at the Center and discovered people enjoyed meeting with me.

I listened compassionately as clients spoke their truth as a way to unravel and let go of painful experiences. Clients shared intimate, often painful details of their lives and began to release the crushing weight of suffering in silence. One client had discovered her father having an affair while she was a teenager and had carried the oppressive burden of this secret by not telling anyone else. Another client remembered being abused as a child and began to understand how that shaped his adult relationships.

I earned the clients' trust with my openness and by holding space for them to transcend the darkness they had experienced. The setting and the circumstances for this work were very new to me and I discovered I also picked up unspoken information. I was often able to validate much of it using delicately-crafted questions.

Dr. Patrick had a huge heart and genuinely cared for his clients. However, that huge heart often trumped good boundaries and smart business practices. I discovered the extent of blurred lines as I studied the financials. Many clients paid very little or nothing at all. Some had barter agreements, but those agreements were unclear. While the office seemed busy, revenue didn't match the flow of people.

As many as five practitioners rented space in the Center and Patrick's fuzzy boundaries carried over into collecting rent. One part-time practitioner owed more in back rent than she typically billed in six months. None had contracts. Patrick had bought the practice years earlier, borrowing from a friend at a ridiculously high interest rate instead of using a financial institution. I saw all this as easily fixable with a bit of structure, attention, and business acumen. I went full speed ahead with the understanding I was creating *sweat equity* and would become a partner in the Center.

In my travels, I sought opportunities to visit other centers and see different business models. I visited Health Touch NC, a collaborative healing center in Durham, North Carolina, where Judith, a banker turned massage therapist turned entrepreneur, had created a beautiful center for thirty healers providing a variety of treatments. She served as both landlord and occasional business coach to the other practitioners who rented space from her. She shared her operational challenges and the nuances of her business, which was very helpful. I loved how Judith used her full range of skills and capabilities in her business, something I sought to emulate.

I visited Duke Center for Integrative Medicine (DCIM), where Eastern modalities like reiki were integrated with Western medicine. Conceived by a group of philanthropists, including a Duke alumna and wife of an executive at Morgan Stanley, DCIM felt more like a spa than a medical center.

From the quiet room with a bamboo garden and water wall, to the use of natural materials like wood and stone, and thoughtful composition of light and space, DCIM felt very Zen and inviting. I walked the labyrinth in the woodlands of Duke Forest inspired and contemplating what we could create back at the Center in Atlanta.

A year and a half later, as our relationship progressed and our lives became more intertwined, Patrick moved in with me. Living with someone has challenges, which were complicated by simultaneously working to formalize our business partnership. I began to have a recurring dream I did not understand. In the dream, I was standing on the sidewalk outside his old house. A U-Haul was in

CHAPTER 6: BLURRED LINES AND A SILVER LINING

the driveway, and Patrick and his friend were unloading the U-Haul and carrying the furniture back inside. I could see intricate details like maneuvering his big sofa up the front steps and then trying to fit it through the door. For many nights, I woke up from the dream wondering what it meant and why I would dream he was moving back into the house where he formerly lived.

After several months, I formulated a plan to expand the Center, add staff, and create innovative programs. I was ready to invest, enlarge the physical space, and grow. Patrick liked my ideas, so we began looking for new office space. I was elated to finally be moving my professional activities toward holistic health and wellness.

I also began writing the terms of our business partnership with plans to incorporate a new business with shared ownership. Despite all previous discussions, verbal agreements, and our romantic partnership, I discovered Patrick was not interested in co-owning a new company, regardless of the conditions. He did not intend to legally share a business with me, and I did not intend to continue investing without equity and a written agreement. Our relationship unraveled quickly, complicated by Patrick living with me.

After a few more weeks of uncomfortable cohabitation, I encouraged him to call his old landlord. He knew his old house, a place he loved, had been rented to another tenant, but I suggested he call anyway. Shockingly, the landlord said the current tenant had already given notice and was eager to move out. Patrick could move back into his old house almost immediately. My recurring dream had foreshadowed exactly what happened.

I felt a full circle moment embedded in my sad realization that while Patrick's loose boundaries facilitated our romantic relationship, once those boundaries were strengthened, we were done.

After months of reinforcing those same boundaries with other clients, colleagues, and vendors; and building a structure to support his business, I suddenly found myself outside it. My time at the Center and with Patrick as my romantic partner ended.

Everything I had poured my heart and soul into crashed at once. I felt angry and embarrassed. I cried for hours at a time, lost my appetite, and could not sleep. I could not forgive myself for unfathomable stupidity. I knew better.

And then, unexpectedly, on a Friday evening I found the silver lining.

CHAPTER 7
As Above, So Below

On a Friday evening two days after ending both my personal and professional relationship with Patrick, I saw I had missed a call from a CEO I had known for a decade. I had led a successful turnaround of one of his billion-dollar companies, a project that provided the basis for my whitepaper, "The Distribution Death Spiral." I had also evaluated multiple acquisition targets for his private equity firm.

I pulled myself together and called him back, hoping he might have a project to distract me from my recent, unhappy ending with Patrick.

He answered and apologized for his unintentional pocket dial. From our past conversations, he knew of my role at the Center and was surprised to learn it had ended. He observed my health habits and thought managing and expanding the Center would be a great fit for my interests and capabilities. He knew I utilized unusual modalities, and while he labeled some of those "*goofy*," I had not had any health insurance claims nor had I used any pharmaceuticals in over a decade. As a CEO running a multi-billion-dollar corporation with several thousand employees, those statistics meant something to him.

His company, CMC, was headquartered in Florida, and his team was in the initial stages of developing a corporate wellness program. Healthcare costs were cutting into profits, and he was eager for solutions. I could not believe the auspicious timing of his pocket dial and my good fortune at following the impulse to call him back.

Two weeks later, I flew to Florida to meet with the Human Resources team at CMC and draft a proposal to consult on the creation of a corporate wellness program for employees and their families. CMC had all the requisite formality the Center lacked. A written contract clearly defined what they expected of me, my compensation, payment terms, and travel expense reimbursements.

I was eager to get started and distract myself from my previous failure.

Corporate wellness programs were gaining popularity at the time, driven by skyrocketing healthcare costs and the price corporations were paying for insurance. CMC wanted to create a consumer-directed health insurance plan for employees and encourage them to use their benefits judiciously with a focus on wellness activities. I crunched numbers from insurance data to quantify potential savings through reductions in small claims and proactive, long-term lifestyle changes and collaborated with the Human Resources team on an array of components for the program.

During weeks I was onsite at CMC headquarters, the hotel where I stayed was situated in an office park with a small lake bordered by trees covered in hanging Spanish moss. An elevated boardwalk kept joggers out of reach of alligators, and a footbridge across the center connected the hotel to the offices. I chose the east side where the rooms had large balconies and I could watch the sunrise while doing yoga. I gazed across the lake, setting intentions for the day as I did sun salutations.

We kicked off CMC's program, which we called "Live Well," with a week of activities, including a health fair with a Wii Fit competition, cooking demonstrations in the company cafeteria, and biometric screening. We launched an online wellness portal with teams competing in walking and running programs. We selected Mayo Clinic for their health risk assessment, and I was invited to attend their key client summit in Rochester, Minnesota. The summit featured presentations from experts and taught best practices from companies with mature wellness programs like Apple, Intel, and L.L.Bean.

While I loved the corporate perspective on wellness in the workplace and building enthusiasm, I found the definition of wellness narrow. We focused on smoking cessation, blood pressure and diabetes management through medication, and screenings for cancer and disease prevention. The *mind-body-spirit* connection was acknowledged, but the timeline to offer alternate and holistic modalities or even a group meditation program felt distant.

The company headquarters building was six stories with the executive offices on the top floor and the company cafeteria and gym on the ground level. One Friday when staff was encouraged to wear casual clothes, we temporarily shut down four of the five elevators. Inside the stairwells, we created a festive environment with balloons, upbeat music, and posters promoting the Live Well program. The stairwells were filled with laughter and people getting a little exercise as they moved between meetings. We left just one elevator running, and those who insisted on using it had to wait a ridiculously long time while suffering playful scorn from passing colleagues.

The next morning, the CEO called my cell phone and barked, "Whose idea was it to turn off the goddamned elevators on Friday?" Then he laughed and said, "That was terrific. I saw people in the stairwells I haven't seen in years!" I breathed a sigh of relief. He went on to talk excitedly about the company's IPO with a potential valuation of more than $3 billion and his latest blood pressure numbers. He was definitely in need of our stress management program.

After developing and implementing CMC's Live Well program, I was hired by another CEO to create a wellness program for a trucking company. I used my relationships with Mayo Clinic and other providers to guide the program's creation.

The opportunity to work in Corporate Wellness reaffirmed my own broader definition that included the mind-body-spirit connection along the role of subtle energy on the physical body. I wondered if corporations would ever move beyond convention to embrace a more progressive definition. I knew they would if we could produce financial results.

Most importantly, these experiences made me eager to stretch definitions and limits while figuring out how I could best serve.

I was hungry for new and different perspectives. I read everything from business and self-help to more esoteric books. One book had beautiful drawings by artist Paul Hussenstamm. I searched online for his artwork. When I found his website, rather than send an email, I called the phone number in Los Angeles. A recorded message said Paul was traveling with Deepak Chopra and was in Atlanta. I laughed aloud as I left a message with my name and phone number, stating I lived in Atlanta and was interested in buying some artwork. This seemed ridiculously serendipitous.

When Paul returned my call, he explained he was at Lanier Islands Resort as an exhibitor at a four-day program called "Journey into Healing." He invited me to come see his artwork and be his guest for a day of the program. The event was promoted as an in-depth exploration of mind-body medicine with world-renowned physicians, authors, a team of guest experts, and Chopra Center co-founders Deepak Chopra and David Simon.

The next morning, I drove north to Lake Lanier and found the Emerald Pointe Resort. Paul encouraged me to take a seat in the audience and enjoy the program. Chopra and others presented from big armchairs on a dais at the front of a huge ballroom. Around the perimeter, a dozen exhibitors were ready to sell their art, jewelry, candles, and gifts during breaks.

I pulled a small pad out of my purse and quickly scribbled notes from two medical doctors talking about prana, chakras, consciousness, and the subtle body. They spoke truths that really resonated with me:

- We create our own reality.
- We are consciousness expressing through a physical body.
- The brain is an editing mechanism for a reality that exists beyond the transient interpretation of the five senses.

Hearing these concepts from speakers with credibility in science and medicine made me feel more optimistic than anything I had experienced in corporate wellness.

When the lights came up and the group took a break for lunch, the exhibitors sprang into action, selling their artistic creations. Outside on the resort patio, participants enjoyed an ayurvedic lunch prepared from recipes in *The Chopra Center Cookbook*. I stayed in the ballroom with Paul and learned the attraction of exhibiting at Chopra's programs was this built-in opportunity to sell to a captive audience. Participants were likely to buy some souvenir of their experience, so artwork, jewelry, and crafts were ideal.

I understood the privilege to be associated with the Chopra brand, but in addition to travel expenses, exhibitors paid a hefty percentage of sales revenue to Chopra's organization. Maybe I did not fully understand the math, but artists giving a sizeable chunk of their proceeds to a group already making hundreds of thousands of dollars from an event dedicated to consciousness and spirituality seemed curious. Chopra's business structure was the certainly anthesis of Dr. Patrick's Center.

Paul's artwork included beautiful, hand-painted mandalas. One in particular, with a bold, colorful design in the center surrounded by the sky and the ocean, got my attention. The painting was framed in a gorgeous piece of intricately carved dark wood. Paul smiled and said the title was *As Above, So Below*. I knew that was the one.

After lunch, Chopra led a guided meditation intended to help participants feel consciousness filling every cell of their bodies. With

Ascension, I could easily drop into a sense of fluidity and love in my heart center to find the indescribable beauty of divine presence. As I listened to Chopra's guided meditation, I felt something more cerebral. The words he spoke were inspiring but what I felt inside was different than with Gomati and Vasistha. It was a subtle distinction but I knew in my heart it was true.

When the meditation ended, I was ready to leave. Paul said goodbye, and as I walked to my car carrying *As Above, So Below*, I smiled at the unexpected serendipity of a backstage pass into a professional seminar designed for spiritual seekers and led by a well-known doctor with his name on the door of his own center. I was grateful to Paul and all the unseen forces that had created another remarkable opportunity for me to explore the intersection of business, health, spirituality, and wellness—and for the colorful reminder of *As Above, So Below*.

CHAPTER 8
Satisfaction and Suffering

I sat sipping a mug of beer and fondly reliving my undergraduate days of the late eighties in a bar called Satisfaction near the Duke campus. The only person I could hear above the music was Jessie, the young woman sitting directly across the table. It was the early 2000s, and Jessie and I were among a group of alumni who had traveled to Durham for a volunteer leadership conference.

Because Satisfaction was iconic among Duke students, our group had chosen it for our evening outing. Over the deafening bar noise, I discovered Jessie had grown up in Atlanta within a half-mile of my condo. She described her family, including her mom, a successful entrepreneur who had built several companies and won dozens of awards. Jessie insisted on introducing us, so when I got back to Atlanta, her mother Claire and I met for coffee.

As Jessie predicted, Claire and I had many common interests and connections. I was growing a small business; Claire had grown and sold two and was well into her third. She was on the board of directors of both private and public companies; I was on the board of one privately held company. She was active and engaged in civic, political, and charitable activities, and I was aspiring to do so. Nearly every month after our first meeting, Claire invited me to an event she sponsored. From charitable and political fundraisers to hosting a visiting dignitary to organizing some new initiative in Atlanta, her invitations were frequent and she was often in the news for receiving another award or accolade.

In addition to seeing each other at big events, we also met for lunch, and I observed the humanness behind her public persona. She talked about the challenges of raising daughters who were both accomplished but not on great terms with one another and her frustration at not being able to heal that dynamic.

By 2009, we had gotten to know one another quite well and we met for her birthday lunch at a trendy spot called Spice Market. I listened as Claire told wonderful stories from her childhood. Her father had been a naval aviator and when Claire was in her early teens, the small, private plane he was piloting crashed and he was killed.

As she spoke, in my mind's eye I saw what appeared to be a storm cloud with thunder and lightning right behind her. It was a sunny day, so I just observed the image quietly. She told me how her father, who had been a naval aviator, had died when the small, private plane he was piloting crashed. She was in her early teens at the time. I again observed the storm image. When she finished the story, I asked if there might be a reason I sensed a storm cloud as she spoke of her father. She smiled and said, "Yes; his nickname was Stormy."

Claire was curious if such imagery was common for me. I said I thought it was an innate capability I was becoming more fully aware of. Claire spoke of her own interest in holistic health, alternative treatments, and metaphysics. She named several practitioners she used in Atlanta and other cities. Then she wrote a name, Shyamala, and a phone number on the back of her business card and pushed the card across the table. Without a lot of explanation, she encouraged me to make an appointment.

Claire's success in the mainstream business world conferred credibility, and two weeks later, I had my first appointment with Shyamala. I had already experienced a medical intuitive, acupuncture, Network Spinal Analysis, energy work, and other alternative modalities. Two weeks later, I had my first experience of CranioSacral Therapy (CST) and SomatoEmotional Release (SER).

In the session, I rested peacefully on Shyamala's cushy massage table as she placed her fingertips in different spots along my back, neck, and head. She seemed to instinctively know exactly where to make contact and just how much pressure to apply.

Shyamala encouraged me to tune into my own rhythms and awareness. Sometimes I was so relaxed I fell asleep. Other times, Shyamala would ask me to describe what I was feeling or experiencing in my body. Often, emotions surfaced unexpectedly and without warning tears rolled silently down my cheeks.

Shyamala made me feel safe and in turn, I trusted her with intimate details of my life. I felt I could speak my disappointments and vulnerabilities and she helped me to release whatever arose.

One year into our sessions, Shyamala suggested I take a class in CST. She was an international instructor and teaching an upcoming course in Atlanta. I saw myself as a businessperson, so taking a class for practitioners seemed entirely illogical. But I felt curiously drawn by Shyamala's invitation, so I enrolled and spent three days with fifty other students, many of whom were using the class for continuing education credits to fulfill licensing requirements.

On the first day of class, we introduced ourselves. Every student was a therapist of some variety—massage, occupational, or physical—but surprisingly, very few had actually received treatment. I introduced myself as an entrepreneur, supply chain consultant, and recipient of CST. Despite having no formal training in anatomy or physiology, I felt comfortable in the group since Shyamala had been my personal practitioner. I knew firsthand how CST was practiced by the instructor leading the training class, and that gave me confidence and a sense of belonging.

After learning the theory and mechanics behind what I had already experienced in private sessions, we practiced the new techniques on our classmates. A year of sessions with Shyamala was like an apprenticeship and a huge head start in the class. I loved contrasting my experience with Shyamala and treatment from trainees attending their first class.

Dr. John Upledger, the founder of CranioSacral Therapy, created a 10-Step Protocol all students used to structure their sessions. I noticed I would rarely complete even a few steps in the protocol before my attention was intuitively drawn to a particular area of the recipient's body. From my sessions with Shyamala, I knew she experienced the same phenomena. As a student, I tried to adhere to the protocol, but I found it more efficient when I followed my intuition and inner wisdom.

We were encouraged to do practice sessions, so I recruited friends. I was delighted to find I enjoyed the experience and they seemed to benefit. When I started the 10-Step, my intuitive instincts kicked in and guided my focus and hands in an utterly mystical and delightful way. I connected with some much larger source of information and a deep sense of extrasensory, metaphysical knowing.

I bought a portable massage table and saw clients in their homes. As my friends began to refer others, I worked with people I had never met. Other than what they told me on the phone while giving me directions to their homes, I knew nothing about them prior to the session. This dynamic of not knowing accelerated my reliance on intuition and enabled me to trust my inner knowing even more deeply. Often, I would perceive information the client had never verbalized, and that led to awareness of emotions, thoughts, or memories ready to be released. Every time I validated this process, my confidence deepened.

One such instance happened with a woman named Laine who was one of my first paid clients and a referral from a mutual friend. When I arrived at her home with my portable massage table, she ushered me into her basement den. I immediately liked the deep, earthy feel of the room. I knew Laine's teenage daughter had passed away unexpectedly a few years earlier, creating a lot of grief and stress.

Laine and I exchanged small talk before she made herself comfortable on the table. As I started the 10-Step, my hands felt rhythms in her body and my extrasensory perception kicked in, providing another stream of information. Several minutes into the session, I felt guided to sit on a stool and hold my hands around her heart. I placed one palm under her mid-thoracic spine (the middle section of the spine) and one hand gently over her thymus (a small gland high on the chest and part of the lymphatic system). As I listened to her talk, my hands felt like they were glued in place. I trusted this sensation. Whenever I got a visceral sense to hold a particular position, I stayed until I felt completion and a release of my hands.

Laine closed her eyes and dropped into a very relaxed state. The room seemed to get very still, and she was silent. I felt her rhythm drop into a *still point*, a time when the body enters its deepest healing state. I felt an odd inner knowing there was something she was not telling me. I continued gently holding one hand over her heart and one beneath it while in a space of deep compassion.

Eventually, I asked Laine in a soft whisper if there was anything more she would like me to know. She opened her eyes as tears rolled down her cheeks. She said she had done something terrible the previous week. She had come home late for a conference call, so she had parked in the driveway and rushed inside. It was a hot, sunny August afternoon in Georgia. After the call, she went back out to the car to discover she had forgotten the family dog, Lucy, in the backseat.

Laine was devastated by Lucy's death and panicked. Rather than admit her negligence and share the tragedy with her family, she dragged the dog's lifeless body out of the car and into the bushes, hoping to make it seem like an accident. For whatever reason, she could not accept responsibility for the mistake. All the emotion and guilt were bottled up and weighing heavily on her.

As I focused on her heart, she accessed her grief and it softened into self-compassion. I don't know if Laine ever shared Lucy's true cause of death with her family, but I do know acknowledging it privately in session helped get it off her chest metaphysically and emotionally.

In my work with clients and in life, I observe people quietly suffering as they hold onto guilt, memories of some painful experience, or belief systems they have outgrown. Part of them desperately wants to let it go, but another part is stuck in an old paradigm, reluctant to acknowledge truth for fear it would require some reorganization of life. This dynamic creates a lot of internal tension even if it remains hidden behind a long list of accomplishments, accolades, and upbeat social media posts. I have seen high-functioning, successful, well-adjusted people hiding deep pain and fear, which has colored their experience of life and eventually undermined their health.

My intuitive insights often center on uncomfortable experiences and trauma that is ready to be healed - as if the subconscious mind is steering my attention to the most potent opportunity.

Sometimes these experiences are buried deep in the psyche, and other times, they are just waiting for a gentle nudge and the right moment to surface and be released.

CHAPTER 9
Integrating Spirituality and Business

At the same time I was honing my skills in CranioSacral Therapy, my company Solertis was awarded a project at Maidenform, a $500 million company selling women's undergarments and shapewear. My colleague Nigel was a rock star with projects involving productivity-based compensation plans for workers in the garment industry and his credentials won us the gig.

Maidenform's distribution campus in Fayetteville, North Carolina, housed four large warehouses with more than 200 employees on a pay-for-performance program and a gain share plan rewarding workers by sharing the savings from improved performance. Maidenform's programs were outdated and overdue for an update.

The project would affect the pay of members of UNITE Local 565, the labor union representing the hourly workers. The union's job was to protect workers' pay. Maidenform management's job was to keep the operation efficient and profitable. Our job at Solertis was to change the pay structure while serving as an intermediary and reassuring both sides of fairness. If Local 565 officers believed we were not impartial, they were entitled to bring in another firm to refute our work.

The first day was typical for a consulting kickoff with introductions and tours of the facilities. Steve, the vice president overseeing the campus, and his staff seemed happy to have us on site to help, but they told us to expect our meeting with union leaders to be contentious. They predicted a highly charged, antagonistic tone with shouting and open hostility. Security officers would be posted outside the conference room. We had been hired to do a supply chain project, but now we were being prepared for a conference room brawl.

The weekend before the meeting, I went to The Light Center, a meditation retreat near Asheville, with Gomati and Vasistha. When I arrived, Vasistha greeted me by saying he was delighted I was becoming a *Oneness Blessing Giver*. What? Apparently, I had misread the event information—this was not an Ascension retreat, but I had driven three hours from Atlanta and knew the power of synchronicity, so I went with it and enjoyed the weekend.

I learned to give *deeksha*, a transfer of energy intended to bring about growth in consciousness, and a chant to invoke the Divine. As always at these retreats, I enjoyed hiking to Meditation Rock and just being in nature with no cell phone service. On Sunday evening, I drove home from Asheville and prepared to fly to the other side of the state of North Carolina and a much different state of consciousness.

Back in Fayetteville, Steve cautioned us the union had unexpectedly flown in some of its top leaders, increasing the likelihood of conflict. In my mind's eye, I envisioned the upcoming meeting and a completely different outcome. Nigel and I had worked together for many years, and clients had always trusted us. Nigel was a tall, stately Brit with a delightful accent, white hair, glasses, and a soft-spoken, endearing demeanor. While distinguished-looking with neatly pressed trousers, classic button-down shirts, and dress shoes, he was also approachable. He had reviewed dozens of gain share plans, and I had done dozens of operations reviews. We certainly had the experience, and we understood the potential effect of our work on people who were making just a few dollars an hour more than minimum wage.

On the morning of the meeting with the union representatives, I sat alone in my rental car outside the main office. I could see the windows of the conference room. I figured there must have been some purpose to accidentally becoming a *oneness blessing giver* over the weekend, so I sat in the car and gave *deeksha* to the entire building. I closed my eyes and dropped into my heart space, chanted the invocation, and gave the blessing. I set an intention that everyone involved would experience the highest and best outcome possible.

Minutes later, I was seated in the conference room with eleven representatives from UNITE Local 565 along with Steve, Nigel, and someone from Human Resources. Nigel and I had a PowerPoint outlining our backgrounds and some case studies. Nigel garnered laughs with some of his stories. The meeting was surprisingly congenial, with none of the hostility or confrontational tone we had been told to expect. I took this as a great sign since our role was to bridge two seemingly conflicting sets of objectives.

After the meeting, it was time to get to work. The project was announced and we were introduced to the workers. We remained approachable because of the project's unique nature and the need to earn the union's trust. Nigel was a time study expert. As a worker moved through a maze of colorful bras and panties, picking and sorting garments into shipping cartons neatly arranged on carts, Nigel followed with a stopwatch and clipboard, timing movements down to tenths of a second.

Workers might have felt intimidated by a tall British gentleman watching their every move, but Nigel was a pro. He explained everything and created a sense of safety by being approachable and dispelling any fears over unfair changes that would hurt their paychecks.

The warehouse held miles of racks with the latest styles in bras, panties, and shapewear already on hangers just like you would see them in a retail store. As I walked the warehouse, I tried not to giggle at the frilly panties, crazy animal prints, or the triple D cup size bras big enough to wear as a helmet. The warehouse made my own underwear drawer look pretty blah.

Fayetteville was home to Fort Bragg, one of the world's largest military installations with 50,000 personnel. When I left the distribution center to go to our hotel or to a restaurant, I went from an environment full of products celebrating sensuality, femininity, and the female body into an environment designed to promote discipline, detachment, and militaristic structure. It was a strange juxtaposition of yin and yang.

Delta Airlines had several direct flights each day from Fayetteville to Atlanta, making travel super-convenient. I often sat next to officers from Fort Bragg who were headed overseas or returning on the last leg of a long journey home from some faraway base.

On one particular flight, I sat next to a defense contractor who was headed back to Afghanistan after a visit home to see his family. He was based at Bagram Air Base where he worked in food service. This was the third time I had sat next to an employee of this same food service company, and this guy was the most talkative of the three. During the flight, he provided a peek into life at a remote military base in the Afghan mountains. He said Bagram was a small city, and he was basically a cook in a restaurant. Although his job took him away from his family for months, the pay was very good and tax-free. On the short flight, I felt a nice rapport with this man and loved hearing about a part of the world entirely foreign to me.

Landing at Hartsfield, I was home, and he was just beginning his long journey back to Bagram. As we pulled into our arrival gate, I had a sudden flash of intuition. I turned to him and blurted out, "President Obama is coming to visit you." He furled his brow and said, "Really? I don't think so."

It was an unexpected, unsought flash of insight.

Just hours later, President Obama did indeed fly to Afghanistan and visit Bagram. *The New York Times* wrote that Obama "swept

CHAPTER 9: INTEGRATING SPIRITUALITY AND BUSINESS

into a dark and windy Afghanistan for a surprise holiday season visit with troops, wrapped in a tight cocoon of secrecy and security." The original plan had been for Obama to fly by helicopter to Kabul to see Afghan President Karzai, but high winds kept him on the ground at Bagram where he spoke to 3,800 troops and gave out five purple hearts.

I loved the mysticality of intuitive awareness and wondered if my seatmate on the flight from Fayetteville got back to Bagram in time to meet the president.

By month nine of our project, I was eager to finish. I had traveled in and out of the country several times and to other client sites in Sarasota, Wichita, and Omaha. I was taking more classes in CranioSacral Therapy and seeing clients. Nigel was finally done chasing people with a stopwatch, and we had two assistants compiling the staggering volume of data for our final report.

Fayetteville was not exactly a culinary mecca, and Nigel was a staunch vegan, so for our last dinner there, we chose Golden Corral. Its "endless buffet" seemed to stretch for miles with some vegetarian options that had not been submerged in a deep fryer. One of us would go to the buffet and load up a plate while the other watched my laptop as we worked on our presentation.

At some point, I looked across the room and was pretty certain Nigel had ladled the meat version of the chili into his bowl. When he came back to the table, it sure looked like there were hunks of meat in his chili. I watched as he took a spoonful, expecting him to grimace and spit it out. By the third spoonful, I was amused and said, "Hey, Nigel, you know that has meat in it, right?" He smiled, and in his lovely British accent he said, "Yes, and it's quite good."

Nigel had relaxed his vegan absolutism long enough to try something different just as UNITE Local 565 and Maidenform management both relaxed and found common ground. The leaders had realized their mutual dependency and shared objectives after years of conflict.

Months later, Maidenform was acquired by Hanes Brands, and as far as I know, none of our recommendations had ever been implemented. Nonetheless, we planted seeds for a new paradigm of leadership with respect for others no matter their title or the size of their paycheck. I sensed leadership dynamics were shifting globally, stretching way beyond Fayetteville.

While we were paid to create a new compensation plan, my greatest accomplishment came from quietly using aspects of spiritual traditions in a mainstream business environment. Those precious moments I spent alone in my rental car just before our meeting showed me how intention and a harmonious field could influence an outcome.

The more I applied spiritual and metaphysical concepts to mainstream business, the more fullness and satisfaction I felt and the more curious I became. Weaving these two seemingly disparate worlds together produced results beyond anything I promised in a contract or wrote in a Scope of Work document. I was being hired to do one thing, but ultimately, I began to realize I was providing so much more.

Although captivating, it was also terrifying to think I might actually reveal more of my unconventional capabilities to conventional business people. I feared clients might scorn or reject me for openly utilizing more of my mystical side, even if it was to their benefit. Little did I know I would spend years learning to cautiously tiptoe into providing more of this combination to all my clients, carefully gauging receptivity and looking for just enough wiggle room to open them to new possibilities.

CHAPTER 10
Egypt: Surrendering to Sekhmet

Despite juggling supply chain projects in several cities in late 2010, I decided to travel to Egypt and Jordan for two weeks on a group trip guided by Isabelle and her business partner, Eugenia. I had been working with Isabelle consistently for two years and was excited to journey with her to an ancient land. The theme of the trip was "Uncovering Your Inner Reservoir of Strength, Truth, and Peace." It was an initiatory journey into the process of conscious evolution of the Self. I was definitely eager to tap into my inner reservoir and flew from Atlanta to JFK to meet our group. I prepared for the trip by reading several books on Egypt along with the twenty-page study guide, but I soon discovered nothing had really prepared me for this adventure.

At JFK, Isabelle and Eugenia found a quiet corner in the boarding area for our flight to Cairo, and we gathered for a ceremony to enter into an "energy time-tunnel." Although I could not see anything with my physical eyes, I felt a geometric structure come into alignment. Once the tunnel was established, I had a certain sense of safety inside a cohesive group of travelers sharing an expansive experience.

We flew overnight, arrived in Cairo, and checked into the Mena House. I had opted to share a room and was matched with a woman named Laura. Serendipitously, I knew Laura's husband from my consulting work. Jim and I had met a year before the trip to Egypt. When I saw him at a conference just a few weeks before my trip, I learned he and Laura had separated and were getting a divorce.

Our first excursion required an early wake up and short bus ride to Sakkara and the Step Pyramid. From inside the massive enclosure wall at the main entrance, the pyramid looked like a giant layer cake with six terraced levels. We walked through a long colonnade lined with tall columns into a huge open space. As I looked at the colossal pyramid across the courtyard, my attention suddenly went to my feet. I was wearing durable Merrill sandals, but I felt like I was stepping on electrical lines. I looked down at the dirt and saw nothing, but I sensed superhighways crisscrossing underground with impulses moving rapidly. I tiptoed around before Eugenia told me I was sensing planetary ley lines and electromagnetic currents. Once my mind had an explanation, my feet were fine.

The pyramid's south and east faces were partly covered in scaffolding, and it looked as if bricks might come crashing down at any moment. I figured the pyramid was inaccessible, but our tour guide, Hatem, led us to an entrance below ground level. Inside, we walked down a dark corridor using just the light from our cell phones. I sensed we had entered a much larger space, and with every camera flash, I could see scaffolding stretching upward inside a tall vertical shaft. Isabelle and Eugenia led us in toning and creating extended vocal sounds without words or melody just to experience the effects on the body. We created beautiful resonance and healing harmonies inside this magnificent sound chamber. I loved toning in pitch black darkness, but I was happy to return to sunshine.

The following morning, we had a private visit to the Sphinx and the Giza Pyramids before other tourists arrived. Standing in front of the Sphinx, Eugenia and Isabelle spoke about the geometry and astronomy of its construction. I had read that when the pyramids were built, Regulus in the Leo constellation had risen a few moments before Ra, the sun. Then Ra arrived at the breast of

Leo, symbolizing the connection between the two realms, celestial and terrestrial. Similarly, our experiences took place in two parallel realms, in the sky and on the earth. Another instance of "As above, so below."

After we posed for photos in front of the Sphinx, I felt guided to walk around to the rear alone. There was nothing much to see, but I kept sensing something like a huge library buried deep beneath the Sphinx. I had read about the Hall of Records and was amazed to actually feel it. Some part of me yearned to journey into the vast repository of this cavernous archive. There was no physical doorway, so I stood alone basking in the sensation. What I felt was very compelling and yet surreal since the archive does not exist in this dimension.

After a camel ride up to the pyramids, we returned to the Mena House for brunch. I enjoyed a leisurely conversation with Bobbie, Lauralyn, Robert, and Diana, during which we shared the life circumstances that had inspired each of us to make the trip. One of the best parts of traveling with this group was sharing stories, and I enjoyed talking about experiences influenced by intuition, synchronicity, and inner knowing. I felt comfortable telling those stories with this group, and I discovered I had many to share.

The following morning, we had a 3 a.m. wakeup call for our flight to Aswan City. After deplaning, we transferred to a bus and joined a small convoy for a three-hour ride through the Sahara Desert to Abu Simbel. Our beautiful hotel had lovely, lush grounds and a swimming pool overlooking Lake Nasser. We went to an evening light show under the stars at the temples of Ramesses II and Queen Nefertari, but the main event was the following morning. We went back into Nefertari Temple for a private ceremony just as the sun was rising over the lake. Isabelle and Eugenia led us as we welcomed the new energy and anchored it in ourselves and into the matrix of the planet. This infusion was about creativity, pleasure, and identity—all aspects of myself I was reconfiguring. I loved anchoring harmonic energy that would benefit all of Earth, her residents, and me personally.

We returned to Aswan and took a small boat to Elephantine Island and the Khnum temple. Elephantine had rough terrain created by a maze of twenty-two previously dismantled temples. The study guide asked us to identify three negative, unresolved patterns we wanted to release.

Early in the trip, I had offered Laura use of my cell phone because hers was not working. She agreed to reimburse me for the cost, but her simply borrowing my phone triggered my awareness of several of my own patterns. Laura was in a relatively new relationship, and since she was using my phone, her heartfelt text exchanges with her beloved came into my account. Observing their devotion to one another helped to amplify a belief I harbored that I was nothing without a man.

Lifetimes of karma were exposed by simply loaning my phone to my roommate. For the ceremony at Elephantine, I ambitiously chose three painful patterns I knew were rooted deep inside me:

- the need to please or care for a man
- the need to be perfect
- the need to help people be better rather than just accepting them as they were

Eugenia and Isabelle held the ceremony on a hilltop. Each of us walked between two stone pillars to symbolize our commitment to piercing illusions and repetitive negative patterns. When it was my turn, I took several steps toward the pillars and felt as if I had walked into a transparent wall. A field of energy like a squishy invisible bubble repelled me. With focus and intention, I pushed myself through and felt waves of emotion. Even though I had simply walked between two stone columns, the emotion told me something significant had just happened.

Later, we boarded the Sonesta Nile Cruiser, the ship that would be our home for the next few days. In the morning, we had another pre-dawn wakeup call, and we were off to Philae, a nearby island, for a private sunrise ceremony at the Temple of Isis. The setting was gorgeous as the sun rose over the Nile between beautiful palm trees. As the study guide noted, it felt like floating in liquid love. I felt a profound sense of serenity in the Temple of Isis. I bent down to pick up a soft, white feather and smiled knowing the feather was an Egyptian symbol for Ma'at, divine truth, balance, universal order, harmony, and justice.

Back on the ship, Laura and I enjoyed the sunshine and stunning views of the Nile from lounge chairs on the top deck. Our destination was Kom Ombo, an unusual double temple—half was dedicated to a crocodile god called Sobek and half to the falcon-headed god Horus the Elder. The former represented darkness and primal feelings like fear. The latter was dedicated to light and the higher perspective. Unifying this duality was represented by neutrality in the center. Legend said initiates swam underwater through a dark, murky pool full of alligators and chose one of two channels. One led to air and life, and the other was a dead-end resulting in death. I winced, feeling a creepy, kinesthetic immersion into reptilian energy and irrational fear. As we walked back toward the boat, I was left wondering if I had been there before.

That night, we had dinner on the ship before a late trip to the temple of Edfu dedicated to Horus. Isabelle and Eugenia led a ceremony in the Holy of Holies. We encircled the Solar Boat, a wooden representation of the boat on which Horus traveled through the sky to his father, Osiris. We were guided to tune in to the lunar and solar energies and balance them within. We also tapped into memories of experiences from other lifetimes to awaken greater intuitive power. As we did this, something spooked the security guards, and we were abruptly ushered out. I smirked, wondering if they had felt our power and gotten nervous.

Outside, we took photos in the courtyard with two huge statues of Horus. Our cameras captured highly intricate geometric patterns contained within spherical shapes not visible to our physical eyes. My photos contained dozens of these small shimmering orbs. One particular orb was very bright and prominent in the foreground. I decided to name it Avi.

Day seven of the trip started uneventfully with breakfast on the ship and plans for an evening costume party. At lunchtime, I had no appetite, so I did yoga alone on the top deck. I loved the lush green papyrus growing along the Nile with dry desert mountains as their backdrop. At that moment, I felt more connected to Egypt than I had at any other time during the trip.

The study guide suggested we ask ourselves, "What are you choosing to become in this lifetime, and what is your innermost desire?" I thought about the possible answers but never settled on just one.

We docked in Luxor in late afternoon and took a bus to Karnak Temple, said to be the second-most visited historical site in Egypt after Giza. The long walkway from the bus into the temple was lined with a double row of sphinxes and packed with tourists. We veered away from the paved area and onto a dusty path where we stepped over yellow caution tape and made our way through ruins to a building not visible from the main part of Karnak. As I stood under scaffolding waiting to enter a chapel that seemed to be off limits, our guide Hatem approached me, looked me straight in the eye, and said, "The next five minutes will change your life."

He was not kidding.

Three of us at a time walked through a dark corridor to a small room and stood opposite an eight- or ten-foot-tall statue. In the dim light, I could see the huge lioness head and slim body of Sekhmet facing me. I knew her to be a fierce goddess representing the destructive energies necessary to break old patterns in order to find and incorporate wisdom and healing. A shaft of daylight from an opening in the ceiling provided the only light. I took a photograph and paused for a moment to sense the powerful presence engaging me from within the statue. I did not dare step any closer because I could already feel Sekhmet's potency from across the dark room.

As I stood mesmerized, someone called out and said my time was up. I went back through the dark corridor out into the warm afternoon sun feeling disoriented, like I might faint. I sat down on a rock overcome with emotion.

Something had touched me in that small room, and I wept. Hatem saw this and told me to sit on the rock while our group moved on to explore other areas of Karnak. He said something in Arabic to two nearby security guards holding rifles and then left. I sat alone weeping until he came back. Hatem was a big, gentle Egyptian, and after comforting me, he told me I needed to go back into the temple alone. I was extremely reluctant, but I knew he was right.

I moved slowly back into the dark chapel and stood cowering in front of Sekhmet. I did not take any photographs. I just cried.

Eventually, I made my way back outside, still unable to understand how a statue could elicit so much emotion. The part of me that was always in control dissolved in the presence of Sekhmet. In my own private initiation, I let go and melted into a river of tears.

Hatem was waiting for me when I came out. He led me through Karnak to an outdoor seating area where I could get a cold soda and stare at Sacred Lake. Isabelle's wisdom helped me see how the perfect set of circumstances aligned to open me to Sekhmet's power. Starting with the introspective time on the boat doing yoga, skipping lunch, and feeling deeply connected to the Nile, I had created the receptivity I needed to feel the full potency of the experience. This kind of surrender was a lesson I would continue learning for many years.

At Dendera and the Hathor temple, we carefully navigated dusty steps down into a long, narrow space guaranteed to aggravate claustrophobia. After we looked at the intricate hieroglyphs on the walls, the lights went out and we toned in darkness in the crypt. I had read about the Hathors in several books and knew they were multidimensional beings attuned to the power of sound. They lived in a natural state of joy. Twenty-foot-tall stone columns had carvings of their sweet faces and very distinct ears. They seemed oddly familiar like old friends.

At Abydos, I was eager to see the greatly revered Flower of Life. I had been introduced to this symbol when I devoured two volumes of writings by Drunvalo Melchizedek. The intricate pattern was formed by interlinking circles of the same diameter touching the previous circle's center. We walked to the back of the complex and the Osirion temple, which had large stone blocks at a lower elevation than the rest of the buildings. To see the carving, we walked down a ramp to the edge of some standing water where the flower was faintly visible under a large beam. I expected the original to be grand and spectacular, but it was surprisingly subdued.

We also had an amazing nighttime tour of Luxor temple where, like Karnak, the broad entrance was majestically lined by a double row of sphinxes lit in the darkness. A nearly full moon shined overhead, and the invisible orbs added their beautiful spherical shapes and geometric patterns to my flash photographs.

I ended the day with another cultural adventure at Pizza Hut with Hatem and two others where we tried the Egyptian version of deep-dish pizza and an orange soft drink called Mirinda. Both were delicious.

The following morning, I awoke and immediately noticed the back of my neck felt hot, sore, and swollen. Laura gasped and took a photo. I had a bright red welt from my hairline down to my collar. It looked like some creature from a sci-fi movie was trying to exit my body through the back of my neck. I went to breakfast and immediately found Isabelle. I was half-expecting her to send me to an emergency room. Instead, she congratulated me, saying this was completely natural and part of my expanding consciousness. She gave me a cool towelette, told me to drink water, and went back to eating her breakfast as if this were entirely routine. I had read about Egyptian mystery schools and wondered if this was related to some other lifetime. I was relieved the current version of me did not need medical attention.

Once back in Cairo at the Mena House, I paused to consider all that had happened since we had checked out eight days earlier. Lifetimes had passed, and I had grown in ways that required softening aspects of myself to allow others to grow. I understood how strengths I had deeply relied on and saw as valuable became liabilities when over-emphasized.

We returned to the Great Pyramid and found the Giza Plateau filled with people celebrating a holiday called Eid al-Adha and the Festival of the Sacrifice. From the same dusty parking area where I had dismounted from a camel just a week earlier, we were led up some exterior steps to an unmarked opening on the north face of the Great Pyramid. I would have never noticed the doorway in the vast, jagged side of the pyramid on my own.

Inside we began a steep climb. There were no stairs, so sheets of wood had been secured to the stone with two-by-fours nailed across them to create small steps. These narrow toeholds provided the only way to get traction up the vertical surface. The stone ceiling was so low we had to stoop during parts of the climb. I paused to take a photo of the steep steps in the darkness, and my flash captured one of the most beautiful orbs of the trip.

The last ten yards into the King's Chamber required crawling through a horizontal stone tunnel. Inside the chamber was a large square room with a high ceiling. The most prominent feature was a stone box, the sarcophagus.

The lights went out as we started our ceremony. We each sensed the configuration of energy and grids before walking across the dim room to the sarcophagus, climbing in, and lying down. I knew in the Mystery Schools of Egypt, the lid was actually placed on the sarcophagus and the initiate stayed inside with no oxygen while journeying into other dimensions and types of consciousness.

My day-to-day life was already a mystery school. As I lie in the sarcophagus, I set an intention to open to the mysteries of life and all the Light that I could possibly hold in this incarnation.

After, I climbed out and went to sit quietly along the wall with the others. Once we had completed our ceremony in the King's Chamber, we descended down to another corridor into the Queen's Chamber. When we took photographs, again it looked as if it were snowing orbs not visible to the naked eye.

Back outside, the sun had set and the moon was glowing brightly over the top of the Great Pyramid. I took a private moment in deep gratitude. I realized if I had continued hellbent to reach some artificial accomplishment, I would likely have missed these truly profound and life-altering experiences.

The next morning, we left Cairo and flew to Amman, Jordan, where the vibe could not have been more different than Egypt. We were required to pass through metal detectors at the hotel to get into the lobby. The flowers and furnishings were gorgeous, but the entire tone was militaristic. Our new tour guide had none of the warmth and friendliness of Hatem. I longed to be back on the Nile.

The Dead Sea Scrolls were among the artifacts we viewed, but more intriguing to me was the Dead Sea itself. While driving south on the King's Highway, one of the oldest trade routes in the world, we stopped at a resort for lunch and a swim. The Dead Sea is like a huge salt bath and its extremely high salinity makes it easy to float.

Rather than going to the spa for a treatment with local minerals, a brave group of us decided to make our own and completely coated ourselves with mud from the shore. I left my pink bikini visible, but every inch of skin was covered in black mud. The very properties that made the mud cling to my skin also made it nearly impossible to wash off, and for days my massive exfoliation continued. Perhaps this shedding was the physical manifestation of a larger process.

The next morning, we started the second part of our mission to anchor an infusion of new energy into the matrix of the Earth. Our journey into Petra began with a long walk through the immense and narrow sandstone gorge called the Siq or shaft. The deep slit in towering rocks was once an aqueduct, the water leaving smooth stones to create the winding pathway.

After almost a mile, we popped out into an open expanse where we could see the spectacular red color in patterns running in horizontal layers of sediment creating a rich tapestry of pinkish red swirls. The study guide encouraged us to connect to the iron in the rocks, in the molten core of the earth, and in our own hemoglobin. Iron oxide was the key ingredient in all three, and red was the color of the root chakra.

We held a ceremony to welcome more of the energies of creativity, pleasure, and strong self-identity into the body of the planet. I could feel this process occurring deep inside me simultaneously. Petra was one of the seven wonders of the world. Other than a few Bedouins raucously riding donkeys, I found it delightfully peaceful and majestic.

We ate our last meal of the trip at a traditional Jordanian restaurant where tall hookahs stood in the center of each table beckoning the brave. After our dinner celebration, we returned to the Amman airport. In the cramped boarding area just before the flight, we huddled together as Eugenia and Isabelle closed the energetic tunnel that had held us during our travels.

As the tunnel dissolved, I suddenly felt bereft. I realized it was up to me to hold that energy all by myself. I found my "inner reservoir of strength, truth, and peace" and stood inside a new energetic structure. This was an initiatory journey, and I was now responsible for holding this new level of sovereignty on my own.

Egypt and Jordan had offered a radical departure from the roles I typically played in my everyday life. Out of necessity and driven by an encounter with Sekhmet that rendered me unable to override my emotions, I had surrendered to vulnerability and the unknown. The cohesiveness of the group and the safe space created by my fellow travelers had empowered me to experience myself in new ways.

Back in Atlanta, Thanksgiving was days away. I typically spent the holiday eating a traditional feast with my family, but I politely turned down invitations and opted to stay home. I did a modified fast and drank tea, meditated, and did yoga. Late in the afternoon, I went for a long, slow walk in my neighborhood. I thought of the beautiful, precious orbs of light and playfully challenged Avi to give me a sign. As I waited to cross the street, I glanced at the license plate of a passing car—AVI 5999.

As my consciousness grew, so did my awareness of the magnitude of what had transpired during the trip and the significance of what was still unfolding. I was happy to be home with some space for integration. What I did not know was how soon the next adventure would begin.

CHAPTER 11
Brazil: "Surgery," and a New Normal

Days after returning from Egypt, I sat across the table from my friend, Anne, at one of our favorite brunch spots, telling stories from my trip and lamenting not having plans for New Years. I was headed to visit family in Kansas City for Christmas, but I had nothing planned after that. Anne looked across the table with a sly smile and said, "Come with us."

I had met Anne three years earlier on a flight to Fort Myers, Florida. We had discovered our homes were less than two miles apart in Atlanta, and we shared interests in spiritual teachings and traditions, holistic health, and alternative medicine. Anne was flying to Florida with her daughters to visit relatives, and I was on my way to Sanibel Island. Over the years, I got to know her family and attended events at her daughters' school. "Come with us" was a familiar refrain.

Anne, her oldest daughter, and one of her sisters were flying to Brazil the day after Christmas to see John of God, Joao de Deus. I had long been fascinated by stories of miracles and spontaneous healings at the Casa de Dom Inácio de Loyola in Abadiânia, Brazil, and I had read an article in Oprah's *O Magazine* but had never considered going. I was not suffering from any chronic illness, but I was curious about the experiences people had there.

I managed to get an interview at the Brazil consulate in Atlanta where I was told it would be impossible to secure a travel visa before the holidays. However, when the clerk heard I was going to see John of God, my visa was magically expedited.

From what I read, most first timers hired a guide to help with protocols and logistics at the Casa. A friend recommended Immanuel, the guide he had used. Immanuel had been in Abadiânia for five years after initially going to the Casa for treatment of self-described brain seizures that left him unable to continue his work in environmental law at Stanford University. He spoke five languages and knew everyone around the Casa. Each time we emailed, I felt a pleasant connection.

Four of us flew together and hired a private car from the airport in Brasilia to Abadiânia. The driver dropped us at a pousada (an inn) called Luz Divina, and once inside the courtyard, I spotted Immanuel. Whatever history we had in some other lifetime, I watched it become apparent to him too as our eyes connected in a moment of recognition.

Luz Divina was completely full, so I was staying nearby at Caminho Encantado. The properties were a few short blocks apart geographically, but worlds apart in other ways. My room at Caminho was big and modern with a cushy mattress, nice furnishings, and sweeping views of a beautiful canyon. While aesthetically pleasing, the vibe felt much different than at Luz. I felt at home at Luz but unsettled at Caminho. The difference was apparent immediately.

The next day, Immanuel took me to visit the sacred waterfall on the Casa's grounds and to get a treatment in the crystal beds. From what I had read, these activities usually took place after a first meeting with Joao de Deus, but Immanuel was an approved guide and could use his own discretion.

The Tuesday after Christmas proved to be a very quiet time. Once on the grounds of the Casa, we followed a dusty road down a long hill and paused at a little flat area where Immanuel gave

CHAPTER 11: BRAZIL, "SURGERY," AND A NEW NORMAL

me instructions. I would cross three small footbridges during the walk to the waterfall. At the first bridge, I was to pause and state everything I intended to release. At the second bridge, I was to state intentions for what I wanted to bring in, and at the third bridge, I was to surrender any outcome to the Divine. As Immanuel gave instructions, a beautiful butterfly circled us, showing its yellow and black colors with bright red tips on its wings. I smiled, knowing butterflies were an omen of transformation.

As I headed down the path alone, a small dog appeared. I looked around but did not see its owner. At the first bridge, the dog laid down crosswise in the middle of it as if to insist I stop. The bridge was narrow, and I was not inclined to try to step over the dog. It lay quietly as if waiting until I had completed my assignment, and when the dog sensed completion, it moved on. While entirely unexplained, I trusted the dog's wisdom.

The sound of the waterfall grew louder until I could see it. Once there, the dog lay down in the shallows as I waded in until I was directly under the icy cold, falling water. I felt invigorated and filled with joy. The falls were beautiful and cleansing. I felt great reverence for the sacredness of this spot and all those who had visited and found healing here. I felt serenity within the power of nature, along with a full spectrum of emotions. When I turned to share my enthusiasm with the dog, it was gone.

I walked slowly back over the bridges and up the hill, this time without the dog. I could see Immanuel holding off other visitors. We walked back up the hill and sat in the gardens. I recounted my experience and the serendipity of the dog in slowing my pace. I learned it was very unusual to get time in the waterfall alone.

Next, I went to a crystal bed in a private room on the grounds of the Casa. Once I was lying comfortably on a table, an attendant lowered an apparatus hanging over the bed so seven crystals were positioned above my body, spaced from my head to my toes and projecting the rainbow colors of the chakras. I relaxed and felt a sense of melting. I cried tears of gratitude with a sense of amazement about everything I had experienced in the past month. When I was done, I sat in the garden and wrote in my journal as I looked out over the hillside.

Back at Luz Divina, I found a lovely lunch spread with organic papaya, fresh vegetable salads, avocado, rice, and beans waiting. Immanuel had made arrangements for me to eat meals at Luz Divina, and the lunch group was eager to hear about my adventures at the waterfall. Conversation ebbed and flowed for hours.

After lunch, I sat under a huge tree and wrote in my journal. I wondered what it would be like to stay here for several years as Immanuel had done, and I quickly realized my greater contribution would be bringing the powerful energy of sacred sites back to my daily life.

Wednesday was the first day of the week Joao de Deus saw people in the Casa. We lined up early ahead of the busloads of Brazilians expected from in country. The line began to move slowly, and eventually, we were inside a large room where dozens of people dressed in white sat silently with their eyes closed. This was the first of two large spaces in the Casa called Current Rooms.

The energy felt very heavy as if the room held the weight of old resentments, burdens, and memories being released. I could also sense a huge column of energy spiraling up and out into the sky. As the line made a left turn into the meditation room, I felt the energy shift and intensify. The benches were packed with people shoulder-to-shoulder in deep meditation. At the front of the room, I glimpsed some of the biggest quartz crystals I had ever seen, and beside them I saw Joao de Deus.

Immanuel had enough experience to know Joao was channeling an entity called Dr. Augusto, but this meant nothing to me. I watched as first timers stood before Joao for a few seconds; he would say some words in Portuguese, and then they would move on. We were each expected to give our handwritten questions to a transla-

CHAPTER 11: BRAZIL, "SURGERY," AND A NEW NORMAL

tor who would read them to Joao de Deus. Immanuel was fluent in Portuguese, and he had barely spoken my first question before Joao de Deus scribbled on a small pad of paper, ripped the sheet off, and handed it to Immanuel. We turned and walked out.

Those few seconds in front of Joao de Deus were brief and rather unremarkable. Immanuel translated the flowing script in blue ink punctuated by a few squiggles and said I had been granted ten visits to the waterfall and would get more instructions later that day.

I ate the special soup provided by the Casa and sat in the garden before going to hang out at Luz. A few hours later, I walked back to the Casa to get my next set of instructions and was told I would have "surgery" the following morning. I had heard about "surgery" and was eager to experience it firsthand.

I awoke to a misty, overcast sky and found Immanuel already at the Casa sipping coffee. He got me a cup and we stood waiting and enjoying the cool, gray clouds. At 8:30 a.m., the surgeries began. I said goodbye to Immanuel and followed the group to a room filled with people sitting on wooden benches that looked like church pews. Everyone was dressed in white, and I noted five mediums standing around the room. I sat down and closed my eyes as a woman began singing and chanting in Portuguese. I could not understand the words, but her voice was angelic.

After a few minutes, I sensed a masculine presence enter. With my eyes closed, I felt a profoundly potent field of energy moving through the room. I sat completely still and sensed activity in the space surrounding my body. I felt as if I were being both tickled and stretched but no one actually touched me. I kept my eyes closed as this potent male presence embodied by Joao de Deus gave an audible blessing in Portuguese. As he left the room, the sensations stopped.

The entire "surgery" lasted less than twenty minutes. I opened my eyes and stood up to walk outside with the others who had been in the room for surgery. While my physical body seemed the same, another part of me felt huge. I had the urge to duck, even though the doorway was more than eight feet tall.

I walked outside and found Immanuel, who insisted I move slowly and take a taxi back to Caminho. I was back in bed by 9:30 a.m. and thoroughly bored. Soup was delivered at 10:30. I read for a bit and fell asleep. I dreamed I was in the garden at Luz Divina. I was awakened by a knock as a staff member brought me lunch. I did not feel hungry, just restless. I checked email and discovered a message from the owner of Luz Divina. We had a rapid exchange online and made arrangements for me to move from Caminho Encantado to a room that had just become available at Luz.

The Casa's post-surgery rules said twenty-four hours of rest, but I figured a move to Luz would support my recovery. I packed quickly and a driver arrived to move me and my bags. By 5 p.m., I was happily unpacking in Room 4 at Luz Divina. Unlike my deluxe room at Caminho, Room 4 at Luz had no windows and was smaller than any of my dorm rooms at Duke—no closet and a small metal cot with a thin mattress. I was delighted to be there. At this point, supportive energy was more important than luxury.

Ten hours had passed since my "surgery," and I felt tired. I ate a light supper alone at a small table while studying the colorful, geometric design covering much of the wall outside Room 4. The exterior was painted a happy yellow with a white triangle inside a circle surrounded by huge, bold rays of bright colors emanating from the center outward. Immanuel stopped by to check on me, and an hour later, I fell asleep listening to him and the musical ensemble in the courtyard laughing and rehearsing for the New Year's Eve celebration.

On the last day of 2010, I awoke before dawn to roosters crowing. Dogs barking during the night had awakened me, yet I was completely relieved to finally be at Luz Divina. I got a cup of coffee and strolled the grounds, enjoying the trees and the labyrinth. I shed a few tears of gratitude thinking how life is such an adventure. Just nineteen days earlier, I had expected a boring end to the year. Now I was in Brazil, energized by possibilities and making new friends.

The kitchen made me a nice plate of scrambled eggs, and I ate in happy solitude while listening to birds sing. I noticed a whiteboard mounted on the wall of the dining area. The board listed all the rooms at Luz Divina, who was staying in each room, their surgery status, and who was assigned to care for them. I smiled reading the names of people who had been strangers a few days earlier and laughed thinking about the lawsuits if a hotel in the United States listed all the guest names and health statuses on a giant sign in the breakfast bar.

As I walked back to Room 4, I saw the resident cat, also called Luz, sunbathing on the stone path. Luz was adored by guests, but I was allergic, so I stepped over her and continued to my room. I managed to create enough floor space for my yoga mat and did a few poses. I felt the preciousness and depth of connection to all life—human, plant, creature, and Earth herself.

Feeling humbled, I began to cry. I heard Luz meowing outside my door and allowed her to come in. She brushed against my legs in a gesture that comforted me. I left the door open for ventilation, and it started to rain. I lay down on my cot watching Luz watch the rain and felt a deep sense of serenity.

During my time in Abadiânia, I intuited there was a book I was to get from Immanuel. Over and over, I imagined him showing me a paperback book. One day, he felt guided to bring me a book by Rudolf Steiner about Egyptian myths and mysteries. Strangely, I felt no inclination to read it. Instead, my attention went to a sticker with the book's price in euros.

At that exact moment, Immanuel's phone rang. It was a Skype call from his fiancée Sylvie, who was in the States. Her call was timed perfectly to offer the missing link. Although the book was about Egypt, they had actually purchased it while in France working with the energy of Mary Magdalene. Immanuel and Sylvie shared dozens of intriguing stories from their time in the South of France.

My intuition about the book had nothing to do with the book's subject, author, or contents. It was one link in a chain of synchronicities. This moment reinforced trust in my intuition even when the logic was unclear. I knew this was a nudge from the Universe to explore Mary Magdalene.

Monday was a business day. I participated in a client call from my cot in Room 4 and felt a tug to get back to work. I knew I was reaching completion in Abadiânia, and I was eager to sleep in my own bed. During the final seven weeks of 2010, I had barely been home. Delta allowed me to change my flight without penalty. Immanuel arranged a car to take me to Brasilia, and Luz the cat meowed endlessly while I packed. I said goodbye to people I had just met but felt I had known forever. I was deeply grateful for the connections that had led me to the Casa and to Immanuel.

We arrived in Brasília early, so the driver suggested a visit to the Temple of Good Will. Dedicated to meditation and introspection, the temple was described as "architecture in the service of ecumenical solidarity." Its dimensions and proportions are based on the numbers seven and one. The building's profile was breathtaking, with its seven pyramids joined to form a cone holding the biggest raw crystal ever found in Brazil. Most of the interior space was below ground, and one of the coolest features was a black-and-white spiral pattern of tiles embedded in the floor of a huge open space.

I took off my shoes and followed the black path in a narrowing spiral, feeling the energy intensifying with each step. When I arrived at the center of the spiral and of the entire pyramid structure, I stood directly beneath the crystal and felt like I was being struck by lightning. I thought I might faint.

I stood there for a moment, then spiraled back out along the white path. The brilliant design and geometry with a forty-pound crystal overhead created a potent vortex and the perfect way to end my time in Brazil.

At five the next morning, after a nine-hour flight, I found myself in Hartsfield airport standing in line to clear customs. A thousand people had deplaned from international flights at the same time. Beyond jetlag, I felt raw and picked up odd information about people as I passed them in the long lines snaking back and forth through customs. I had a new level of empathy for empaths. I could not wait to get home, unpack, integrate, and figure out my new normal.

NOTE: In 2018, eight years after I visited Abadiânia, allegations of sexual abuse by João Teixeira de Faria, the man called John of God, were made public. In 2019, he was sentenced for abusing multiple women. As written in this chapter, I was only in the presence of John of God for a few minutes during my visit. My experience in Abadiânia was about the community created there more than any single individual. I am deeply sorry for anyone who suffered while seeking care at the Casa.

CHAPTER 12
Rebirth in Berkeley

After Egypt and Brazil, I continued to straddle two worlds, keeping one foot planted in my supply chain consulting business as the other pivoted to different types of work in wellness. I had tried the Center for Holistic Health, corporate wellness, and seeing private clients one-on-one for CranioSacral Therapy. I knew I was heading in a new direction professionally and I trusted my next steps to be revealed.

In the meantime, a consulting project in Omaha had been my focus for several months. One upside was traveling with Bill, one of my favorite industrial engineers. A consulting project in Omaha had been my focus for several months and one upside was traveling with Bill, one of my favorite industrial engineers. I first met Bill in the 1990s when his office was across from mine at Ingram Book Company. He had a great "can do" attitude and always had me laughing. After he retired, I hired him to do contract work. We had known each other so long we often finished one another's sentences.

Bill was not much into holistic or alternative therapies, but after working all day in Omaha, and grabbing a bite to eat, he often agreed to be my practice patient for CranioSacral Therapy. I had learned to work inside a client's mouth to resolve trauma in my most recent class, and Bill was a great sport as I donned blue medical gloves and honed my skills.

Our final project presentation was at the client's headquarters in Greensboro, North Carolina, and after we finished, I felt a sense of finality beyond just this one project. I was eager to find my way into wellness and had a meeting at Duke Center for Integrative Medicine the following day. I dropped Bill off at Greensboro airport and drove across I-85 while listening to the audiobook *Ancient Hermetic Secrets to Alchemy* and wondering *What next?*

The following week I stood in Hartsfield airport waiting to board a flight, gazing mindlessly into space. I did a double-take when I spotted a woman wearing a shirt with a familiar logo. I got closer, and sure enough, it was the logo for Upledger Institute.

I introduced myself to Mysti, the international education coordinator at Upledger Institute. She was on her way to a training seminar. I took this synchronicity as a nudge and went online to register for the SomatoEmotional Release 1 (SER1) course. I had already been considering expanding my training to include SER, and seeing Mysti was a wink from the Universe.

I had experienced my own SomatoEmotional releases dozens of times during sessions with Shyamala and the practitioners I visited during my travels to other cities. In his books, Dr. John Upledger defined SER as the spontaneous expression of emotion retained, suppressed, or isolated within the body. When an injury, trauma, or pattern was ready to be released and the physical body sensed an environment conducive to this, it would spontaneously move to a position to facilitate release. As this release happened, tissues softened, energy was expelled, and the body returned to greater health and performance.

One of the benefits of taking classes after dozens of treatment sessions with Shyamala and others was I knew firsthand what it felt like, and that gave me confidence as a practitioner.

I already had the prerequisites for SER 1 and selected a class in California taught in a hotel ballroom in the Berkeley Marina DoubleTree. Fifty-seven students attended the four ten-hour days of training. Prior to the seminar, I had only met two of them. One was a teaching assistant I knew from Atlanta. She and I flew together to San Francisco and went to lunch at Café Gratitude before heading to the hotel. The other was a classmate from CranioSacral 2, a Catholic nun from Louisiana, Sister Francanne. I really admired her because she was both committed to her faith and open-minded enough to peek beyond conventional wisdom.

The course started with introductory remarks. The instructor's first words were, "Throw out everything we taught you in CST 1 and CST 2." Everyone laughed as he chuckled and clarified we should add our intuitive insights and instincts to the foundational knowledge we gained in CST 1 and CST 2.

Beyond precise techniques with specific hand positions and linear, step-by-step procedures, we were taught to follow our inner wisdom and guidance. The course introduced Dr. Upledger's concept of *Therapeutic Imagery and Dialogue* defined as any form of communication whatsoever from the subconscious to the conscious. That meant abstract symbolism like a mental picture, thought, sound, movement, or feeling and a seemingly random, synchronistic event in the environment. A skilled therapist would evoke helpful information from the client's subconscious mind, and imagery was often the vocabulary of that realm.

I was elated and relieved because I was being encouraged to trust imagery and direct knowingness I had received spontaneously throughout much of my life. Beyond trusting it, I was now emboldened to utilize it. Here in a formal training class, I was encouraged to develop my capabilities and use extrasensory perception as a skill.

Not knowing my classmates left me reliant on whatever information I received during our practice sessions. I actually preferred this because the less I knew about the person, the more I trusted the abstract symbolism in whatever form it took.

In one session where I was the lead therapist, the practice patient slipped into an SER fairly quickly. She was lying flat on a massage table and spontaneously raised her right arm, as if fending off an attacker. She made some odd sounds and movements, and I sensed something was unwinding. When the practice session ended, she said she had entered a childhood memory of being badly bitten by a dog. The arm that had been bitten was the one she had raised defensively.

This was just the beginning. The incident with the dog was actually an access point to some beliefs she had created at the time. Her father and brother had been nearby but did not do anything to protect her. Her psyche wanted to assign blame, and these two men were her targets. She held this disappointment in them for much of her life and created a bigger belief that all men were unreliable. This belief had played out in many of her relationships. The spontaneous movement of her arm into the position it was in during the trauma indicated her subconscious was ready to reexamine this experience and release a limiting belief. I loved how this all unfolded, starting with a simple, spontaneous movement.

Far away from my Atlanta identity and responsibilities, relative anonymity gave me freedom to explore aspects of myself both on and off the table without caring how it might look to those around me. Each day we worked in teams of three and rotated so we were never with the same group twice. The last day of the seminar, I was the practice patient receiving treatment on a massage table and Sister Francanne was the lead therapist while a woman I did not know was the second practitioner.

I quickly relaxed and went into a semi-hypnotic space. My right leg came off the table and started spontaneously making a circular motion. Sarah, a teaching assistant, was observing our group, and she came over to our table. She used her hand to provide gentle resistance and slow the rotation of my leg. Strangely, my leg kept urgently pushing harder and harder against Sarah's hand until I was

CHAPTER 12: REBIRTH IN BERKELEY

moving headfirst off the massage table and onto the ballroom floor. Another assistant saw what was happening and came to help. I was wriggling and gasping for breath with four clinicians supporting my movement and preventing me from hurting myself. I had entered a process beyond my control.

After thirty minutes, I came back into conscious awareness and found myself lying on the carpeted floor of the ballroom with a group of practitioners encircling me. I sat up, blinked, and whispered, "How did I get on the floor?" Sarah gave me a sip of water and softly asked me to describe my experience. I said it was like being in a tight, dark space and knowing I had to get out…as if my life depended on it. She smiled and waited for my brain to catch up.

I had just experienced my birth, or perhaps a rebirth of some kind. Some part of me had been in utero kicking frantically to get out so I could take my first breath. I could recall wanting to scream, "Someone get me out of here!" Or maybe I really had screamed it. The possible interpretations were plentiful. I had outgrown aspects of myself and was stuck in patterns that had become too tight and limiting. I knew some part of me was ready to be birthed into the next dynamic of this incarnation. Perhaps my subconscious had just signaled it was happening.

At the end of course, I felt utterly exhausted. Beyond my spontaneous rebirth experience, we completed forty hours of intense training. I had managed to get a hotel room with a spa tub and dumped a few cups of lavender sea salt in a warm bath. Later, I took a stroll around the marina and enjoyed looking at the beautiful boats. I hiked up a trail in César Chávez Park and enjoyed the view of San Francisco. I walked out on Berkeley Pier and watched the golden sunshine glistening on the rolling waves as I sat in deep gratitude for all the synchronicities and grace that had guided me to this moment.

Before flying back to Atlanta, I met up with Melanie, one of the friends I had made during my time in Abadiânia. Melanie had contributed to some of the most meaningful conversations during the long, leisurely meals at Luz Divina. She was an intelligent, professional woman, extremely resilient and not afraid to wade through life's messiness to find a higher expression of herself. I always found her stories captivating and inspiring. She lived in the area, and we met for a great dinner overlooking San Francisco Bay. We caught up on everything that had unfolded for each of us since returning from Brazil.

I left California feeling both confident and uncertain. I was learning to use intuitive insights professionally and for the benefit of others. I also knew that with access to more intuitive information came the urgent imperative for great discernment in how and with whom to share it.

CHAPTER 13
The Power of Intuition and Emotions to Heal

When I left California after the SomatoEmotional Release course, I had no idea I would be back again just six weeks later. During a reading binge, I stumbled on the books of Dr. Judith Orloff and devoured *Intuitive Healing*. I found she was on a book tour promoting *Emotional Freedom*, so I made a point to be in Atlanta when she visited.

On a rainy Thursday evening, I drove to a bookstore in Buckhead for her talk and book signing. A dozen of us sat in neat rows of uncomfortable plastic chairs in a back corner on the second floor. Judith was interrupted intermittently by loud whooshing sounds from a barista making frothy drinks at the coffee bar. I loved her quiet, unassuming presence. I sat listening and felt a field of energy around the table and chairs as if we were sitting in our own transparent cube. The field was well defined in one sense and yet entirely invisible.

I also sensed Judith was seeing each of us beyond our hairstyles and clothing, and I played with the idea of seeing the audience from her perspective as if I were able to look through her eyes. I quietly wondered if this was another type of empathic capability I could develop and if so, to what end.

Two days later, Judith presented a three-hour workshop called "Achieving Emotional Freedom" at Unity Church. The program was held in the main sanctuary, and the audience was much larger. This time I sensed an energy field with a layered quality. I thought my perception of layers might represent the ever-present energy in the church, some magic Judith brought with her, and something I created for myself. I took two pages of notes, recording all the truisms she spoke that day.

Judith mentioned she would be teaching at Esalen in Big Sur in late October. I had heard The Esalen Institute mentioned in spiritual circles and knew it as a retreat center and intentional community focused on humanistic alternative education. As I waited in line to get a book autographed, my mind raced ahead, planning a trip.

Days after these two events with Judith, I made a presentation to 150 business school students. As I put together my PowerPoint, I found myself weaving Judith's truisms into my presentation on entrepreneurship. I felt an intuitive knowing that I would one day write a book and this presentation contained some of the material for it.

I also had a phone conversation with my mom and told her about meeting Dr. Orloff. I emailed Mom some of my favorite sound bites from the workshops, and she went to her local library and checked out *Emotional Freedom* and *Positive Energy*. Mom was totally intrigued and began sending emails with questions about the books. I sent her a link to the Esalen workshop, and a week later, we were planning our trip to California.

Mom's brother and his wife, who lived in San Francisco, hosted us at their beautiful home in Pacific Heights on our way to Big Sur. I stayed in the guest room on the top floor and had to lug my bags up several flights of stairs. It was well worth the effort when I discovered I could see the Golden Gate Bridge extending over to Marin County. We walked in Crissy Field, and I took a few moments to linger among the big trees I had seen in my aunt's beautiful paintings of the Presidio.

CHAPTER 13: THE POWER OF INTUITION AND EMOTIONS TO HEAL

A decade earlier, Aunt Nancy had recommended *The Tao of Physics: An Exploration of the Parallels Between Modern Physics and Eastern Mysticism* by Fritjof Capra. That book was my introduction to quantum theory and the cosmic web of life. Looking back, I understand how it foreshadowed many great experiences to come.

Mom and I drove south and spent one night in Carmel at the Pine Inn, which had luxurious rooms and plentiful amenities. We strolled to the beach, took pictures of the cypress trees, and enjoyed sunset over the water. We shopped in lovely boutiques along Ocean Avenue and dined at Il Fornaio.

The next day, we arrived at Esalen where I waited in a long line to get our room assignment. The first room was so tiny I sprinted back to the desk before Mom could even get out of the rental car. Fortunately, we were able to switch to a larger room with two double beds and a view of the organic vegetable garden. The room was clean but austere, a stark contrast to the luxury of Carmel and Pacific Heights. The walls, doors, and desk were all made of wood. The headboards and chairs were wicker. I thought of the five elements of Chinese medicine. The element wood was associated with the liver, springtime, and the energy of growth, change, and pushing through. The liver was associated with the emotion of anger, and in the cycle of elements, wood fed fire. I silently wondered how sleeping in a wood chamber might influence us.

Esalen was perched on a cliff high above the ocean with spectacular views. I was happy to sit quietly in the afternoon sunshine under a huge tree and just watch the ocean. People were getting settled in, and occasionally, someone would walk by and say hello.

Esalen promoted itself as an ideal setting to "reconnect with yourself," so there was no cell phone reception and no internet access. We had planned for this by telling Dad we would only be able to communicate from a public phone in the lodge, but we had not planned to be unable to communicate with one another on Esalen's sprawling campus. I was accustomed to being adventurous and independent. Mom had lived her entire life with a comfortable network of friends in Kansas City. A spiritual retreat in an unfamiliar environment among a group of strangers was new territory.

Judith Orloff's workshop was titled "The Power of Intuition and Emotions to Heal," and it was held in Leonard Pavilion, a huge platform covered by a canvas-like structure that made it feel like a big tent. I had already made friends among the sixty participants and sat with them on cushions on the floor while Mom chose to sit in a chair at the back of the tent.

This was one of many times when I was consciously working on the balance of my inner masculine and inner feminine. Many of the strengths that had gotten me through life and contributed to my success, like tenacity, grit, and determination, were traditionally associated with masculinity. I was working on softening into more of my femininity and was curious to see who and what I attracted.

I found myself sitting between two men, Garry and Gary. While their first names were pronounced the same, the similarities ended there. To my right, Garry was a good-looking, polished attorney who had achieved material success. And to my left, Gary wore his hair in a ponytail, was soft-spoken, and worked as a shaman. I thought the Universe was pretty funny positioning these two on either side of me as if to remind me of the value in combining yin and yang energy. Interacting with Garry and Gary became my own mini-seminar within the workshop.

One morning, I ran into Garry in the lodge, and he suggested we take our coffee and go for a stroll. We were gone longer than planned, and when we got back to the lodge, Mom was furious. I watched as Garry used his masculine charm and charisma to smooth things over.

The previous evening, Mom had walked back alone after the workshop and gotten lost on a dark path without a flashlight. She had to ask someone for directions, and it was very uncomfortable. I did not see a problem with asking for help, but she felt neglected and was angry with me. The next morning at breakfast, we sat at separate tables. Garry walked in with a tray of food from the buffet, looked over at me, and said, "Uh oh. Are you in exile?" I nodded and he sat down next to Mom. I giggled as I heard him say, "Okay, Helen, what's the problem here?" He was handsome and attentive, and his strong masculinity soothed Mom. I watched as he had her smiling in about two seconds.

Later that night, we went to the firepit to sit outside under the stars. Gary the shaman was there, and I observed a certain fluidity to his energy, like we were cuddling, even though I was sitting two feet away. Gary was eager to talk astrology, tarot, and how I could embrace my feminine goddess within. Mom had no interest in this, and the other Garry was not there, so she went back to the room to read a book.

I told Judith my mom was attending her first spiritual workshop at seventy-seven. Judith was very kind and made a point to sit with Mom for a few moments and praise her for bravely trying something new.

Mom was so overloaded that she did not attend the final hours of the workshop. She was sleep-deprived from stewing over my inattentiveness and seemingly unaware of the energetic influence of Esalen and the seminar. We packed up the rental car, said our goodbyes to Gary, Garry, and several other new friends, and headed north toward my aunt and uncle's house in San Francisco.

Mom slept most of the way, and I enjoyed the silence. I reflected on the experience and all the people I had met. As I drove, I enjoyed the views of the agricultural area of Salinas Valley where miles of cauliflower grew in farms along the highway. I marveled at dozens of workers stooping to hand-pick big, white, flowering heads of cauliflower growing close to the soil. I stopped for gas and a few things at the Whole Foods in Cupertino while Mom continued to snooze. Once we got back to the familiarity and comfort of my aunt and uncle's home, Mom perked up and was back to her happy self.

The next day, Mom and I flew back to our respective cities. During the four-hour flight, I journaled and revisited many valuable insights gained during the trip. I learned Mom went from living at home to a junior college to a sorority house at a university and back to living at her parents' home before marrying Dad. She lived within the cultural expectations of the 1950s and never had her own apartment or the type of independence that required a deep sense of self-reliance. In three days at Esalen, I gained appreciation for the chasm between her life choices and my own. I felt fortunate to be in a position to explore lots of possibilities and live beyond expectations that might have kept me from pursuing the fullest expression of myself.

As my flight landed in Atlanta, I thought about the choices I was making and how those were changing with a new sense of freedom to explore myself. I set an intention to use "The Power of Intuition and Emotions to Heal" and smiled, wondering how that might unfold.

CHAPTER 14
Check Oil

Before the seminar at Esalen, and for six weeks after, I had been on a dead run. When I was home in Atlanta, I made time for yoga classes led by my favorite instructors. John used the vigorous Ashtanga sequence, intensified with heat and his own unique twists. His studio doubled as a laboratory, enabling me to study my physiological and psychological responses to challenges, as well as the responses of others.

I learned to use my breath to relax my body and mind and how to hold the tension of opposites in a delicate dance of strength, flexibility, and balance. Some days, I powered through with vigor, and others, I honored my body with a gentler practice. Yoga gave me unexpected insights into myself. What I discovered while sweating on my mat was often applicable and highly beneficial outside the studio too.

Many friendships were created during the ninety-minute practice on Saturday mornings. One yogi invited me to a sweat lodge in the North Georgia mountains led by a shaman with twenty-five years of experience. It was December, and we huddled around a bonfire for a ceremony and drumming. I was happy to be outdoors in the crisp mountain air, and the synchronicity of a lunar eclipse brought an added depth to the event.

The lodge was a small, dome-shaped structure covered with blankets and pelts. The top was so low it was impossible to stand or even kneel inside. Fifteen of us crawled in and sat on the ground shoulder to shoulder around a sandpit. Fires outside heated massive rocks called *The Grandfathers*. They glistened with red cinders that flared and popped almost as if speaking to us as the *fire keeper* moved them into the lodge using huge metal tongs.

There was a sudden flash, sizzle and smoke as the shaman threw water, sage, and eucalyptus on the glowing rocks and then closed the flap, creating total darkness inside.

I had greatly underestimated my tendency for claustrophobia and my heightened empathic sensitivity to the fear I felt in others. The smoke, darkness, and intense heat made it much worse. I was freaking out. After an invocation, I asked if I could leave. As soon as I spoke, all fourteen people in the lodge with me said, "Awwww," as if empathizing with my fear. With that heartfelt sound something shifted, and I suddenly felt committed to staying.

The shaman led us in four rounds, honoring each of the four directions of the compass along with the four themes of awakening, healing, tribute to ancestors, and transformation.

In the first round, I felt my own fears existentially amplified beyond what was happening in a sweat lodge in the North Georgia mountains. It was as if everything I had ever felt fearful about was intensified inside me. My brain could not begin to keep up with the catalogue of experiences that flashed in my mind's eye. I breathed through it, aware of my commitment to stay.

Between rounds, the fire keeper opened the flap and added more sizzling Grandfathers before quickly closing the flap, plunging us back into total darkness. In the brief moments the flap was open, I felt the cool outside air offsetting the cruel heat. I tried not to look at any of the other faces.

CHAPTER 14: CHECK OIL

In the second round, I felt the fears of those around me, particularly the two men seated on either side of me. I could not escape it, so I chose just to be present to their unspoken fears.

In the third round, I made a conscious decision to hold a higher vibration, and I immediately experienced the immense beauty of the glowing rocks and the beauty of my fear itself. With that choice. I found instant balance and neutrality in the tension of those two opposites, beauty and fear.

In the last round, I sensed my role in our larger collective and wondered if I could hold a high-enough vibration to support others in transcending their fears, not just here in a sweat lodge but in other settings as well.

Every round had provided a deeper level of self-realization.

When the fourth round ended and the flap opened, two fire keepers carried me across a stream to the bonfire, sat me on a log, and covered me with a towel. I was weak, lightheaded, and dripping with sweat. I sobbed as I shivered next to the fire. My conscious mind was still processing but deep inside, I knew I had just completed one of the most unexpectedly profound experiences of the year.

Some part of me had just melted and been replaced by something much more potent and valuable. I wept, wondering that was.

Two days later, I flew to a client site in Philadelphia. I had worked with this client intermittently for fifteen years, and this trip marked an opportunity to coach a female operations manager named Irene who had been promoted from within the organization. Coaching was something I often provided, even though I was not explicitly being paid to do so.

I had known Irene for 15 years and watched her rise through the ranks of the company. She was extremely capable but she had few if any models of good management. We had always communicated honestly with one another and over the years, I had become an occasional mentor.

Irene knew I had studied holistic healing modalities and, on this visit, I went beyond conventional coaching and mentorship into the world of metaphysics and healing work. Irene privately admitted she was challenged by several men on her staff. I closed the door to her warehouse office as she began to offer specifics and I began to get intuitive information.

After a few minutes, I asked Irene if I could put one palm just below her collar bones and another on her mid-back as she continued to talk while sitting at her desk. Instantly, I felt lifetimes of old karmic patterns begin to release as her tears flowed. Thirty minutes and a few tissues later, Irene was done and we went back to work in the warehouse.

Later that evening, I headed back to the Philadelphia airport contemplating another profound marker in my evolution from mainstream to mystical. Seemingly disparate professional interests had overlapped organically again, leaving me eager for more.

The Universe often speaks to me in metaphors, and in every car I had rented in every city for a month, the *check oil* light had come on while I was driving. The low oil indicator had also come on in my own SUV in Atlanta. Automotive oil is needed to reduce friction, and without it, an engine will seize up. I got the message. I was overdue for personal maintenance.

Flying home to Atlanta, I dozed and meditated, feeling deep gratitude as I was ending an amazing year of growth and transformation. I was relieved this was my last flight of the year and looked forward to rest. The passenger sitting next to me lamented she was connecting to another flight that same night.

As we deplaned, she smiled and wished me "Happy holidays." Then she said, "If you happen to be in Manhattan on New Year's Eve, Central Park South has the best fireworks!" Her comment seemed odd given I had just said this was my last flight of the year, but I nodded politely and thanked her. As I walked through the concourse, I tried to shake off the curious weight of her words.

CHAPTER 14: CHECK OIL

My holiday gift to myself was going to be rest, yoga, Netflix, and a spiritual practice called Varadeeksha Mala, which Gomati and Vasistha had told me about. It was a way to connect to Divine Consciousness through eleven days of practices. I liked the idea of a simple, self-directed spiritual activity I could do alone during the holidays. Each morning at sunrise, I lit a candle, sang the mantra, and prayed for myself, for all sentient beings, and for the Earth. The last practice of each day was to express gratitude to people who had helped me.

On the first evening of the practice, a bit of serendipity occurred. I was making the last of three payments buying back all shares in Solertis. Two years earlier, my shareholders had expressed concern about the amount of time I was devoting to what they perceived to be extraneous activities. They were particularly concerned about me working in the holistic health center I planned to co-own, and they demanded I buy back their stock. From a rental car in Florida, I called my attorney and he drafted a formal Stock Redemption Agreement.

While shockingly abrupt, this flash point was a wakeup call. My shareholders were correct. I was not committed to my company's financial performance above my other pursuits. I was committed to maximizing my personal potential across a number of categories, and Solertis had become more of a platform for exploration than a means to generate shareholder value. We had experienced some wildly profitable years, but my aspirations had shifted since their original investment.

The buyback was the right thing, but the demands were delivered during a family vacation. My parents were among the original investors and two of my biggest supporters. My dad had followed in his father's footsteps and been a small business owner all his life. Both my parents encouraged my independence and celebrated my determination. As shareholders communicating to a CEO, their request was entirely valid. As parents to a daughter, their disapproval stung.

Now, on the first night of Varadeeksha, I lit a single candle and signed the final checks to my former shareholders. I wrote a heartfelt letter of appreciation for their investment fifteen years earlier. I had bought back the full rights to follow my dreams, and I was ready to grow again. I laughed when I realized the stamps I chose for the envelopes were Liberty Bells. I said a prayer of gratitude, sealed the envelopes, blew out the candle, and smiled in the dark wondering what adventures were ahead.

One of the few friends I did plan to see over the holidays was my college classmate Michael. He, his wife, and three children came to town from New England every year for an extended Christmas visit with his wife's family. Michael emailed me his schedule, including his plan to purchase a car and drive it back to the Northeast.

Michael had a mature yoga practice, and we had a tradition of going to class at one of the studios where I practiced in Atlanta. The holiday snowball picked up momentum and one yoga class became three. Another friend joined us for yoga and brunch on December 30. As we sat talking over cold-pressed juices, raw cultured veggies, and vegan burgers, Michael said, "Annie, if you're not doing anything, why don't you drive with me?"

I flashed back to the 1980s and heading to North Myrtle Beach for a few days of fun after final exams at Duke. One year I ran into Michael at Myrtle and ended up giving him a ride back to campus. The stereo blasted Dire Straits as we drove back to Durham with the windows down in my little Honda.

Now twenty years later, in a moment of spontaneity, I went to my condo, packed a bag, and jumped in Michael's new Volkswagen Jetta. We laughed and reminisced about college and everything that had happened since our time as undergraduates as we drove 800 miles through six states in perfect weather conditions.

We finally arrived in New York City about 9 p.m. on New Year's Eve. Michael had an apartment on the East Side because he commuted from his home outside Boston. I used Hilton points to book a room at the Waldorf. I checked in, changed my clothes, and then walked ten blocks to his apartment. After a little champagne, we decided to take a walk. Michael strode with purpose, seeming to have a destination in mind. We ended up in a throng of people on the street near Columbus Circle.

As fireworks went off at midnight, I smiled, suddenly remembering the passenger on the Delta flight who had made a seemingly random recommendation about Central Park South on New Year's Eve. I had brushed off her comment, and now, fifteen days later, I was in the exact spot she had recommended.

I completed Varadeeksha Mala watching the Golden Ball meditation on my laptop in the Waldorf and left New York realizing I could have never imagined where the year would take me and how it would end. Synchronicities and winks from the Universe seemed to be coming faster and more curiously as I opened myself to the flow.

CHAPTER 15
The Liberating Quality of Truth

As a new year started, I reflected on how my priorities and the structures I used to define myself were shifting. Many of my volunteer roles were ending either due to their own inherent timelines or because I was consciously opting out. I was creating space to explore new capabilities while squirming in the uncertainty of my pivot from mainstream, status quo to something more unconventional. Globally, supply chain was becoming more important as an industry, and my professional expertise funded my ongoing exploration of the intersection of business, metaphysics and holistic health.

Between visits to client sites for supply chain projects, I continued my sessions with Shymala. She mentioned a conference hosted by the Upledger Institute called "Beyond the Dura." The event was in West Palm Beach and celebrated Dr. John Upledger's eightieth birthday and the thirtieth anniversary of his groundbreaking book. Leaders from around the world would be speaking, so I decided it would be interesting to interact with the best and brightest practitioners.

For two days senior practitioners gave polished presentations showcasing their research while also sharing heartwarming stories of their work with patients. Several speakers started with a simple practice to bring us all into harmonic resonance at a biological level. I smiled, thinking how adding this simple practice to business meetings would provide a new dimension in corporate wellness.

One presenter, Tad Wanveer, was a practitioner whose office I visited during a business trip to Raleigh-Durham. He spoke about trusting whatever showed up during a session and trusting in your own ability to perceive it. I smiled knowing I was building that trust inside myself.

Another presenter, Chas Perry, had worked with Dr. Upledger since the 1970s and encouraged us to learn to be in the client's reality without judgment and in total acceptance. He suggested we "follow from inside rather than fix from outside." I found myself adding material to my own PowerPoint presentations based on principles I heard during the conference.

Two weeks after "Beyond the Dura" and between trips to client sites, I flew to Seattle for a weekend workshop called "Rebirth of Humanity" hosted by Isabelle and Eugenia, who had led the incredible trip to Egypt and Jordan. I immersed myself in an advanced metaphysical workshop and rekindled friendships with fellow travelers.

For years, I had reflected on the many roles I had played in my life, and this workshop took that a step farther, presenting life as a simulation we enter for the purpose of growth during the soul's incarnation in a body. We can choose to make our experience a prison or a playground through the situations we create.

Many of the concepts were esoteric and multidimensional, but I always found something pragmatic and applicable to my day-to-day existence. I was in a rebirth myself, and the workshop helped me sense my place within the greater rebirth of humanity. My life and work were bringing together the mainstream and mystical, and each day brought some new experience to highlight this dynamic.

I returned to Atlanta where I had been asked to speak at a Chamber of Commerce luncheon. I was promoting the annual conference of the Council of Supply Chain Management Professionals (CSCMP), the premier group for industry networking and education. Over fifteen years, I had served in a dozen volunteer

CHAPTER 15: THE LIBERATING QUALITY OF TRUTH

leadership roles including President of the Atlanta Roundtable, Roundtable Advisor, and Finance Chair of the annual conference with a $5 million budget.

The luncheon was hosted inside the Federal Reserve Bank of Atlanta, a massive marble building constructed like a fortress with layer upon layer of security. Once inside, the interior was dripping with old Southern charm, ornate furniture covered in opulent fabrics, heavy draperies, and expensive-looking art. It was an odd juxtaposition of *Gone with the Wind* inside a museum capable of serving as a bomb shelter.

A hundred industry leaders were served a four-course lunch on elegant china with white linens. When we finished dessert and coffee, I was introduced and walked to the dais to promote the upcoming CSCMP conference.

As I moved to the front of the room, I suddenly felt like I was back in the airport in Amman, Jordan, at the moment when Eugenia and Isabelle had dismantled the energetic tunnel, leaving me holding that energy on my own. I approached the podium and felt some part of me extend downward far beneath the massive building toward the heart of the Earth while the space above me extended upward with a spiraling flow in a vertical column.

I stood in front of a hundred colleagues, paused, and felt deep reverence and compassion. Perhaps it was the result of the sweat lodge and two recent workshops I had attended, but I felt profound respect for every person in the room and the challenges they faced along their path. I smiled in the stillness, feeling the intensity of the moment in every cell of my body.

To the audience, it probably seemed like I was simply waiting for everyone to look up from their electronic devices and stop talking. I sensed this field of energy I was holding as it expanded to include everyone in the room.

For a few seconds, I felt harmonic resonance just as I had at spiritual events. Now I was experiencing this with a group of businesspeople at a Chamber of Commerce event. I thought about how we could change the world if we could get more people vibrating together like this.

After announcing the dates and keynote speakers for the upcoming conference, I walked back to my chair and sat down, wondering what had just happened. I silently set an intention to replicate what I had just experienced and to share it with everyone who might possibly be open enough to receive.

Three weeks later, I flew to Chicago to speak at another CSCMP event called the June Forum. Volunteers from roundtables around the world gathered each year for a two-day symposium where best practices were shared among leaders. I was invited to speak about the successes of the Atlanta Roundtable, the second largest in the world.

After my presentation, I sat in the audience next to a man named Ralph. Ralph had worked in supply chain for years, but our paths had never crossed. We had several casual conversations between speakers, and he laughed when I snacked on carrots and raw tahini. His mom had fed him tahini as a child, and he hated it. Tahini somehow led him to reveal his mom was very spiritual and believed in energy work.

Throughout the day, when Ralph coughed, I would immediately feel pain in my own chest and lungs. It was early summer, an unusual time for a cold. Ralph confirmed the restriction in his chest and lungs and said it came and went intermittently. When he coughed, I observed a female presence energetically connected to him, but it was not his mother.

He was curious so I offered that the woman associated with his cough seemed like she was of some ethnic descent, not American. He said his wife was from the Philippines, and they were already in the process of ending the marriage. I privately guessed his lungs would clear once he was free of the relationship.

CHAPTER 15: THE LIBERATING QUALITY OF TRUTH

After the June Forum, Ralph scheduled a coaching session to help him evaluate a business opportunity and his relationship with the company's owner. I loved combining my business experience with my capabilities in the metaphysical realm as I offered Ralph insights into the interpersonal dynamics I predicted he would find with the owner.

Earlier in the year, I had attended a Duke fundraising event where I watched President Richard Brodhead interview former President Jimmy Carter. I was heartened by the humility, kindness, and compassion these two leaders shared as they discussed the history and challenges they had each faced in their respective roles. I was inspired by the humanness and generosity in their approaches to their constituents and colleagues.

That evening, George from Alumni Affairs mentioned an international leadership conference being planned in Barcelona to coincide with the US Olympic basketball team playing tune up games before the London Olympics. Duke's own coach, Mike Krzyzewski, was leading the US Olympic team. With the event just two weeks away, I decided to go, and George emailed me the details of the logistics with a *déjà vu* reference to my impromptu trip to London he had also arranged on short notice.

Duke had blocks of rooms at two hotels in Barcelona, and despite being sold out, I had figured out a way to get a reservation at the Ritz-Carlton where the Olympic team was staying. Just as I was pressing the button to confirm my online reservation, intuition stopped me and instead, I booked a room at the overflow hotel, Pullman Barcelona Skipper, a block away and also on the beach. I trusted the guidance even though some part of me would have preferred the Ritz.

The leadership conference was held on the forty-first floor of the Ritz-Carlton overlooking the marina. Popular NBA players were staying at the hotel and a mob of hopeful fans was being restrained by armed security officers. I had to go through multiple security checks, show my passport and my invitation just to get into the lobby. I wondered if this chaotic vibe was why I was guided to choose the Pullman. I smiled as the elevator stopped and Kobe Bryant got on, followed by other players. I suddenly felt like a dwarf among giants.

At the leadership conference, two professors from Fuqua School of Business presented their extensive research showing how a CEO's word choices could predict a company's financial performance. Choosing words to justify one's actions versus taking ownership for mistakes was a key predictor of corporate performance.

I smiled, knowing word choice and how one aligns with their assertions creates an energy field. When someone says something that they know is untrue or that doesn't align with who they are, I feel the disharmony. I once did a double-take because in my mind's eye, it looked as if the liar's nose grew like Pinocchio's in the children's story.

After a packed forty-eight hours, including the leadership conference, two basketball games, a walking tour of Las Ramblas, paellas, and pitchers of sangria on the beach followed by iced Cristal with Duke friends at a discotheque high above the Mediterranean, I hugged George goodbye and hopped in a taxi to the airport with another guest from the Pullman.

We were each tired for very different reasons. She confided she had met her lover for the weekend and winked as she said they never left the room. He was a well-known *avocat* (lawyer) in Paris in the throes of a divorce. She was CEO of a company in Lyon, France. They had come to Spain where they would not be recognized.

After not answering calls all weekend, she was rehearsing her alibi. I smiled, thinking about the research study showing her word choices could predict her company's performance and I recommended she choose the liberating quality of the truth.

I bought three liters of Evian in the airport, anticipating a long flight and knowing I was sitting in Delta economy comfort with no upgrade to first class. Just after takeoff, the seatback entertainment system and the electrical outlets failed in my row. The flight attendant reset the system several times, which irritated all the passengers already watching movies, but it did not fix the problem.

With no way to power my laptop and no entertainment for the ten-hour flight, I was teetering on indignant rage. Instead, I chose to surrender to the circumstances and meditate. I put on my compression socks, earplugs, and eyeshades, and got as comfortable as I could. I used *Ascension Attitudes* and envisioned myself in an energetic cocoon of soft pink angora. I relaxed my way into a complete state of bliss and an altered state of consciousness. Part of me left the plane and flew elsewhere as my physical body headed home to Atlanta.

CHAPTER 16
Lessons Learned

Starting in the early 2000s, I was invited to speak each spring at the Executive in Residence program in the business school at Georgia Southern University. Entrepreneurship and Supply Chain provided the backdrop for my presentation titled "Lessons Learned." Each year, I found myself adding material to my PowerPoint based on wisdom gained from spiritual travel, principles I learned during the holistic health seminars, and deeper truths gained on my journey through life.

I took the students through the twists and turns of my professional trajectory using logos and mascots. I started all the way back with the red umbrella logo of Rainy Day Books, where I had a part-time job in high school working alongside an amazing female entrepreneur who started a successful chain of independent bookstores and showed me how to use passion, perseverance, and pride to create a thriving business.

The Blue Devil represented my time at Duke University where I designed my own major with courses from a dozen different academic departments, did five independent studies, served on the undergraduate judicial board, managed the student health insurance office, and mastered the drinking game, Quarters.

Snoopy represented my first job after college in the Humor Department at Hallmark Cards. I turned down prestigious offers with higher salaries to work with Charles Schulz, Jim Davis, and the Peanuts and Garfield product lines.

The logo for Ingram Book Company represented my fortuitous foray into logistics when I was hired to oversee relocation of a distribution center. I was good at project management but knew nothing about operations, so I spent long days in jeans, picking, packing and stocking books to learn ops before returning to business attire as a liaison to the state's economic development office. At Ingram, I was again fortunate to work for another amazing female boss.

Tony the Tiger represented the grueling year I endured as operations manager at a Kellogg cereal distribution center run by Exel Logistics. As a twenty-something, I supervised fifty forklift drivers and one-million square feet of warehouse with eighty dock doors and a rail spur. I eventually discovered I could only work so many consecutive sixteen-hour days before I burned out. I grew from the challenge, leveraged the experience and found a better job.

A bright blue pallet represented my time at CHEP USA, where I managed twenty-three contract warehouses in five states and spent most of my workweek driving back roads from one remote warehouse to another in a company car. As an operations manager, my job was to ensure inventory was deployed effectively and to make friends with the local fire marshals in small towns. Warehouses stacked full of wood pallets burn quickly.

The last image was the original logo of my company from when it was first incorporated in 1996. Our original business plan was based on my partner Joe's vision to optimize truckload shipments for companies, including Kimberly Clark, Procter & Gamble, Kellogg, and Campbell Soup, and profit from the savings we helped them achieve. It was a complex model, and that complexity along with our entrepreneurial naivete meant we did not generate revenue as quickly as we had predicted. In the meantime, synchronicities brought unexpected opportunities.

CHAPTER 16: LESSONS LEARNED

In the 1990s, when I worked at Ingram, my boss had asked me to give two visiting executives a tour of our distribution center. I was proud of our operation and eager to show it off. My enthusiasm must have made an impression because years later, just as I was starting my first company, those two executives tracked me down and asked me to evaluate their distribution operations.

This opportunity led me down the entirely new path of consulting and started a decades-long relationship with the client. I enjoyed being deeply embedded in tactical operations while also advising senior executives and formulating strategy, and this unusual range became one of the key differentiators in my consulting.

Joe eventually made the difficult decision to return to a corporate job and a steady paycheck. I lamented losing a dear friend and business partner but his departure somehow seemed to accelerate opportunities. The original idea for optimizing truckload freight was simplified, so rather than running a complex optimization algorithm, we created strategic alliances between big consumer products companies. Our *Collaborative Transportation Network* thrived once we honed the business model.

During the mid-2000s, my work developed a natural rhythm with periods of adventure travel and spiritual retreats interspersed between intense projects. I rode this ebb and flow as new clients appeared serendipitously.

Jacob, a mergers and acquisitions advisor I met while watching Duke basketball, called me from the parking lot of a hot startup that manufactured accessories for personal digital devices like iPhones. Digital Lifestyle Outfitters (DLO) had grown from the founder's basement to their first warehouse, and they were rapidly outgrowing their second. Jacob had pitched his M&A advisory services to the CFO and noted distribution operations were not able to support growth.

I flew to Raleigh-Durham, met with the CFO, and started a supply chain strategy project the following week. In my first few days on site, DLO discovered a design flaw in a new product manufactured in Asia. All 50,000 units needed a slight modification to a circuit board, and that meant disassembling every unit to make one tiny fix with a simple soldering iron.

DLO had planned a coordinated launch at big box retailers like Target and Best Buy. They didn't have time to ship the products back to Asia or to manufacture new ones, so for five months, I served in an interim management role at DLO's distribution facility in Durham. I hired dozens of temporary workers from several agencies and ran two shifts, disassembling and reassembling 50.000 new boom boxes, just to make a teensy connection with a $10 soldering iron. With creativity, a little luck and thousands of man hours, we averted a crisis, saving the retail launch and ensuring the young company's future.

This project came with an added benefit. I spent an entire collegiate basketball season commuting to the city of my alma mater and living a few blocks from campus in a trendy loft apartment paid for by the client. Every morning, I got coffee at Fosters Market and walked to Ninth Street to grab something for lunch from Whole Foods. I spent more time watching Duke basketball in Cameron than I had since my undergraduate days. I also managed the crisis and completed the project on schedule.

During my last week at DLO, the CFO gave me the opportunity to promote four temporary workers to full time with a significant pay increase and benefits. One choice was obvious—Eric Pittman. Eric was the most reliable and hardest working of all the temps. When I got to the facility early in the morning, Eric was sitting in his gray Dodge Neon, sipping a thermos of Folgers coffee and waiting for me to unlock the building. For ten hours a day, Eric endured monotony, folding cartons and neatly stacking them before stretch wrapping and moving the pallet to a storage bay.

Eric was diabetic, and I sensed he was in physical pain most days, but he never complained. He consistently had the highest productivity rates and the best attitude. He embodied the qualities and work ethic I wanted to reward.

The CFO and I held a facility-wide meeting where I spoke about the person who exemplified an attitude that made the project successful. Eric received a standing ovation from his co-workers. I could feel how much it meant to him to be acknowledged and promoted.

I loved the human side of my work with clients, and this was one of the most cherished moments in my career.

The day after the project was completed, I moved out of my loft apartment and shipped five months' worth of accumulated household items and clothes back to Atlanta. I always felt a letdown when I finished a project, and I had really poured my heart into this one.

A week later, I was copied on a group email to employees at DLO. Eric had slipped into a diabetic coma while asleep. After four days with no brain activity, his family made the difficult decision to remove life support, and Eric passed away.

I wept. I couldn't eat. I was just devastated.

I sought counsel from the medical intuitive who helped me after Susana's death. She assured me that being acknowledged and honored was one of the things that had helped Eric complete his time here. Thankfully, he did not suffer and his death seemed to be guided by a hand of grace. I had advocated for Eric to get his health insurance activated immediately because he had been working as a temporary for more than ninety days.

Serendipitously, that health insurance enabled him to get his final medical care at Duke University Medical Center without putting any financial burden on his family during his coma. I felt some reassuring symmetry in this along with deep gratitude for my time working alongside Eric, a man whose attitude belied his circumstances.

The business school students who attended my "Lessons Learned" presentation also saw my lifestyle and the aspects of running a small business I found most appealing. After the DLO project, my romantic partner and I bought a sailboat and cruised Long

Island Sound for the summer enjoying coastal towns like Mystic, Newport, and Woods Hole. Living aboard a sailboat taught great lessons about conservation and deep respect for nature. I learned to enjoy the calm seas and sunshine one day while being prepared to ride ten-foot swells the next.

Over the years, my presentations expanded to include highlights of my projects in corporate wellness and my interest in holistic health modalities and self-care. I began to weave in ideas about balancing intellect with intuition and allowing space for unexpected synchronicities.

I was always the last speaker of the spring semester and was invited to the class cookout. In a tremendous sign of respect, the students grilled eggplant and squash for me alongside their hamburgers and hotdogs. They also quizzed me about intuition and how to cultivate synchronicities.

Each year, my PowerPoint chronicled my path to aligning my natural skills, interests, and lifestyle with my professional activities. Rather than chasing expectations imparted to me by well-intentioned family, friends, and institutions, I put forward my own definition of success and presented it for students to see. I encouraged them to watch for opportunities that seemed unconventional but felt intriguing.

Each spring, the Executive in Residence program provided an opportunity to reflect on all that had unfolded; milestones, opportunities, choices and decisions. My presentation became a celebration of the grace and guidance steering my career and life in new directions.

CHAPTER 17
Morocco: Tea in the Sahara

In late 2012, I traveled again with Isabelle and Eugenia, this time to Morocco and the Canary Islands. The theme of the trip was consciously evolving the Self through choices and internal changes to accommodate new levels of consciousness. After what I had experienced in Egypt, I figured this would be another stretch for my psyche.

The group was again meeting at JFK for our flight to Madrid and on to Casablanca. I felt a bit skittish when the Delta agent in Atlanta checked my luggage all the way through to Casablanca on Iberia Airlines. I watched as my blue duffle bag covered in neon yellow priority stickers and Delta Medallion credentials disappeared down a long conveyor out of sight. After clearing security, I went to the Delta Sky Club and checked the Delta app on my phone, but my bag was not tracking. I boarded the plane already feeling uncertain, and I had not even left Atlanta. At JFK, I deplaned and went to terminal seven to meet the group for our Iberia flight to Madrid. I still had no information on my checked bag.

In the gate area, I hugged some familiar folks from the Egypt trip. Isabelle and Eugenia moved us to a quiet space to prepare our energetic travel tunnel. I saw nothing with my physical eyes, but I felt an energetic structure like a big vertical column and the powerful coalescence of energy as we silently honored our intentions.

My first intention was to learn about the infinite supply of the Universe, a metaphysical idea that there is always enough if we choose to experience abundance rather than fear scarcity. My second intention was to become a more benevolent leader starting with compassionate inner leadership. I knew I would spend the next twelve days discovering what those intentions really meant.

We flew overnight and arrived in Madrid at 7 a.m. on a Sunday with three hours before our connection to Casablanca. Eventually, Starbucks opened, and we sat in groups at bistro tables in the terminal. I passed the time with Mira, Marge, and two women named Nancy, and we compared notes about how we had each met Isabelle and Eugenia.

Once in the air again, we flew south over the coastline of Spain. I thought back to a vacation in Marbella in 1999 and how much more inner contentment I felt now. I was an entirely different person because I had made choices and changes to accommodate new levels of consciousness. I sat happily scribbling thoughts in my journal as we flew over the Strait of Gibraltar.

We arrived in Casablanca and deplaned into bright sunshine. Everyone's checked luggage arrived except for Marge's and mine. Fortunately, I had packed a few days' worth of clothes in my carry-on bag. We met our guides, Mustapha and Said, before boarding our tour bus for a ride to the Sheraton. After a refreshing shower, I went to the pool and fell asleep in the afternoon sun. Later, I ran into Mustapha, who said Marge's luggage was on its way from Madrid but mine was still missing.

While I was happy for Marge, I was furious with Delta. I mentally catalogued the items in my missing bag, including my yoga mat, jeans, scarves, shoes, a magenta windbreaker, and my lightweight mini-backpack filled with my favorite Pure Bliss granola bars and supplements.

The next morning, I awoke at 6:45 a.m. I had borrowed a yoga mat from my friend, Robert, and despite having everything I needed in the moment, I was unhappy and fired off a few sharp emails to people at Delta.

After breakfast, we boarded the tour bus to one of the largest and most beautiful mosques in the world, Hassan II. Inside the mosque, the retractable roof opened, providing rays of sunlight to illuminate the colorful tiles and a unique view of the tallest minaret in the world. The mosque was absolutely stunning, but my favorite feature was the foundation. Hassan II was built on a platform that extended out over the Atlantic, and I welcomed the sense of gently undulating movement under the rock-solid foundation.

At the next stop, we walked through the lush courtyards of a government building. Isabelle took me aside and suggested I allow myself to go into the pain about my lost luggage and the sense "I do not matter." My fury was growing exponentially with every passing minute, and Isabelle hinted it would be productive for me to cry. I was really uncomfortable crying, let alone crying in a group of people happily taking photos.

Suddenly, I had an idea, a sort of *déjà vu* from an earlier conversation. I recalled something Nancy had said while I had been arrogantly proclaiming my Delta Platinum Medallion status and how lost luggage never happened to me. Nancy had said, "So you are not as independent as you think you are." I had been conditioned to be self-reliant and organized. I vigilantly warded off vulnerability and helplessness with independence, assertiveness, and control. Nancy's comment stung, but I had only allowed it to register briefly.

Now I replayed it and discovered it deeply triggered my emotions.

With my lost bag, the Universe set up circumstances for me to experience exactly what I feared; a meltdown that would expose any hint of weakness or emotion fragility. Surrender was not in my repertoire, but all the Delta priority stickers, Platinum Medallion status, and emails to executives had done nothing to locate my bag, so I let go and cried.

The general manager of the Delta SkyMiles Medallion program emailed me that my bag had been found in Madrid—still a continent away. No one could explain why Marge's luggage had arrived but mine had not. I knew this was a spiritual exercise beyond logistics. Mustapha smiled and said it was *destiny*. We were still laughing about my destiny when Iberia called with news that my bag was en route to Casablanca.

The following morning, our tour bus made several stops in Rabat, including Kasbah des Oudaias, which was originally a fortress at the mouth of a river. I loved the narrow maze of whitewashed corridors with quaint blue and white buildings and amazing views of the ocean amid lush flowers and ornately painted doors. Far from the bustle of Casablanca, we enjoyed traditional hot mint tea before moving on to Touarga and Meknes.

By dusk, we were at Volubilis, once a royal residence. All that remained were ruins of a magnificent structure in the middle of the countryside. Huge stone columns and massive archways hinted at what had once been a prosperous city centuries earlier. The panoramic views of pastoral scenery in the soft light at the end of the day felt magical. In the golden glow of sunset, Eugenia and Isabelle gathered the group in a circle to support us in processing the growth we were each experiencing in our own unique ways.

After a sleepless night, I unrolled the borrowed green yoga mat and held several yoga poses, including downward facing dog, while feeling gratitude for my friends' support. In the hotel lobby, I watched as people came to breakfast in various states of unhappiness. Many of us were in an unexplained funk. Cherie made me a delightful mocha coffee, and I forced myself to eat a small bowl of cereal. Mustapha said my bag had arrived in Casablanca and was on its way to the Fez airport. I was reluctant to get too excited.

After breakfast, we loaded up the bus to go sightseeing at one of the royal palaces. At the palace, I was drawn to a beautiful, twenty-foot-tall door with a traditional, ornately tiled arch. I walked to the door and stood on my toes, reaching up toward the beautifully carved metal handle. The towering door made me look like a character from the movie, *Honey, I Shrunk the Kids*.

When our long day of sightseeing was winding down, Mustapha and I left the group and headed for the airport. We endured Fez traffic in a black SUV. With the windows down, the warm dry breeze smelled exotic.

We finally arrived at the airport, which was beautifully lit but completely deserted. We could see dozens of bags locked inside a room, but to get in, you needed two keys—security had one and the airline had the other.

When we finally got in, I spotted my bag partially zipped with the handles splayed open. It had a long string of tags indicating all of the stops it had made. I had to sign a damage waiver and show my passport. When I finally got to examine the bag myself, the contents looked like someone had put them in a Cuisinart. Every pocket of every garment and every pouch in my small backpack had been opened. My jeans were turned inside out. My scarves were wadded up. My supplements had been opened.

I felt violated, as if I had been personally touched by dozens of strangers.

Back at the hotel, I unpacked the bag. Every item was accounted for, including every single granola bar. Despite getting my bag and all my things back, I could not shake the negative energy leftover from people who felt entitled to touch my belongings with such insensitivity. I left the clothes hanging in the bathroom, hoping that energy would dissipate.

When I arrived in the dining room late, the only empty chair was beside Isabelle. I could feel her helping me release the energetic residue of the bag debacle as I ate a few bites of dinner. I celebrated the end of a very long saga with a half-dozen mini éclairs from the dessert tray.

We left Fez and drove up into the Atlas Mountains, stopping in a quaint town called Ifrane that felt like a Swiss ski resort. The alpine climate was a stark contrast to the dry, desert conditions throughout much of Morocco. The fresh air, greenery, and sense of spaciousness made me feel like I could breathe again. Our tour bus stopped, and we walked up the gentle slope of a hillside. We stood in a circle while Isabelle and Eugenia led a ceremony to honor our beautiful host, Earth, and helped us connect to the holographic reality supporting our existence. I felt my own presence within this larger system and was reminded that everything I experience helps me learn—including lost luggage. After taking photographs at a scenic outlook in the warm glow of the sunset, we continued on to Erfoud.

In the morning light, our hotel, Kasbah Tizimi, was gorgeous. It was built around an inviting swimming pool with beautiful, lush palms and traditional Moroccan architecture. I grabbed some coffee and jumped on the hotel Wi-Fi to email a client in the US. While I was a half-world away, Solertis was awarded another supply chain project that would start when I returned to the States.

After breakfast, we loaded up the tour bus and headed for Merzouga, the last bit of civilization before our journey into the Sahara Desert for an overnight stay at a remote Bedouin camp. We each packed a small bag before mounting camels for a two-hour ride through the bright red-orange sand to the campsite. I had seen pictures of Erg Chebbi, a massive expanse of dunes formed by blown sand, but being in it was beyond words. We meandered through miles of dunes that glowed in the late afternoon sun and arrived at our camp to be welcomed by dozens of friendly Moroccans playing drums.

Our Bedouin hosts prepared a delicious traditional meal, and we lingered around a long, low table for hours. After dinner, we stood in a circle looking up at the beautiful stars glistening in the dark sky from one edge of the horizon to the other. The Milky Way

CHAPTER 17: MOROCCO: TEA IN THE SAHARA

was directly overhead and looked like something from a NASA photograph.

I sensed something just under the surface of the Earth moving and sparking in a grid pattern. It reminded me of the open courtyard at Sakkara in Egypt. When everything got still, Eugenia said we had all reached another level of coherence—a quality of unified wholeness. Oddly, it felt like what I had experienced standing at a podium in the Federal Reserve Bank. With my bare feet in the sand of the Sahara Desert, my body vibrated like a tuning fork. After the ceremony, we moved to a roaring fire where our hosts played drums, and we danced into the wee hours before making our way to our tents.

Several of us chose to pull our mattresses outside and sleep under a blanket of twinkling lights. In a universe of 100 billion stars, I felt tiny—like a single grain of sand in the vast Sahara. I felt energy and excitement as if those brilliant stars were transmitting their magnificent wisdom. The energy was so intense that I only slept a few minutes at a time.

I arose at the sound of our hosts making us their traditional hot mint tea. A group of us hiked to the top of a tall dune to watch the sunrise in silence. The vastness of the desert was profound. As the sand began to warm under the sun, we got back onto our camels for the trek through the dunes to Merzouga.

Back in the bus and driving toward Ouarzazate, I felt tired and a little off. By the time we arrived at our lunch spot, I was feeling completely drained and nauseous. The restaurant was inside a guesthouse high atop a hill too steep for the bus. I felt a bit abandoned as I watched my friends climb the winding road while I stayed in the bus and snoozed.

Eventually, I needed to use the restroom, and as I walked up the hill, I discovered how weak I really was. My body had always been super-strong and reliable, but now I had to go slowly and rest every ten steps. I stopped twice and got sick as local children watched, hoping I might give them a few dirhams. I felt completely humiliated. When I reached the guesthouse, I needed to lie down. I found a staff person who let me use an unoccupied guest room. I was dehydrated, hallucinating, and too weak to make sense of what was happening.

After some time, I got up and followed the sound of voices. The group was now leaving for Todgha Gorges. When we got there, I still felt awful, but I was happy to be in the fresh air as we strolled along the river with the canyon's steep walls towering above us.

After another few hours in the bus, we finally arrived at our hotel, Berbere Palace. I was barely functioning and could not wait to lie down again. My room seemed to be in a remote part of the hotel. I tried to call the front desk to ask if someone could bring me a cool drink, but the room phone was dead, and I was too weak to walk back to the lobby. I was miserable and helpless, two conditions I had rarely experienced before this trip. I cried.

The next day, we continued our drive through the Atlas Mountains. Winding through the Tichka Pass while nauseous was one of the trip's more unpleasant experiences. The scenery was spectacular, but I was too delirious to enjoy it. We finally arrived in Marrakech, and I was relieved to have three consecutive nights at the same hotel.

As a teenager, I had kept a book called *Mystery in Marrakech* in the top drawer of my nightstand. I had loved the descriptions of the exotic Moroccan capital city in the 1960s, the strong young heroine, and her forbidden romance. I could still picture the cover of the book and feel the spicy anticipation of exploring a city with an intoxicating mix of African, French, Indian, and Arabian influences.

That afternoon, we went to the Menara Gardens where the main feature was a large, square water basin with a green-tiled pavilion. Isabelle and Eugenia led us along dirt paths into an orchard of olive trees where we formed a circle to support integrating the changes we had experienced. They said the unconditional energy of grace allowed us to experience even unpleasant circumstances with some degree of equanimity. I seemed to be getting daily opportunities to practice experiencing unpleasant circumstances with equanimity, and I was certainly not good at it. I was trained to spring into action and fix things. I privately thought to myself such a capacity sounded ambitious and would probably signal one was approaching enlightenment.

Later in the day, we visited Marrakech's souk, a huge, open-air square with snake charmers, magicians, and acrobats. The souk was loud, colorful, and bustling with crazy characters creating spectacles. At sunset, just gazing at the beautiful Koutoubia Mosque offered a welcome bit of serenity.

The following morning, I indulged in a massage at the hotel and relaxed poolside under tall palms blowing in the breeze. My body was feeling good again, and my energy was back. I journaled, noting the judgment I had once felt toward others who were weak or had some infirmity. I was accustomed to having a strong, resilient physical body, and what I experienced had provided a healthy dose of humility.

I asked Mustapha to walk me to the famous La Mamounia hotel, which was every bit as grand, elegant, and Moroccan as I expected. We sat on the terrace, and I thanked Mustapha for his support and humor during all of my challenges.

The next day, we said goodbye to Mustapha and Said and left Morocco for Gran Canaria, in the Canary Islands, 150 miles west of Africa. I had recovered from my nausea and intermittent malaise, and now I was experiencing neck pain. Never one to mince words, Eugenia observed I had been trying to control life and make it match what I thought it should be. Now, as my old beliefs collided with my new ones, I experienced internal conflict. She diagnosed my pain using the language of chakras and the levels of my energy field.

When I asked how to reconcile wanting to have my luggage with loosening control, she reminded me that desiring and demanding are two different things. Pleasure came from desire, but in my paradigm, if I allowed myself to want something and it did not happen, it was a personal failing. Rather than risk the perception of failure, I would fire up my afterburners and do whatever was necessary to get what I wanted.

I knew Eugenia's assessment was accurate, which made it that much more painful to hear. She suggested I let go of my win-lose mentality. I could win by *choosing* to learn in every moment, and that way I would never lose.

This was a new perspective. My experience had taught me if I wanted something, I had to take action and go after it. My family, school, sports, my career—every system I had ever participated in rewarded me for taking control and taking action. Now I was being encouraged to apply curiosity rather than sheer will, determination, and brute force. I could feel my neck relax as Eugenia smiled and said, "Let go, m' dear."

Isabelle and I had had regular sessions over several years, and they allowed her now to reflect on the difference between the version of me that went to Egypt and the one in Morocco. She saw my commitment to personal growth as demonstrated by my choices and my approach to life, but I still had much work to do. Between flights, Isabelle spoke with me about my tendency to flatten and tighten my chakras in situations I could not fix. Crying softened my resistance, and when I was able to release the tension in my chakras, my physical pain began to abate.

When we landed in Las Palmas, I was delighted to find my checked bag intact at baggage claim. Whatever lesson I needed to learn from my luggage was apparently complete for now.

Our first full day included a tour of most of the island, starting with Agaete, a seaside town on the northwest shore. We also visited Los Azulejos de Veneguera, an unusual rock formation with layers of turquoise stone embedded in the steep hillside, and our last stop was the Maspalomas Dunes, which formed millions of years ago when crushed shells from an offshore marine shelf blew inland and spread along the southern coast of the island. Isabelle and Eugenia found a quiet spot in the dunes, and we gathered again to honor the *soul of the earth*, our beautiful home, and to anchor new lifeforce energy into the planet.

Our travel tempo in Gran Canaria was decidedly more relaxed. I reflected on the intentions I had set, and after ten days, I knew being a more benevolent leader meant starting with a deeper level of acceptance of my imperfections and humanness.

Like in Egypt and Abadiânia, the group was eager to share stories. I enjoyed a leisurely breakfast with a steady stream of fellow travelers coming and going from the buffet at Hotel Santa Catalina. Eventually the dining room closed, and a group of us relocated to a beautiful outdoor lobby area to continue our conversation. These moments of raw, honest conversation were precious and gave me an opportunity to reflect on the changes in my life and career.

The following day, I took a long walk in Doramas Park with one of the other travelers. We meandered on the gravel paths through colorful flowers to a waterfall and from park bench to park bench, alternating between bright sunshine and cooler shade, comfortable in both silence and sharing. These moments of deep heartfelt connection were some of the most treasured of the trip.

From my room in the hotel, I could hear children laughing and playing in the park and splashing in the swimming pool just outside my windows. I watched a gorgeous pink sunset, happy to have a few moments of solitude to savor the experiences of the trip.

After four relaxing days in Las Palmas, we started the long journey home. I had an ocean's worth of flight time to journal about what I had learned during twelve days in a living laboratory. With support and encouragement, I had allowed vulnerability to be a doorway to receptivity, creating a new connection with life as a partner rather than me as its master.

My flight was barely on the tarmac in Atlanta before the Universe brought me opportunities to demonstrate how my evolution in consciousness would be embodied in my day-to-day routine.

CHAPTER 18
The Physics of Miracles

Several days after returning from Morocco, I was still exhausted and incorporating what I had learned during my adventures overseas.

I had really been looking forward to my first advisory board meeting at the Center for Entrepreneurship and Innovation at Duke's Fuqua School of Business, but in a nod to benevolent self-leadership, I chose to rest rather than attend.

After two long weeks in Atlanta, I was ready to travel again. A tropical vacation in the Caribbean did not materialize as expected, and I found myself surfing the web looking for "What's next?" I came across a podcast on the website of a publisher of metaphysical and spiritually-oriented books. It was an interview with Dr. Richard Bartlett. He talked about quantum science, the field of the heart, and some pretty wacky experiences that led to the creation of his book *Matrix Energetics*. Within hours, I had listened to the podcast, purchased the book, registered for a level one seminar in Asheville, and reserved a room at the hotel where the seminar was being held. My next adventure was officially in progress.

The weekend of the seminar, the weather forecast called for an unusual dusting of snow across the Southeast. I had barely driven from Atlanta to the South Carolina border before seeing several accidents caused by ice on the interstate highway. I sat in a long line of cars waiting to get past an overturned eighteen-wheeler. I realized driving through a winding mountain pass in dark, icy conditions was ill-advised. I was fortunate to get a hotel room in Greenville and hunkered down for the night.

The following morning, I drove through the mountains on I-26 with sunshine illuminating icicles glistening on the trees and pristine snow creating a vibrant crystalline tunnel.

I arrived in Asheville shortly after class had started and quietly took a seat at the back of the room. A hundred participants sat in chairs arranged around a dais. Dr. Bartlett was already onstage teaching with his partner, Melissa Joy Jonsson.

I learned Melissa had been a top salesperson for a pharmaceutical company before becoming a student of Matrix and client of Dr. Bartlett's. She was articulate and able to distill esoteric concepts and techniques into something I could follow. Melissa and Richard taught in a natural tag-team style with lessons interspersed with demonstrations of fundamental Matrix techniques using audience members who were invited onstage. The mood was light and fun.

We were invited to question consensus reality, access morphogenic fields, and purposefully master subtle energy for transformation. The only rule was there were no rules. Matrix had a certain playfulness and levity meant to engage one's inner child and expand a sense that *Anything is possible.*

After demonstrating a technique, Richard and Melissa had us pair up to practice with our classmates. I had come to the seminar alone and arrived late, so I stood at the back of the room and waited. When the crowd of twosomes parted, a man approached me. His nametag read Larry from Durham, NC. We quickly discovered we were both Duke graduates. This seemed like an amazing synchronicity in a ballroom full of one-hundred students.

Larry was a classically trained medical doctor and radiologist. He was also one of the original founders of the Duke Center for Integrative Medicine (DCIM). I was astonished at the serendipity since I had just visited DCIM and met with the executive director as part of my continuing interest in corporate wellness. Now I was practicing *Matrix Energetics* with one of DCIM's founders.

Larry spoke on dreams and hypnosis at conferences while working in mainstream medicine. He had come to the seminar with friends and invited me to join his group for dinner.

On the last day of the seminar, Melissa invited me onstage. I cannot explain how, but I had an inkling she would. She asked what I would like to work on, and I said, "I would like to get out of my own way." I don't know what she thought I was holding back, but she was very gracious and said to the audience, "I'm going to put everything Ann may want to work on and doesn't want to say aloud on a holographic clipboard." I had seen Melissa use this technique before, and I knew it might let us include the stuff my ego was reluctant to share.

For the next twenty-five minutes, I was able to track subtle sensations throughout my energy field. Similar to my experience with John of God in Brazil, I could feel where energy was being directed even when it was five or ten feet from my body. I had also experienced a similar phenomenon with healers who would direct my focus to a particular area of my body or a chakra, and a nanosecond before they spoke their instructions aloud, I felt my attention already there. Maybe this was the quantum field I had read about. It was amazing to connect my awareness to hers and track subtle energies.

During the first two days of the seminar, many participants were overwhelmed by the transformative energies and simply could not stand upright. They were helped to the floor so they could lie down. This looked sensational, but I knew the participants' dense physical bodies were simply integrating a new level of coherence. After a few moments of integration, they were up talking and laughing again.

Whatever happened when I was onstage I was both a witness to and a participant in. I felt I was engaging dormant capabilities simply waiting for me to rediscover them. At one point, Melissa found an energy pattern in my field, and I could feel where she had connected with it. She counted aloud and said it had sixty other patterns associated with it. I felt an uncanny sense of things shifting as I stood onstage under bright lights.

When we were almost done, I spotted Richard sitting just below the dais in the front row with his arms folded and his eyes closed. He looked like he was asleep, but as we finished, he suddenly popped his eyes open and said, "Wow, that's a lot! She can handle it, but that's a lot." He had his microphone on so the whole room heard it. Melissa said the experience had been like "a private session on steroids" and suggested I would continue processing our session for twenty-one days.

The class broke for lunch, and everyone left the room. The seminar was being recorded by a simple video camera on a tripod at the back. I was eager to see what the session looked like from the audience's perspective, so I asked the videographer if I could watch a replay while everyone was at lunch. After a firm "No" to my request, I started to leave the room when the man suddenly reversed his position and motioned me over to the camera.

The video guy turned out to be Richard's son, and it seemed he had received some divine guidance to let me watch. He rewound the video and handed me a pair of headphones. I stood and watched and took notes with a pen and pad. I had been onstage for twenty-five minutes, but I only consciously remembered about half of it.

Asheville was an amazing experience in every sense. Richard's suggestion to give ourselves extra credit for noticing anything outside normal programming felt expansive and added another level of depth to what I had learned in SomatoEmotional Release in Berkeley. Matrix took a crowbar to the logical practicality of my left brain and made space for the non-sensical. This environment of unfettered wackiness while practicing techniques with fellow participants gave me more confidence in my ability to read and interpret extrasensory information.

CHAPTER 18: THE PHYSICS OF MIRACLES

Meeting Larry seemed like a wink of serendipity related to my fascination with the intersection of mainstream and mystical.

Two months later, I attended Matrix Energetics Level 3 in Fort Lauderdale with Larry and several others from the Asheville group. Late on the last day, I was invited onstage. Richard asked me, "What can we help you with?" As if in an altered state, I felt my mouth open and words tumbled out. "I'd like to deepen my experience of the *morphic field* you are teaching us about."

Richard looked at me like an alien had just landed and said, "Whoa, that has power!" He demonstrated a few techniques and drew patterns on notebook paper with a blue ink pen. I have no idea how long I was onstage, but this time Richard said to allow six months to integrate what we had just done.

Over Easter, my family gathered in Kansas City, and my sister and I decided to go to the metaphysical bookstore to look for a gift for my ten-year-old niece, Vivian. Viv wanted to come with us, so I entertained her while my sister shopped for a gift.

I told Viv we were going to play a game. We went to the nook at the back of the store where books were shelved in no particular order. I suggested we both close our eyes and allow ourselves to be guided to a book that would serve us in our spiritual growth. I barely got my eyes closed before I began moving toward a particular shelf. Without looking, I pulled a book from among dozens and laughed. I chose *The Physics of Miracles* by Richard and Melissa. I explained to Vivian I knew the authors and had studied with them in Asheville and Fort Lauderdale.

Vivian did the same exercise and was guided to the *Encyclopedia of 5,000 Spells*, a $35 hardback book on spell-crafting. I thought it was pretty funny, but I got a scowl and a raised eyebrow from my sister.

After reading *The Physics of Miracles*, I looked for upcoming Matrix seminars and went to one in Seattle titled "Unplugged," which included a celebration of Richard's sixtieth birthday. Melissa invited me onstage, and with no specific problem to address, she connected some new patterns and said my consciousness was already expanded; I just needed to move more fully into who and what I already was. I smiled, knowing that was a lifelong process.

I stayed in touch with Larry and attended a program on paranormal studies he organized a few blocks from Duke's campus at the Rhine Center. I was also invited to his dream workshops at Monroe Institute.

I knew there was more Matrix Energetics in my future, but it would be a few years before I was guided back, and by that time, much had changed.

CHAPTER 19
Waaaay Past the Edge

In the early 2000s, I was among a small but growing number of women working in the rapidly expanding field of supply chain. I was also an entrepreneur, having founded a consulting company, and I was building a collaborative transportation network serving some of the country's largest consumer products companies. With these achievements, plus a long history of volunteer leadership in the Duke University Alumni Association, I was invited to join an advisory board at Duke's Center for Entrepreneurship and Innovation (CEI) in the Fuqua School of Business.

I had missed the fall board meeting after my adventures in Morocco, so my first meeting was in the spring of 2013. The meeting started with a group dinner at the Washington Duke Inn, and after dinner, several of us—Reid, Mike, Marty, and I—gathered in the hotel's Bull Durham bar. They were highly accomplished in their respective fields, and we chatted late into the evening.

The next morning, the board met in a beautiful, wood-paneled conference room where Duke staff made presentations about curriculum and programming. Marty, the most successful entrepreneur in the room, sat directly opposite me across a large, round, walnut conference table. Marty had started and sold two technology companies, reportedly for tens of millions of dollars, and now he had his own venture capital firm. He had something of a celebrity status in the group.

As we discussed ways to attract more students to entrepreneurship programs, I looked across the table at Marty, and in my mind's eye, I saw his tightly puckered anus squarely in front of his forehead. I was accustomed to receiving intuitive information and unsolicited images in client sessions, but nothing quite like this had ever happened in a board meeting. This image was disruptive and annoying. I looked around the room at other board members and staff and did not see body parts or images hovering in front of any of them. I knew the image was meant to convey information. I just did not know *what* information.

I had met Marty at the board dinner the night before and enjoyed our conversation. He did not seem to be an asshole or a tight ass or any other metaphor that might possibly be symbolized by this image. In fact, he seemed just the opposite. While intelligent and successful, he seemed to be laid back and reserved, but the image of the anus persisted as if to make a point of its significance.

Shortly after the meeting ended, we left the conference room uneventfully. I stayed another night at the Washington Duke Inn so I could go to campus for a jazz concert and visit with friends. Reid joined me for the concert, and as we returned to the hotel that evening, we joked Marty was probably in the hotel bar with an entourage of people hoping to make a pitch for his money.

We were right. The hotel bar was crowded and noisy on a Friday night, and as expected, Marty was surrounded by a group of friends and aspiring entrepreneurs. Reid and I ordered wine and found some comfortable club chairs just outside the bar where it was quiet enough to enjoy a conversation without shouting.

Marty spotted us, came over, and pulled up chairs for himself and another friend of his. As we sat in a circle talking, I was relieved the persistent image of a tightly puckered anus was no longer present in front of Marty's forehead.

Being a California tech entrepreneur, Marty was usually clad in jeans and an untucked shirt, and by this late hour on a Friday night, he was now in his sock-feet with no shoes. We sat in the club chairs and spoke about holistic health modalities, herbs, and some spiritual festivals Marty had attended. He had been an early pioneer in developing apps for cell phones and tablets. I did not know any of the ones he named and was clearly not his target demographic. I handed him my iPhone and winced as he scrolled looking for apps and discovered my embarrassingly scant use of technology.

When I looked away for a moment, Marty must have opened my photos. He held the screen toward me and asked who the people were in a picture. I was surprised that out of hundreds of photos he asked about one I had taken while hiking in the North Carolina mountains with Gomati and Vasistha. I said they were my meditation teachers.

Marty perked up and said meditation had always eluded him because of his busy mind. He asked about my experiences, and I told him about meditation's benefits, including the ability to quiet my mind and access my intuition.

"Ah, so you're intuitive?" Marty said.

I smiled and replied, "Um…about some stuff…."

Marty leaned in and asked, "Like what?"

I took my phone back and paused, knowing I was approaching the edge of a metaphoric cliff. I could play it safe and offer a general answer, or I could take a leap of faith by owning my intuitive capabilities and sharing the image I had received during the board meeting.

I started my response with my observation that people who are in discomfort will often transmit messages non-consciously in such a way that the information can be picked up intuitively. I lowered my voice and explained information often came to me in images or some knowingness that just popped into my awareness.

Marty was still attentive, so I went on to say I knew he must be experiencing significant discomfort because his body had transmitted images throughout the board meeting earlier that day. Marty cocked his head and looked quizzical. I softened my tone and said I was very sorry he was in pain and believed it was probably caused by a hemorrhoid.

Marty choked on his sip of red wine and then stuttered, asking how I could possibly know this. While stunned, he validated the accuracy of my information and his corresponding level of discomfort. I described the vision I had received consistently throughout the meeting and how that correlated with his level of discomfort and body's desire for relief. Marty confirmed the discomfort and said it was his first hemorrhoid. I spoke about metaphysics and my belief that physical conditions begin in the energy field before they fully manifest in our dense bodies, so metaphysically, over-pushing or feeling pressured to push toward his next success might have led to the hemorrhoid.

At 1:30 a.m., our group finally headed to our respective rooms. As Marty got off the elevator on his floor, he looked at me and said, "Thanks for watching out for my asshole." Everyone else on the elevator seemed confused, and I just shrugged.

Our conversation continued in an exchange of text messages. Marty said he was glad we had met and hoped to experience my CranioSacral expertise one day. I texted back that I hoped our paths would cross again soon.

I sensed the amazing divinity in our chance meeting at the hotel. I had left the board meeting Friday afternoon thinking I would never have any opportunity to mention the tightly puckered anus hovering in front of Marty's forehead or understand its meaning. Ten hours later, my path serendipitously crossed Marty's again and his question about a photo on my iPhone created an opportunity to actually talk about the image I saw I my mind's eye. I marveled at the precious synchronicity required to bring all this into

CHAPTER 19: WAAAAY PAST THE EDGE

perfect alignment so I could offer my intuitive insight and validate its accuracy.

The next board meeting I attended was a year later with dinner in the same dining room at the Washington Duke Inn. I sat talking with colleagues at a long table with white linens and elegant place settings. Marty came in and quietly took the chair beside me. I sensed a shift in Marty. He had always been laid back, but I sensed a deeper, truer, inner calm.

When we spoke, he said our encounter a year earlier had inspired him to make some life changes. He had revisited a class he had taken on meditation and tried it again. He said he didn't know how I knew what I knew and described it as "way past his edge." And then he smiled and encouraged me to share anything I might pick up during our time together.

The next morning, the board and Duke staff met again in the same beautiful, wood-paneled conference room. Marty and I took the same seats as the year before directly across from one another at the large, round, walnut conference table. Despite the meeting's formality, we could barely make eye contact without smirking or even laughing out loud. As at the previous meeting, Marty's internal system transmitted very clearly. Thankfully, this time, the transmission did not include the tightly puckered anus and what I did receive was much less intense.

After the meeting, four of us went to the university gift shop to buy some Duke sportswear before catching our flights home. Marty and I maneuvered around racks of Blue Devil sweatshirts trying to find a private place to talk. I conveyed the impressions I received during the meeting and Marty again validated their accuracy. Because our colleagues were also shopping nearby, the conversation was short.

Marty and I continued to talk via email, with him offering suggestions for apps and me offering encouragement to rest his busy mind and tap his own intuitive capabilities. Our email exchanges were candid and revealing. Months later, Marty left the board and I did not see him again.

I was grateful for the opportunity to share my impressions. The validation he offered was an added benefit, helping me understand and refine my perceptions and translations. I had always picked up information in ways I could not explain, and I wanted to encourage others to explore their own capabilities. Perhaps most importantly, something about our exchange led Marty to make life changes, and while they were perhaps not apparent to anyone else, I felt them firsthand.

Such instances of direct knowingness continued to manifest in mysterious ways at unexpected times. My reality became filled with synchronicities and unseen support requiring me to develop the finesse to know what, when, and with whom to share my insights.

CHAPTER 20
Art and Tom

My seemingly separate careers continued to overlap in surprising ways. I encountered curious synchronicities as I explored new aspects of myself, leading me to wonder if the evolution within was being perceived by others. Supply chain clients expressed interest in my wellness practices and intuition, so I allowed myself to be more open in sharing my interests and capabilities.

Solertis had worked with one company in Sarasota, Florida, for a decade. Visiting their headquarters several times each year, I got to know the executives. The company was publicly traded, and I had purchased shares as we began our first project. As both a vendor and shareholder, I made a point to attend the investor and analyst meeting each year. I enjoyed interacting with Art, who headed the Investor Relations department. From our conversations, I learned Art had studied philosophy, Ken Wilber's Integral Theory, and Amos Tversky's work in cognitive bias and intuitive judgment.

One day, I was talking with Art on the phone in preparation for an upcoming meeting when he mentioned he was limping around the office in a medical boot after breaking his ankle. He had been visiting family in Ohio and slipped on black ice. As he spoke, I winced, intuitively sensing the clean break in his right fibula just above the ankle. From there, my attention was drawn to his right hip where I felt a torque or twisting energy.

Art described the accident, but it only involved his ankle, not his hip. He went on to say he had recently been through a particularly difficult time. He had lost three people he loved, including his best friend who had committed suicide, a martial arts master with whom he had studied, and one of his business mentors. These men had been father figures and meaningful contributors to his life. Since the loss of these friends, he felt he had been "stumbling around." I thought his choice of words was interesting given he had just literally stumbled, fallen, and broken his ankle.

I asked if he had also injured his right hip and he explained he had already scheduled hip replacement surgery, but he'd had to delay it until his right ankle healed.

My question about his hip piqued his curiosity. We had discussed my interest in alternative modalities previously, but this was the first time our conversation turned to him personally. Art mentioned he would love to have a session sometime when I was in Sarasota.

Weeks later, I flew to Florida and spent a few days on Sanibel Island visiting friends and paddleboarding before driving up to Sarasota for the annual shareholders meeting. Thinking ahead to Art and his interest in a session, I borrowed a friend's portable massage table and put it in the trunk of my rental car. Art and I went to our usual seafood spot for lunch to catch up. Art enjoyed studying and discussing leadership styles, including those of the company's executives. I loved his candor. He had a quick wit and brilliant intellect that masked his more sensitive side. I knew a lot was going on just below the surface.

At the end of lunch, Art again said he would like to do a session sometime. I said if he was serious, I had a friend's massage table in the trunk of the rental car and was ready to go. He loved the synchronicity, and we had more than enough time for a session the next meetings back at company headquarters.

CHAPTER 20: ART AND TOM

Once our session started, Art mentioned that besides the deaths of three mentors, his father had died when he was age seven, so he became the "man of the house." I felt the pain he held in his heart. He used the metaphor of a vault. He kept his emotions tightly contained and was afraid if he put the key in and unlocked the vault, he would be overwhelmed by what he had stuffed inside over many years. I assured him he could safely lock and unlock his metaphoric vault on his timeline and at his discretion.

With that assurance, he began to cry. I held one hand over his heart and one hand beneath it as Art accessed the deep pain around the loss of his father and his three mentors. Not having to hold it all in allowed him to release years of pent-up emotions. I felt deep reverence for his braveness in allowing himself to be vulnerable.

As I put the portable table back in the rental car, I got a text from the CFO, who was ready to meet. Before driving back to headquarters, I spent a silent moment in gratitude for all we cannot possibly know with our logical minds that is readily available when we drop into our heart space. Experiencing a person in their most basic human messiness beyond titles, roles, and accomplishments is simultaneously respectful and healing.

I knew that creating an environment where a client felt safe to express vulnerability was what I wanted to do professionally.

A month later, I flew to Chicago for a supply chain leadership forum and lunch with a client between meetings. Tom led a multi-billion-dollar consumer products company and had also run supply chain at a global consulting firm. He was well known in the industry and had hired my company for numerous projects over fifteen years. Tom always was curious about my life outside supply chain and often quizzed me about wellness and my interest in holistic health. At lunch, I mentioned I had trained in CranioSacral Therapy and SomatoEmotional Release and was seeing clients in Atlanta.

While explaining these techniques, I told Tom I had always thought he might benefit from work on his jaw, particularly on the right side. As I spoke, I had a sudden flash of Tom in a terrible accident many years earlier—I saw him as a passenger in the backseat of a car. I saw a slow-motion movie in my mind's eye. At the moment of impact, Tom's head hit the back of the seat in front of him, and a line of energy traveled down his spine. I grimaced at the feeling of whiplash.

In the context of explaining my training, I told him I sensed trauma to his head and jaw in the car accident. He looked up from his plate, set his fork down, and said, "Yes, that car wreck was seventeen years ago."

Tom is a lifelong super-achiever, so while waiting for paramedics, he had triaged everyone else in the vehicle. He was probably in shock, but he had sprung into action to help his friends who were badly injured. Now, his system was signaling he could benefit from releasing whatever trauma was still stored within.

Tom said he would love to have a session and suggested Denver since we were both planning to be there for a conference a few weeks later. As I walked back to finish the afternoon meeting at the leadership forum, I smiled thinking about how the disparate parts of my professional life seemed to be organically overlapping so regularly.

Weeks later, I flew to Denver for the annual conference of the Council of Supply Chain Management Professionals. At its peak, the three-day event attracted 7,000 professionals, and as with most events of this type, the activities ranged from educational sessions and networking activities to lavish evening receptions.

Tom and I planned a session at 7 a.m. on the Monday of the conference. Without any coordination, we both booked rooms in the same hotel near the convention center. I knew the hotel had a spa, and I arranged to borrow one of its massage tables. Tom showed up in a T-shirt and shorts right on schedule. After getting comfortable on the table, Tom dropped into deep stillness. His physiology relaxed as I held my fingertips along his spine. In my mind's eye, I again saw the slow-motion movie of the car accident and the

CHAPTER 20: ART AND TOM

wave of energy that traveled down his spine. I felt his body slip into SomatoEmotional Release and a subtle movement of energy as he appeared to nap on the table.

In my experience, the subconscious mind is capable of transmitting more information than the ego will ever allow. One hour resting on a massage table might appear inconsequential, but in the right circumstances, a transcendent field of energy is created and a transformative experience occurs, even if unbidden by the client. Tom's session included unconscious transmission of patterns, themes, desires, and challenges.

As Tom napped, I held a space of deep compassion for his soul on the journey of human experience. I watched his system sort, sift, and reexamine experiences almost as if flipping through a Rolodex holding Polaroids of his entire life. The experiences I saw told a different story than his public persona.

After forty-five minutes, I was guided to move to Tom's head and work with his jaw. He was alert for this portion of our session and aware of an impulse to move around. Trauma releases can be uncomfortable, but clients often feel better, and the release is enhanced if they squirm, even if they don't know exactly why they are squirming.

When we ended the session, Tom had no sense of anything happening while he was snoozing on the table. I encouraged him to drink water and try to make some time to be still, although this was unlikely since we would be at the conference all day.

Ten hours later, I saw Tom again at the elegant reception his company hosted for several hundred guests. Hosting duties required him to mingle, so we only spoke briefly, and he did not mention the session.

Working with Tom, I learned if the client is entirely new to subtle energy work and is engaging primarily because of rapport with me personally, I need to proceed with caution. My tendency is to cover as much ground as possible, but that style is not always optimal in deeply transformative work. It is impossible to know where a session might take us because the subconscious is extremely powerful when the ego is silent. Part of Tom was completely unaware of what had happened and part knew exactly what had transpired.

I thrive on navigating a vast range of experiences, but not everyone is comfortable moving from the intimacy and vulnerability of a session to a professional networking reception in a matter of hours. By most measures, Tom had previously held much of the power in our relationship. The session created a subtle new dynamic.

I saw Tom several times in Denver, but no mention was made of the session. With the changes in my life and professional aspirations, our paths never crossed again.

CHAPTER 21
Odd Sense of Foreboding

During the twenty-plus years I ran my consulting company, I experimented with different approaches to sales and marketing. Early on, I hired a telemarketer, made cold calls, deployed a part-time sales force, tracked a pipeline of prospects, and used many traditional sales techniques. Those techniques felt like an impersonal numbers game. I preferred relationships and referrals based on reputation and the quality of my work.

My business model facilitated a lifestyle of adventures, spontaneity, and the ability to move quickly to take advantage of both personal and professional opportunities. Scale was important to me as it related to expanding human consciousness but not much else. I trusted myself and synchronicities, and when it was time for another project, one showed up. I knew this mentality would never fly in mainstream business, but my sales process was guided by something larger than myself.

In the summer of 2013, I visited friends at their home on Cape Cod. Between sailing in Wellfleet Bay and paddleboarding on Gulf Pond, I took a call from a colleague in Atlanta who worked in business development for a big consulting firm. This firm was a competitor, but we had collaborated on projects. The sales guy had recently met with a prospective client who needed support beyond his company's capabilities. He called thinking it might be a fit for

Solertis. The timing was perfect. The potential client company, Vail Brands, seemed like a good size, and it was the type of operational work I loved.

Vail Brands was a party favors and gifts company started by an ambitious entrepreneur named Kate. While working from her basement, Kate tapped a niche and sales skyrocketed. Creative product design, an attractive website, and the ability for customers to personalize gifts led to explosive growth and complexity. The business had outgrown both her basement and her first warehouse.

Days after returning from Cape Cod, I met with Kate and her team. The meeting started in the conference room with five staff members describing their challenges. After an hour of discussion, Kate offered to give me a tour of the warehouse.

We walked among high bay storage racks filled with pallets of products. It was August in Georgia, and the warehouse was not air-conditioned. We stood at an open dock door where a warm breeze was blowing as a forklift loaded a tractor trailer. As we turned to walk toward the shipping office, I had an odd flash. I sensed people of Asian descent. Ethnicity was the most defining characteristic I perceived, but I had not seen any Asian-looking people on site.

We entered the air-conditioned shipping office, and Kate introduced me to the staff. Again, no Asians. We discussed my team's capabilities as we walked back to the main office area.

In the conference room, we sat down to discuss a proposal and the next steps. Still pondering the flash of intuition, I drove back to my office to write a proposal.

We were awarded the project and began work on site two weeks later. The project scope and deliverables included operational process improvements, potential changes to warehouse design, assessment of key warehouse employees, and a high-level assessment of the warehouse management system (WMS).

Within a week, I knew the warehouse manager, John, did not have the skills to support operational growth and was not a good

CHAPTER 21: ODD SENSE OF FOREBODING

leader. He created turmoil and divisiveness, hurt morale, and then positioned himself as the hero sweeping in to fix the problems he himself had caused. John had been an employee since the early days, and Kate was extremely loyal and reluctant to let him go. We planned a timeline to fire John, and I assured her I could step in and manage the warehouse if necessary.

I knew Kate's pain firsthand. In Solertis' early years, our business ebbed and flowed. I had a very small, close knit staff and had to terminate a loyal colleague whom I considered a friend and brother. It was excruciating. When I saw Kate come back into the main lobby after saying goodbye to John, I felt her pain. I reassured her it was the best path forward.

Most of my time on site was spent working on warehouse operations. The executive offices, Human Resources, Accounting, and IT departments were on the second floor. After several days, I had questions about the technology driving operations. In twenty-five years of supply chain consulting, I had studied dozens of warehouse management systems (WMS). In a company the size of Kate's, it was common for the WMS to be "homegrown." Systems were created and continuously updated by someone inside the company because it was cost-effective during early growth stages.

At the scheduled time, I went up to the second floor and Kate walked me to the last office on the hallway and introduced me to the man who wrote the WMS' software code. I felt the hair on my arms go up as we shook hands. JD was Asian.

Kate left me with JD so we could talk systems functionality. I had a list of questions about why the system operated in particular ways, and I offered some suggestions. JD's expertise was in technology, not warehouse operations. He showed little interest in a consultant with a dozen suggestions for improvement and modifications based on best practices in the logistics industry. We had a spirited discussion, but I sensed subtle resistance to my input and observations.

The most important thing I discovered during this meeting was the software behind the entire multi-million-dollar business was effectively controlled by one person. JD knew every line of code and how it worked because he wrote it. With changes to a few lines of code, he could shut down the entire enterprise.

A few days later, I met with Kate. I politely pointed out the risk and vulnerability of having one person in control of the software, even though two other employees reported to JD. Kate said she doubted JD would do anything to sabotage the system because he was one of the two minority partners in the company.

My heart sank. The other minority partner was JD's wife, Sharon, who managed relationships with overseas suppliers. I suddenly understood the flash of insight I had on the loading dock during our first meeting.

I got to know most of the staff over several months on site. Everyone in the enterprise loved Kate and looked to her for leadership. She was friendly, creative, and passionate, and Vail Brands was her baby. I attended a company picnic and saw firsthand how Kate interacted with each person. I sensed how loyal they were to her. I also noticed JD was not at the picnic and largely isolated himself in his office.

Kate had brought JD and Sharon into her company early on because they had needed expertise in their respective areas. To conserve cash, Kate had given them an equity stake rather than paying a big salary.

I completed the project and provided Kate with a report. In addition to dozens of tactical and operational recommendations, my report again highlighted the risk with JD and systems.

After the project ended, Kate and I occasionally met for lunch and stayed in touch. I continued to provide intermittent support, interviewing candidates for key warehouse positions and visiting their new, bigger warehouse.

One Sunday afternoon, Kate called me. The situation with JD had become untenable. Kate wanted to bring in a chief operating officer, but JD refused. They had differing visions for how to grow the business. Kate was planning to offer JD and his wife a buyout, which would trigger a corporate buy-sell agreement already in place. JD and Sharon would have sixty days to come up with a counteroffer or buy Kate out and take ownership of the company.

And that's exactly what happened. JD got millions in investment capital from Asian investors and took ownership and control of Vail Brands. After ten years of heartfelt investment growing her business into a thriving enterprise, Kate was pushed out. She profited financially, but losing her company and the team she had built was crushing.

I continued to revisit the flash of insight I received while outside the shipping office in the heat of that August afternoon. I had no idea what would happen two years later. As was the case with Susana and the house in Taos, my intuitive flash had carried an odd sense of foreboding.

With the Vail Brands project, I had satisfied all the deliverables and completed work. I had pointed out vulnerabilities and risks, but I continued to wonder if I should have said more.

I thought back to times when I had felt a loss but ultimately came to see how it had cleared the way for something greater and helped me to evolve. I knew even a painful experience could become a net positive.

I continued to encourage people to develop their own intuitive capabilities as I refined my own inclination to jump up and down on the conference room table versus simply accepting and embracing the Universe's greater plan.

CHAPTER 22
Simply Spooky

The following year, 2014, brought more shifts and changes in my priorities. I had been a volunteer leader with the Council of Supply Chain Management Professionals for twenty years, serving in roles at local, regional, and national levels, and I had won awards for doing so. Volunteer leadership was something I truly enjoyed, and supply chain management was growing in notoriety. The CSCMP board of directors had a plan to expand beyond memberships sold to individuals and create a corporate membership program. I offered to use my Rolodex to sell the association's services. I loved CSCMP and could provide a heartfelt testimonial. What I underestimated were the nuances of becoming more than a volunteer.

After putting a contract in place with a commission structure, I sold a $50,000 internet-based course called "Supply Chain Essentials" to a company CSCMP had never been able to sell to. I made the sale in just a few months by working with an executive I knew from the Duke Alumni Association. The CEO of CSCMP celebrated and called it huge, but my excitement was quickly dampened by a misunderstanding about the terms of our agreement. After weeks of unpleasant discussions, we agreed to a compromise and terminated our contract.

Before the commission issue, I had managed to get a meeting with the vice president of supply chain at Chick-fil-A, and since I had initiated it, I intended to be there despite terminating my sales contract. The meeting was scheduled for a Monday, and the CEO of CSCMP was flying in to co-present with me. On Friday, I was told the CEO was sending Jay in his place.

Jay was relatively new to CSCMP, so I offered him my notes, an update call over the weekend, and to pick him up at the airport. Jay declined all my offers. When I arrived at Chick-fil-A Monday morning, Jay was already set up in a conference room and did not want any of my thoughts.

When the meeting started, I introduced myself as a volunteer and spoke of how my career and professional network had benefited through CSCMP. Jay had no such experience, only a formal PowerPoint presentation. He went through the entire deck without a pause and presented statistics I knew to be misleading. He dropped names and attempted to boost his own self-importance while sitting in the headquarters of a corporation that valued humility, ethics, and faith above profit. He made no attempt to learn about any of Chick-fil-A's supply chain challenges.

I kept my heart open but felt sad because Jay's presentation was not representative of the organization I had known and loved.

Jay refused my offer to drive him back to the airport and insisted on using a black car service. One of the Chick-fil-A guys, Mike, overheard the conversation and asked if I could drop him off at another building on campus. Mike and I had a friendly conversation, and he shared some of the company's initiatives, including sustainably sourced coffee.

Later, I sent a thank you email with a short recap of the meeting to an executive at Chick-fil-A. I got an out of office auto-reply and then a kind personal message saying he and his family were on vacation and he looked forward to hearing more upon his return. His warmhearted email was a stark contrast to the tone set by Jay.

Weeks later, I was at an Atlanta CSCMP luncheon seated next to the CEO of the company that had spent $50,000 for 100 user seats for "Supply Chain Essentials." The CEO was totally disinterested in talking supply chain. Instead, he observed I had passed on the calorie-laden chicken parmesan with penne pasta, choosing a romaine salad with grilled chicken instead. He spent the entire lunch asking about my health and wellness practices. This interaction seemed like another wink from the Universe about my professional direction, and for the first time in fifteen years, I chose not to attend the CSCMP annual global conference.

The choice felt both odd and yet entirely natural at the same time. While I was sad to be ending an association that represented decades of history, I knew I was opening space for opportunities more aligned with my current consciousness and more supportive of my growth. Any fear and uncertainty were outweighed by a sense that everything was happening in divine order.

For several months, I had been meeting with two girlfriends, Cam and Marcia, who had recently left a digital media agency and were in various stages of professional exploration. Cam had been managing director of a large agency where she led projects for Fortune 500 clients. Marcia was an award-winning creative and content strategist. I loved the synthesis of our skills and backgrounds.

After weeks of meeting in restaurants and coffee shops, we decided to rent an office in a trendy coworking space called Industrious. Coming up with ideas was fun and energizing, with a lot of metaphoric spaghetti being thrown at the walls and notes scribbled on whiteboards. I was still traveling regularly for supply chain projects, but I was eager to see where this collaboration might lead.

During one week in 2015, I was in a different city every day. One project was an operations assessment for an iconic brand with a multi-national retail presence. The company was under new ownership, and the CEO asked me to visit some of their highest-grossing stores in Manhattan. I flew to New York, arrived at LaGuardia, and stood impatiently in a long line of travelers waiting for taxis. It started to rain, and as the rain got heavier, the line of cabs got shorter until only one was left.

I happened to overhear the man ahead of me say he was headed to SoHo, and that's where I was going too. I approached him as he was getting into the last taxi and asked if I could share a ride. He agreed, and I jumped in as the downpour intensified. His name was George, and he was friendly, talkative, and had just gotten off the red eye from Los Angeles. George was a celebrity hairstylist who had used his background to launch a startup catering to clients looking for a personal, in-home beauty experience. We had a lively conversation about life and entrepreneurship before the driver dropped him outside his apartment. After thanking George and riding another three blocks in the taxi, I arrived at my client's flagship store and met the chief operating officer.

My client's brand positioning was high-end gourmet with products imported from all over the world. Operations were complicated by the huge diversity of products, from finely aged cheeses to luxury linens. Sales were good, but operations were inefficient, and I wanted to see stores in action. The flagship store anchored a prestigious street corner in SoHo. It featured fresh flowers, a popular coffee bar and bakery, made-to-order sushi, and staff in crisp white uniforms with all the polish of a truly upscale shopping experience.

But what I saw next was shocking.

Behind the elegance and sophistication of the retail floor, the freight elevator was out of service, the loading dock was far too small to handle delivery trucks, and employees were running up and down flights of stairs looking for inventory. The constraints of the historic building were causing extreme inefficiencies that would not be corrected with a few process improvements or a little investment in automation. My day was getting complicated.

The COO and I took a cab to their store on the Upper East Side and then another to the New York Times café at 40th and

CHAPTER 22: SIMPLY SPOOKY

8th. It was mid-afternoon, and I was thoroughly engrossed in the challenges that grew in complexity with every behind-the-scenes peek into store operations.

As the COO and I stood in the café, I heard a male voice say, "Ann?" I looked up from my notepad to see SoHo George standing in line waiting to order lunch.

Stunned and delighted, I introduced George to the COO and explained how he had saved me from a torrential downpour at LaGuardia just a few hours earlier.

In a city of nine million people, it was remarkable to randomly meet the same stranger twice in one day. George explained he had a meeting nearby and had just stopped in to grab a sandwich.

I saw this incredible synchronicity as a wink, reminding me we live in a magical universe of infinite possibility. George's help at LaGuardia followed by his repeat appearance hours later, provided some odd sense of reassurance in the midst of an increasingly challenging day.

The COO simply called it "spooky."

I flew back to Atlanta late that night and took a cab home from the airport. The driver was blasting music punctuated with a deafening chant of, "In the name of Jesus!" I asked him twice to turn it down, but he could not hear me. I felt guided to jot down the name of the cab company, phone number, and vehicle number from the decal on the window. I could not imagine I was really going to file a complaint, but I followed the impulse.

When I got home, I tipped the driver and got my luggage out of the trunk. Once in my condo, I began to unpack and repack for another trip the following morning. I reached into my purse for my cell phone and discovered my wallet was missing. I had tipped the driver cash, so I must have left it on the seat. I called the phone number I had jotted down, and the dispatcher asked for the vehicle number. At 1 a.m., the driver returned with my wallet. I was again grateful I had followed an impulse even without knowing its purpose.

I travelled to Southwest Florida every few weeks for work. When I was there, Sanibel Island provided a quiet place to slow down and immerse myself in nature. Paddleboarding in Tarpon Bay, walking the beach, and looking for crocodiles in Bailey Tract were among my favorite ways to relax.

Sanibel had a holiday tradition called "Luminary" when a two-mile stretch of bike path along Periwinkle Way was lined with candles in paper bags creating a magical trail for a leisurely stroll under the stars with stops at shops offering refreshments. As I walked with my friends, Lee and Andy, I felt drawn to look back in the direction we had just walked. The edges of the path marked by luminaria stretched as far as I could see, and the full moon, perfectly aligned between two palm trees, was just rising. I smiled to myself in a private moment of gratitude, took a quick photo, and walked briskly to catch up with my friends.

The morning after Luminary, I drove across the Everglades to Miami Beach where Duke was hosting an event for Art Basel. The registration list was available online, and among the 400 guests, I spotted the name of an old friend, Evan, who had graduated a few years ahead of me and married his Duke sweetheart. I got a warm feeling when I saw Evan's name. Then I noticed his guest for the event was not his wife.

I arrived at the Bass Museum of Art and immediately ran into Evan. He introduced me to his girlfriend, who complimented my skirt and excused herself to use the restroom. Evan quietly told me his wife had died exactly two years earlier. After ten years of treatment for cancer and a brief remission, she had a recurrence that took her life.

As Evan spoke, I felt the strong cords of connection between him and his wife, and while they were endearing, I sensed they were no longer beneficial. As he finished his story, Evan exhaled deeply, almost like a sigh, and with his exhale, I felt something shift. I did a double-take as I watched a shimmer of white light rise from behind him and dissolve.

Seconds later, Evan's girlfriend returned and our circle widened to include more friends. I embraced people I had not seen in decades and reconnected with an old friend from freshman year, Lance, whose wife was a New York art dealer. Lance, his wife, and another friend of theirs provided a guided tour of the main exhibition and a beautiful poolside lunch at a hotel on the beach, but I didn't see Evan again.

The sun was setting as I drove back across Alligator Alley toward Sanibel thinking about all that had happened. I had seen a lot of amazing artwork at Art Basel, but whatever had happened with Evan and the shimmering light was far more interesting and extraordinary.

CHAPTER 23
Stretching in New Directions

Back in Atlanta, I attended the Georgia Logistics Summit where I watched a panel discussion hosted by James, the CEO of the consulting company that had connected me to Vail Brands. James and I had started our companies around the same time, and early on, we had compared entrepreneurial ambitions and philosophies. James was on an eighty-hour-a week trajectory working to build an empire, and I was working to fund my next sailing trip or spiritual adventure. He had once called mine a "lifestyle business," meaning it as a diminishment.

More recently, James's firm had needed a subject matter expert for a project with Apple. One of the guys on my team, Bert, was a perfect fit. James had sent me a legal agreement, and I had forwarded it to my attorney, who sent back a long list of objections that included indemnification standards, non-circumvention clauses, and payment terms. In a nutshell, James's contract was grossly disadvantageous to my team.

While going back and forth on revisions, James made derogatory comments and told me I was "running nothing more than a glorified dating service." I did, indeed, have some exceptionally talented subcontractors, and James needed one of them to secure the Apple gig.

In another instance of amazing serendipity, I was on a flight with a colleague and mentioned the deal with James and Apple. This colleague was actually familiar with the situation and was certain James had been unable to find anyone else with Bert's expertise. That information reassured me holding out for an equitable contract was the right thing to do. James and I came to agreement and signed the contract the evening before the first scheduled trip to Apple.

At the Georgia Logistics Summit, I watched James moderate a panel discussion with executives from Macy's, Chico's FAS, and Home Depot. After the panel, James spotted me, smiled, and motioned for me to come over. He looked older and more tired than I remembered. He was also surprisingly friendly and introduced me to the panelists. His usual condescending tone had shifted. He was gracious and treated me as a peer rather than a pawn.

I was suntanned and rested after a long weekend in Sanibel, and I privately wondered if he was having second thoughts about my "lifestyle business." I knew this new level of respect was a direct reflection of my growing ability to hold myself sovereign, heal old patterns and gain authentic, inner strength. My external world was finally reflecting years of attention to inner growth and investment in personal transformation.

Back at Industrious, Cam, Marcia and I had not come up with any viable ideas worth pursuing. Because Cam and Marcia had worked at a prestigious digital agency, I was able to get my client in New York City to allow us to pitch a project to design and implement an e-commerce platform. I was still under contract on a supply chain project, and e-commerce dovetailed nicely with that project.

We put together a capabilities presentation for the CEO and CIO who came to Atlanta to meet with us and other agencies bidding on the project. In our meeting, Cam gave a brilliant, polished presentation and demonstrated she had perfect credentials for the project. Marcia had talent but lacked the sophistication of a managing director.

CHAPTER 23: STRETCHING IN NEW DIRECTIONS

I could read the CEO's body language and thoughts during the meeting. He was impressed by Cam and impatient with Marcia, who talked unnecessarily and nervously.

Sitting with the group in a conference room, I saw the entire project laid out in my mind's eye. Cam went to a whiteboard and drew that same vision. I quietly smiled feeling the alignment.

Later, as we wrote our first proposal, Cam insisted on including a role for Marcia. I knew the CEO's target price for the first phase, and we were 25 percent over budget. The most expedient solution was for Cam to run the first phase and bring Marcia in later. Friendship trumped good business sense, and after weeks of frustrating discussions, the CEO hired another firm. The ordeal did not reflect the way I ran my supply chain consulting company, and fortunately, the CEO knew that.

Months of enthusiasm fizzled quickly after our failed attempt to land the e-commerce project or find a viable business idea to pursue. The potential I perceived in our collaboration never materialized. Over-estimating potential and over-hoping for results were lessons the Universe had provided dozens of times and I was clearly still learning.

Just as things fizzled with Cam and Marcia, new supply chain consulting opportunities rolled in. Almost immediately, I got a call from Rich, a colleague at a $300 million logistics company looking to hire someone to facilitate a two-day meeting. Rich said the CEO, Karl, needed twenty of his senior staff to agree on strategies and tactics to achieve sales and operational targets as part of their acquisition by a larger, publicly held company.

When I met with Karl, he was very clear about his objective. He wanted a spirited discussion leading to a coherent strategy, actionable steps, and an implementation timeline, and he wanted to challenge assumptions and identify innovative ideas while refining a plan to quickly scale to $1 billion in revenue. I had been certified as a facilitator in the 1990s, but I was hired because I knew supply chain and had good rapport with Karl.

Staff from across the country converged on a hotel near company headquarters. I was told to expect an unruly group who liked to talk over one another and required firm discipline.

The evening before the meeting, I visited the hotel, and a manager showed me the conference room, which was already setup with tables configured in a large square with an open space about twenty feet wide in the middle so all the participants would see each other. The manager was called away, and I sat in the meeting room alone. I meditated on the harmonic I believed we could create and set an intention for highest and best outcomes for all involved. I wanted everyone to get some benefit in some dimension. I silently reconfirmed my commitment to offer my best and to be offered the best from others.

As participants arrived the next morning, I introduced myself to each, shaking hands and making direct eye contact. Seats were not assigned, so people chose their spots organically. Without planning it, I sat directly across from Karl, and his executive assistant sat immediately to my left.

I facilitated the discussion for two days while one person furiously typed notes into her laptop and a second wrote on whiteboards. The group was spirited and eager to share ideas and opinions. Moments of silence were rare, and the discussions were respectful and collaborative.

Sitting across the room from Karl, I could easily observe his expressions and read his body language. When he made eye contact with me, I instinctively knew whether he wanted to go deeper or move on to another topic. During short breaks, Karl would ask for my input and seemed to want to confirm we were making progress. He was definitely the alpha in the room, the one people looked to for leadership, but privately he showed vulnerability, and I provided reassurance.

CHAPTER 23: STRETCHING IN NEW DIRECTIONS

At one point during the discussions, someone asked Karl for his prediction on sales within a certain market segment. Karl answered in a slightly indignant tone, "What, do you think I'm clairvoyant?" I looked down and tried not to laugh. I had no doubt we could get an intuitive answer if we wanted one.

Beyond facial expressions, nonverbal cues, and clairvoyance, what really got my attention was Karl's heart. While accessible and good-natured, I sensed the underlying stress in his life. He used chewing tobacco and was overweight, but I had no evidence of any medical condition. At one point, the team discussed the exorbitant cost of a particular type of software they wanted to purchase. When talking about the staggering cost of buying this pricey technology, Karl said, "You guys are going to give me a heart attack." I looked down and quietly thought to myself, *Oh, no. Please, don't say that!*

That evening, I texted Karl to make sure he had gotten the details and actionable information he desired during the first day. He immediately replied, "Absolutely. You'd have to have experienced the previous attempts at this to appreciate how productive this has been!"

The meetings ended the following afternoon, and everyone seemed pleased with the results. Karl enthusiastically praised my work. As the room cleared and I packed up my briefcase, I noticed Karl's assistant nervously checking her phone. I asked if everything was okay, and she said she was trying to get Karl's doctor to phone in a prescription so he could pick it up on his way to the airport. I casually asked what the prescription was for, and she confirmed my intuitive awareness when she answered, "It's his heart medication."

I drove home thinking about how much I enjoyed stretching in new directions. I loved combining my business expertise, my metaphysical awareness, and my ability to hold coherent energies. This unique combination gave me great satisfaction and produced tangible results. I appreciated the Universe winking in recognition with confirmation of an intuitive insight, a kind word, a heartfelt connection, and a very nice payday.

CHAPTER 24
Extrasensory Perception at Work

Sharing a co-working space with Cam and Marcia had been a great experiment. One of the many benefits was the new friendships I developed at Industrious and spending time with dozens of entrepreneurs. When Cam and Marcia moved out, I downsized to a small office directly across from the coffee bar where there was a steady flow of traffic.

In corporate America in the early 1990s, we had cubicles, so I heard my colleagues but could not see them. In the modern glass offices at Industrious, I could see body language and demeanor but could not hear conversations. Working at my desk, I could sense the energy fields and interpersonal dynamics of those around me. Industrious became a laboratory for studying energetics and using extrasensory perception.

Beyond appearances, I sensed who was truly secure in their capabilities and who was posturing in a way that was not entirely grounded or authentic. Often my observations were validated.

One day, I arrived to find a nearby office entirely empty. Five busy workstations had been reduced to dust bunnies and rental furniture. The well-dressed CEO of this flashy startup was nowhere to be found. After hiring talent and trying to appear successful, the company never gained traction and their funding got pulled. I had never understood the product or the premise and ultimately, neither did their intended customers. The CEO's personality and posturing had carried the company for nearly a year but I sensed a lack of depth and capability. His investors finally figured it out.

In office #26, I created a bright, inviting, Zen space with a sisal rug and a beautiful lamp. I used feng shui to arrange my furniture, plants, and crystals. I kept a bouquet of fresh lilies on my desk, and my guest chair was an open invitation for colleagues to come in and chat. I left metaphysical books on my desk and waited to see which ones started conversations.

My office invited intimate conversations, and I had a few regular visitors in my guest chair. Clay talked about perilous dates with thirty-somethings. Kris discussed the latest self-improvement book he was reading. I laughed when he told me I made a good "consigliere," a term popularized in The Godfather. He meant I was a trusted confidant and he was right. I had played this role informally for CEOs, professional athletes, and many others—and these conversations were happening more frequently.

One afternoon, five of us gathered in a conference room to discuss a possible project. One colleague at Industrious, Brian, was in talks with a company that had developed supply chain software to support their core business and believed it had commercial value beyond the company's main enterprise. They wanted to look into the possibilities and needed supply chain expertise.

As we wrapped up discussion of one project, Brian wanted to talk about another business idea related to integrative sports medicine. He got the idea as a result of having to run around to numerous specialists after hurting his back. Driving in metro-Atlanta was time-consuming, and each provider billed separately. Brian saw an opportunity to consolidate and manage services using a concierge model.

I asked if his plan included services to address the mental, emotional, and metaphysical aspects of injuries and briefly described my personal history with chronic pain, which was ultimately resolved

CHAPTER 24: EXTRASENSORY PERCEPTION AT WORK

by using a mix of alternative treatments. I explained CranioSacral Therapy (CST) and described treatment using Brian's recent L4-L5 injury as an example.

Brian interrupted to ask, "How did you know it was L4-L5?" He had never mentioned specifics of his injury, so he was surprised when I knew the exact discs. I explained I sometimes felt or knew things. I just knew without any effort or thought. I acknowledged it was inexplicable.

A man named William was also in the conference room that day. I had met him briefly right before the meeting. He was sitting to my right at the table. As I spoke about extrasensory perception, William stood up to leave and said, "So, where am I injured?"

I immediately felt my jaw tighten, but my attention was drawn to something that appeared as a lightning bolt at his right hip. In my mind's eye, I saw a very subtle line of bluish silver energy like a tiny laser zap the front of his right hip. I grabbed my jaw and said, "You have a lot of tension in your jaw, but my focus goes to your right hip."

William looked around the table and said, "Who told her?" Unbeknownst to any of us, William was scheduled for hip replacement surgery a few days later. Years of pushing limits in his workouts had caught up with him, and he was in a lot of pain. The Universe had provided another opportunity to offer intuitive insights in a business environment, and I took another leap of faith.

I spoke with William during his recovery, and six weeks after his surgery, he stopped by my office. He had read dozens of books on business leadership and was always thinking about human behavior and motivation. William often said he was inspired to be a part of creating something or revealing things hiding in plain sight. That day in my office, he smiled and said, "Maybe I should say the ability to make obvious to myself that which is already apparent to Ann Elliott." We both laughed.

One morning, I felt guided to go to the office unusually early. As I sat staring at my laptop, Hank, one of my regular visitors, stopped by. He had sold his first company and was busy with several other startups. On this particular morning, he was at Industrious on his way to therapy. He and his wife had separated and were giving their marriage one last shot by going to couples therapy. He was not looking forward to the session because he and his wife had recently argued, and it ended with Hank declaring, "I will spend every last dime scorching the earth you live on!"

Hank admitted he was angry at himself for allowing himself to be baited into an emotional response and regrettable choice of words. I empathized with him and suggested he offer this honest explanation to the therapist and his soon-to-be ex-wife.

As Hank was leaving, he mentioned he had moved into an upscale apartment in Buckhead. He was paying more for the apartment than his mortgage, and his three children were unhappily schlepping back and forth between homes. I suddenly recalled a conversation with another friend, Len, who had privately confided he was leaving his marriage, too. Serendipitously, both men chose the same luxury apartment complex. When Hank heard Len also had kids, he asked if I thought Len might be willing to give him some advice. I said I would ask, and Hank left for his *paid* therapy session.

A week later, Hank, Len, and I met after work for drinks. I noticed no one ordered alcohol. I intentionally spoke very little and simply held a clear field of energy. I listened as these savvy, successful men talked about the pain they had caused and the pain they felt in ending their marriages. They each spoke of infidelity, how hurtful it was, and how it had damaged trust irreparably.

I felt the immense power in their honesty and vulnerability. I was amazed by the level of intimacy and knew I had validated my ability to hold space for the connection that had made it possible. I set an intention to replicate this and felt a powerful wave of knowingness sweep through me as if to confirm my direction.

CHAPTER 24: EXTRASENSORY PERCEPTION AT WORK

A few weeks later, I was cleaning up hundreds of unread emails and noticed Dr. Bartlett was teaching a seminar titled "Master Energy Dynamics." The course description called it "a journey into holographic physiology," but I could not find MED in any of his books. I was eager for a change of perspective and decided to fly to Minneapolis where the seminar was being held.

It had been more than a year since my last Matrix Energetics seminar, and I immediately noticed a lot had changed. The seminar setup was pared down, and the vibe was raw and completely different than it had been in the big hotel ballrooms with bright lights, a booming sound system, and several hundred participants. Richard was no longer teaching with Melissa. He had longer hair and wore a fedora with casual pants and a black T-shirt.

Despite the different physical appearance, he was still wacky, personable, and created plenty of what he termed *holographic roadkill*. After seven Matrix seminars, I had catalogued some of Richard's maxims, like, "When we can embrace the *nothing*, we gain access to the *all*."

The first day of class ended an hour later than scheduled. After decades of travel, I had status with Hilton that included access to the concierge lounge on the top floor of the hotel with the usual spread of crudités, cheese cubes, and snacks. As I nibbled carrots and read email, the door flew open and Richard walked in. He loaded a plate with Swedish meatballs and chicken wings, nodded to me, and sat down at an adjacent table. We ended up talking for two hours, and this serendipitous meeting began the first of several over the next three days as our paths crossed at breakfast and again in the evening.

I was in the lounge drinking coffee one morning when Richard passed my table and said, "Don't drink your own Kool-Aid." After getting a plate of breakfast sausages at the buffet, he sat down and explained that was the title of a book he was recommending.

For three days in Minneapolis, Richard was accessible in a way he had not been in past seminars and told deeply personal stories that I had not heard previously. Long hours of class were bookended by conversations in the concierge lounge giving the weekend a *Wizard of Oz* quality. Richard was the wizard in class, and the more vulnerable, ordinary man behind the curtain in the concierge lounge. In class, he offered quips like, "Create a structure that unstructures you," and in the lounge I saw a man with bills to pay, responsibilities he may have preferred to ignore, and someone in need of a partner to help anchor his brilliance.

On the last day of the seminar, we were preparing to practice a new technique. Richard passed by my practice partner and said, "Good luck. Her system is so well organized that you probably won't find much to work on." I interpreted his comment as a nod to a decade of personal transformation through energy work with gifted healers. For years, one synchronicity or chance meeting had led to another as if the sequence had been guided by a divine force leading me to programs and teachers as part of my evolution in consciousness. I had learned much through working on myself, and I was eager to support others.

I flew home from Minneapolis thinking about people I had met who confided the most private details of their lives. Something allowed them to be raw, open, and vulnerable and these intimate conversations were happening more regularly.

I was working to embrace more of my humanness and knew that was a bridge to supporting the humanness in others. I derived a lot of satisfaction from these interactions and wondered how they might represent a new direction professionally.

CHAPTER 25
Manatees and Metaphors

One of my first business deals as a newbie entrepreneur grew into the Collaborative Transportation Network, which was a lucrative residual income stream providing me the freedom to work from a sailboat, the players' lounge at the US Open, or on a spiritual pilgrimage to a foreign land. When the income stream dwindled to a trickle, I knew the Universe was nudging me in new directions.

In the months leading up to the end of CTN, I watched as men at two companies I had brought together in strategic partnership twenty years earlier got into an ego-driven disagreement. Locked in a stalemate, neither could yield, and in the process, they destroyed a decades-long business arrangement benefiting all of us. Neither was willing to soften enough to find a solution, and I could not do it for them.

It was the end of an era. Perhaps the most surprising aspect of the whole ordeal was my calm acceptance. I had relied on this income, yet somehow, I knew the end was part of some divine order. I trusted myself, my resourcefulness, and all the serendipity that brought grace to my life. I was certain something better was coming.

Days after the end of CTN, I flew to Florida still feeling change in the wind. For eighteen years, my company had provided supply chain consulting to HydraSolis in Sarasota. In the late 1990s, my young company was one of four firms invited to submit a proposal to improve operational efficiency. I had flown to Sarasota and made a capabilities presentation to the selection committee. As I was packing up to leave, the CFO motioned for me to sit down.

The CFO told his seven colleagues in the room, "We've had three good presentations, and now we have the *Queen of Logistics* here. I know my choice. Do we need to have any further discussion?" In all my years in business, I had never been in the room while a prospective client deliberated about which firm to hire.

We were awarded the project that day and went on to work for HydraSolis every month for eighteen years. The company's culture had been the subject of several Harvard Business School case studies. I enjoyed the executives, their insights into the challenges of running a public company, and the CEO's impeccable taste in red wine.

I also bought stock. Over the years, the company grew both organically and through acquisitions. The CEO and CFO who had hired us both retired as HydraSolis grew into a new company. As a shareholder, I was delighted. As a vendor-partner, I knew our time was ending. I met with one of the bright new leaders and listened as he laughingly said he was trying to get the consultants under control. A week later, we were notified our contract was not being renewed.

Again, I felt calm acceptance.

I always felt soothed by nature, and it had been easy to begin and end business trips to Southwest Florida with a few days on Sanibel Island. Starting in 2012, I made an average of fifteen visits and spent sixty days a year walking along the beautiful white sand beaches, watching dolphins play, riding my bike to the lighthouse, paddleboarding, and enjoying a slower pace. With no buildings taller than four stories, no stoplights, and miles of bike paths, Sanibel provided a welcome contrast to my home in Midtown Atlanta. I always stayed at the Ocean's Reach condominiums, so rather than hauling beach

CHAPTER 25: MANATEES AND METAPHORS

clothes, sunscreen, and a yoga mat back and forth, the condo manager Andy allowed me to keep a duffel bag of my gear in storage.

Over the years, I made lots of friends. One was Charlie, who worked at Tarpon Bay Outfitters where tourists rented kayaks, pontoon boats, and paddleboards. Tarpon Bay is known for dolphins, stingrays, pelicans, turtles, and manatees. On my first visit, Charlie said if I happened to spot something that looked like a gray sofa floating just under the surface, to kneel down on the paddleboard immediately. Manatees sometimes mistake paddleboards for potential mates and gently bump the board as a friendly hello.

One Sunday morning, Charlie, his girlfriend Laurie, and I met early to get out on the water before it got too hot. I was already sweating just walking from the car to the dock. While Charlie prepped the boards, Laurie and I went to the gift shop to buy water and snacks. While we were browsing, I told her about a funny dream I had awoken from at 4 a.m.

In the dream, I was inside my own reproductive system. It looked like a cartoon version of Santa's workshop at the North Pole. A bunch of elves wearing stocking caps worked at long wooden tables. Tools and toys were strewn everywhere, and it seemed a bit chaotic. Every few minutes, Santa would run out of his office and yell, "Make eggs!" The elves would pick up their tools and start feverishly working. Moments later, the office door would fly open again and Santa would yell, "Stop making eggs!" This cycle repeated until I awoke from the dream.

When I got out of bed, I discovered I had started my menses for the first time in months. At the time, I was experiencing odd cycles and infrequent periods. The metaphor in the dream was insightful. Some part of me was sending subconscious signals to my ovaries to make eggs and another part of me was ready to stop. Laurie and I laughed at the crazy dream. I was not particularly thrilled with the uncomfortable cramps.

The hot sunshine beat down on us as we paddled a mile out into Tarpon Bay with rarely a ripple or a puff of air. When a dolphin surfaced fifty yards away, it was audible in the stillness. Birds diving to catch fish sounded like someone doing a cannonball off the high dive. I loved quietly propelling myself with a single oar while standing on a piece of fiberglass just inches above the water.

Manatees were plentiful, and one in particular spent time circling us and putting its fin and head onto each of our boards as we knelt down to avoid falling into the water. Of all my paddleboard outings, this was the biggest group of manatees and the longest they had ever stayed around.

I allowed my board to float away so I could observe the manatees circling Charlie and Laurie. I sensed a magical exchange of energy as mammals silently communicated with one another. I felt deep compassion, harmony, and love. A manatee swam over and put its flipper up on my board. For the first time ever, I saw its tiny little toenails, like those of a child. The moment was precious and felt otherworldly. Physically, this was the closest I had ever come to a manatee. Psychically, this was the closest I had connected to any oceanic creature. I was deeply moved.

As we paddled back toward the launch area, I realized we had been out in the hot sunshine for almost two hours. The experience with the manatee felt so serene and beautiful that time seemed to stand still. I had been mindful to stay well-hydrated, but I realized I had not eaten since the previous night and knew my blood sugar was too low.

By the time I got the paddleboard beached, I was weak and lightheaded. I walked ten steps to the hut and opened my cooler bag. I took two sips of a cold drink and watched Charlie walk by carrying our paddles and life jackets. We made eye contact, and I called out, "I am going to faint *now*!"

I'm not sure I got the last word out before everything went black. I don't recall anything after those words and feeling my knees

CHAPTER 25: MANATEES AND METAPHORS

buckle. Charlie caught me and kept me from hitting my head. He and another staff person laid me on the ground in the shade of the hut. Apparently, my eyes were rolling around in my head, and I was not breathing. Someone went to call 911 and get ice. Charlie propped my head up on towels, and I snorted and got myself breathing again, but I lay unconscious for another few moments.

While unconscious, I went to a beautiful place I did not recognize. Everything was in swirly pastel colors, and I felt an incredible love I had not known as a human. I experienced the preciousness of all life and a reverence for every minnow and piece of kelp playing its part on the planet.

I was just beginning to explore the swirly colors when I sensed someone waking me up. I did not want to leave this beautiful place, but I knew I couldn't stay. I came back to consciousness lying in a pile of seashells with four panicked faces peering down at me. My first words were, "No, no. I want to go back. I want to go back." Of course, this led to further concern.

It felt like I was gone from the third dimension for a long time, but I had no frame of reference. I did not recognize the place I had journeyed to, but I knew it was not of this earthly plane. I felt the most surreal sense of serenity and love, even though my physical body was lying awkwardly on the ground. Eventually, I sat up and drank water while my friends put ice on my neck and wrists. I said very little because I was still in a cocoon of bliss.

At my insistence, they called off the paramedics. Laurie and Charlie took me back to my condominium. I felt deeply peaceful and stared out at the ocean most of the afternoon with very few thoughts. I had been to many sacred sites, but few had caused an impact as profound as this.

On the surface, it appeared I just did not eat enough, got overheated, and fainted. At a deeper level, I appreciated all the circumstances that aligned and enabled me to safely let go enough to *pass out* into another dimension.

I also understood the significance of my dream about Santa's workshop. A lifetime of reproductive cycles was ending along with the old business deals. Everything was shifting hormonally, biologically, and professionally. Some part of me was sorting through endings to establish a new sense of validity, legitimacy, and value, creating a path forward. If my next phase included the beautiful place with the swirly colors, I was all in!

CHAPTER 26
Finding the Path Inward

With many doors closing, I felt a nudge to look for a place to offer CranioSacral Therapy (CST) and SomatoEmotional Release (SER) more regularly. I decided it was time to rent office space. I looked on Craigslist and other websites. I sent messages and made calls. Occasionally, I allowed myself to feel excited about this unlikely trajectory and wondered how it was all going to unfold.

One night, I dreamed I was in the parking lot of a familiar building. The architecture and gray metal exterior were so distinct I knew exactly where I was because twenty years earlier, I had practiced Pilates at a studio there. Later that morning, I drove to Zonolite Road, about two miles from my home, and wandered through the breezeways between offices looking at the placards, reading the names of businesses, and looking for some connection to the dream.

I saw a familiar name listed on a placard outside Suite 10. Claire, the woman who led me to CranioSacral Therapy, had once mentioned a professional psychic named Jamie. Now I stood looking at Jamie's name and felt the dots connecting. No one was in Suite 10, so I drove to my office at Industrious and searched online until I found Jamie and the Center for Love and Light. The website said the center had multiple practitioners sharing treatment rooms. Within two weeks, I met Jamie and agreed to a sublease with Corey, a massage therapist, who rented me her room several half days each week.

The week I started, I met the other practitioners, some of whom took me up on my offer for a sample session. One of those was Kate, who owned a physical therapy practice in an adjoining office. She was friendly and familiar with CranioSacral Therapy. We ate lunch together periodically, and she helped me get acclimated to this new environment.

One afternoon, Kate was training a new physical therapist, Lee, and wanted to use Corey's room for a practice session. I happened to be at the office and decided to observe as Kate coached Lee, who was using Corey as his practice client. I silently observed, and when Lee finished the practice session, I said, "Corey, what in the world happened to your back right molar?" Corey had indeed cracked her tooth and was waiting on a dentist appointment. Lee did not understand how I could possibly know about Corey's tooth pain by simply observing from ten feet away. Kate knew exactly how.

Kate referred several clients to me, and one day, she texted an invitation for me to come down the hall to her treatment room when I was available. She introduced me to the client on the table, Warren, a triathlete working on a decade of intermittent pain in his left leg. Kate told him I was "an intuitive trained in CranioSacral Therapy."

Physically, I noted a long, winding scar on Warren's left kneecap and another scar running laterally across his left thigh. I grimaced while watching Warren moan in pain as Kate dry-needled his left calf. He said he'd had something like a cyst removed when he was just a year old. As he spoke about his surgeries and scars, I started getting intuitive information.

I asked Warren, "Who are the three most important women in your life?" He said, "My wife." After waiting a moment to see if he would continue, I asked again. This time, he said, "My wife, my wife, and my wife." I joked, "That's a lot of wives." He asked if his most important women needed to be alive, and I said no. The room got still, and Warren confided that his mom was important, but she had died when he was three.

This confirmed the intuitive information I had received moments earlier. The ongoing pain in his left leg was connected to the loss of his mother. As Kate continued her treatment, I sat on a stool and held my fingertips on Warren's left hip bone and neck. I felt his entire system relax. This was the first of a half-dozen sessions where we worked with both his physical and emotional pain.

Warren knew his father had internalized the grief and turned to alcohol for comfort. His father had passed away soon after Warren graduated from college. Warren described several instances when he knew his dead father was present, and he had said "Hello" as if his father could hear him. When I asked if he communicated with his mother the same way, he said, "That would be like talking to a stranger." Since she had died when Warren was so young, he had never gotten to know her. I felt the tenderness of young Warren's yearning for his mother as he cried a bit.

My offices at Industrious and at the Center were only a few miles apart geographically, but they represented two distinct parts of myself I wanted to bring closer together. I wanted to integrate my intuitive capabilities, my curiosity about metaphysics, and my love of consulting and business strategy.

As I thought about how to integrate these disparate paths, in my mind's eye, I saw a book with a mosquito and an elephant on the cover. I recognized the image and knew it was a book I'd read years ago, *The Medici Effect: What Elephants and Epidemics Can Teach Us about Innovation* by Frans Johansson. The book was about intersectional thinking and bringing concepts from one field into another to create breakthroughs.

Much of what I had highlighted when I first read the book in 2006 covered principles from Harvard Business School I had also explored through metaphysical teachers. I knew this book had come back into my awareness for a reason. I was in the process of my own intersectional thinking and figuring out how to integrate disparate paths and passions. The convergence was already happening organically. I wanted to formalize and monetize it.

I also owned Johansson's second book, *The Click Moment*, featuring "actions you can take to increase your exposure to serendipity, luck, and random events." I found the Medici Group, Johansson's consulting company, online. They were hiring, and their application questions were the same as the ones I was asking myself. Two of the questions were, "What is your idea of success?" and "Describe an accomplishment you're proud of." I loved that they drew a distinction.

To answer the first question, I wrote, "Success is continually creating and redefining life based on personal growth and expanding consciousness to find new levels of meaning and purpose along with vehicles for authentic self-expression." As for accomplishments, I described several that had propelled me along a mainstream trajectory like graduating with honors from Duke, pursuing jobs with increasing levels of responsibility and starting my own company.

Ten days later, I got a lovely email from Chantal, a woman whose name I recognized from *The Medici Effect*'s acknowledgments. Chantal indicated I was beyond Medici's original target for new hires. We discussed possibilities for other strategic positions, but all required relocating to New York City. Despite some disappointment, I was grateful for the opportunity for self-reflection required by the application and eager to continue exploring intersectional thinking.

As I pondered what to do next, more curious synchronicities occurred. A client at the Center asked if I could do a remote session with her friend in San Francisco. I had done phone sessions with people I already knew but never with a total stranger. It went well, and the client seemed pleased, reassuring me of something I already knew; my intuitive work did not require an office. I giggled, feeling a new kind of freedom in knowing I could work from wherever my adventures took me.

CHAPTER 26: FINDING THE PATH INWARD

Next, Industrious raised my rent by the maximum allowable amount. Several of my favorite people were moving out, and I was spending less time there, so I gave notice, rolled up my sisal rug, packed my lamp and my crystals, and said my goodbyes. Another era had ended.

Corey sent me an email saying she had to have unexpected surgery and encouraged me to use the room full time while she was recovering. The timing was perfect since I had moved out of Industrious and was not traveling as much for consulting gigs.

I emailed all of my CranioSacral Therapy clients and offered a special price for sessions that month. It worked. I did more sessions and saw more new clients than I had in any previous month. I experienced what it was like to have a busy practice and found it intriguing to use my intuition with new clients and see how it matched up with whatever they chose to share.

In one case, the new client, Marc, was an attorney and entrepreneur. The session started with him providing a list of his physical pains, ailments, allergies, and medications. Then he told me about his chaotic work life, stress, and how he used alcohol to numb himself. Marc admitted he was lonely and found himself in intense relationships that only lasted a few months. At one point, he raised his head off the table and asked if everyone told me so much in a first session. The irony was we hadn't even gotten to the intuitive information I received before he arrived yet.

Marc said he could feel more "stuff" wanting to come up. I sat on a stool beside the table with one hand under his back and one hand on his chest over his heart. He said he had been thinking back to his late teens and twenties and the girls he had dated then. He rattled off the first names of dozens of women he had been with twenty-five years earlier. He seemed remorseful as he spoke each of the names.

I sensed we were finding the path inward since the intuitive flash I had prior to the session was that of many women vying for

Marc's affection. The imagery was valid, but my interpretation was not. The issue was not infidelity; it was denial. In dating women, Marc said he had denied and concealed his homosexuality from his friends and family, particularly his parents.

Marc acknowledged self-hatred over hurting many caring women, including one who attempted suicide after he broke up with her. Speaking this truth allowed him to begin to release pain he had carried for decades. I felt his physiology relax as he allowed himself to melt into compassion and self-forgiveness. For me, this was another reminder that the interpretation of intuitive information is nuanced and delicate.

As the session ended, Marc expressed his gratitude and said the way I had combined my heart, mind, and intuition was amazing. I smiled, thinking that was exactly what I wanted to do and encourage in others.

CHAPTER 27
Jungle Love

In the weeks between endings and new beginnings, I registered for SomatoEmotional Release 2 at Upledger Institute in West Palm Beach. Since my last SER course in Berkeley, I had read eight of Dr. Upledger's books, including *Inner Physician, Lessons out of School*, and my favorite, *Cell Talk*. I had also watched an entire set of instructional DVDs filled with endearing videos of Upledger teaching in the 1990s. I loved his caring way and his teaching style. When I worked with my own clients, I often imagined Dr. John with his curly white hair sitting at the end of my table watching and coaching me.

In Florida, it was the off-season, so I booked a room at a luxury Marriott resort hotel on the beach. The nearest bridge from the mainland out to the Marriott required a drive through John D. MacArthur Beach State Park, a narrow isthmus separating Lake Worth from the Atlantic Ocean. I checked into the Marriott and discovered I had been upgraded to a two-bedroom suite with a full kitchen. The suite had a big balcony with an unobstructed view of both sunrise over the ocean and sunset over the intracoastal waterway.

After unpacking, I drove back to MacArthur Park and paid the entry fee. The parking lot was empty, and I found myself walking alone under a canopy of trees, past a gift shop that was closed, and across a long boardwalk over a marshy lake. I spotted two kayaks off in the distance but no other humans. It was a warm, sunny day, and I walked silently through a labyrinth of hiking trails in a lush jungle of trees and plants. The park was delightfully deserted, so I listened to birds and jumped out of the way of lizards scurrying past. Nature always calmed and connected me to something greater than myself.

The next morning, I drove back through MacArthur Park, over the drawbridge, and a few blocks South to the Upledger Institute. Thousands of people had sought care at this office complex. I learned Dr. John and Chas, our instructor, had worked together for decades in the room where the course was being taught. I was eager to soak up all that experience along with whatever magic might be held there.

Twenty students from across the world had registered. The registration materials conveyed a philosophy I believed:

It is not possible to treat at this level without doing our own work. Find an experienced CS therapist and get on the table as much as possible. If you cannot find such a person in your area, good CST is worth traveling for!

I had been a client of Shyamala long before I started my own practice and looked for practitioners wherever I went. I knew self-care was vital before trying to help others.

The first student I met, Gretchen, said she lived on the other side of the state and described the tiny island she and her family lived on. In two sentences, I recognized Sanibel and smiled at the serendipity. Sanibel had become my second home, and Gretchen knew all of my favorite places on the island.

Chas, four teaching assistants, and twenty students sat in a big circle and introduced ourselves. Chas spoke about the many group therapy sessions held in the room in the past, including a program for Vietnam veterans. He told stories of the rare depth of intimacy with vets who attended two consecutive weeks of daily treatment with multiple practitioners. I resonated with many of Chas' philosophies, including his belief the therapist served as a facilitator and not a director or doer of anything. The practitioner never led the client. They followed the client's reality from a neutral, supportive position and helped them to let go on their own terms. That precious balance required discipline and finesse.

Chas said a practitioner should not share any information until the client shared it out loud. I said if I had adopted that style, I might have missed opportunities to facilitate releases, and I offered an example: I receive intuitive insights in unusual ways, and while one client, Patricia, was lying peacefully on the table, I started hearing a polka in my head. I recognized "The Chicken Dance" from wedding receptions, but I ignored it until the tune played in my head so insistently I finally asked Patricia if it had any relevance to her. She laughed and said she was flying to California and would attend a polka party in a friend's barn.

Then she said, "Full disclosure…" and went on to describe how she had been deeply hurt by this friend. I watched her body squirm on the table, presumably releasing some pain she had stored with the memory. If I had not said anything about the polka, we might have missed the opportunity. Those insights were threads I cautiously followed. I trusted my process and knew it took finesse to decide what and when to share. My flashes of insight were often a direct conduit to something transformative for my clients.

Chas said he did not advise this, but he agreed it had worked well in my example.

After class, I drove toward the Marriott and found the street leading to the drawbridge closed. The city was having its annual holiday boat parade with dozens of boats of all types in a festive flotilla moving north along the Intracoastal Waterway. All the bridges for several miles were raised so the tall masts could pass under. I decided to park and watch.

One sailboat had long strings of green lights extending from the top of the mast to the bow, stern, and mid-ship, creating the appearance of a floating Christmas tree with twinkling stars hanging from the forestays and strings of red lights running the length of the hull. I stood on the bridge feeling the warm breeze and recalling dozens of sailing adventures I'd had.

When the parade ended, I drove along the water's edge through MacArthur Beach State Park and back to my sanctuary.

In class, we took turns being the practice patient while two other therapists facilitated a session. When it was my turn to be the patient, one of the most-experienced teaching assistants, Agnieszka, joined our group. She sat with her hands gently on my head, and I felt myself slip into an altered state. A few minutes later, she moved to my side, put her hand on my chest, and pushed firmly. As I lay on the table with my eyes closed, I said, "Someone is standing on my chest." Demonstrating proper technique, Agnieszka quietly asked if I knew who it was. I suddenly felt disoriented and uncomfortable.

Somehow, I was in my four-year-old body in the office of my childhood pediatrician, Dr. Blim. I could see the maroon-colored examination table with a white sterile paper covering it, a blood pressure cuff hanging on the wall, and the long fluorescent light bulbs in the fixture above. Dr. Blim was standing beside me, pressing a cold stethoscope against my tiny chest and explaining something to my grandmother. My chest hurt badly. A nurse came in and gave him something that he showed me. It was a jungle scene with perforated paper dolls in the shape of animals like giraffes, lions, and zebras. My four-year-old self wondered why he was acting so dumb. Had he forgotten how to be a healer? I wanted to scream.

Some part of me was remembering a lifetime where Dr. Blim and I were in a desert doing healing work with animals. I could see the reddish-brown dust under our primitive sandals. We would call a giraffe, lion, or zebra, and they would use their noses, hooves, and energy to support our healing work. In one reality, an animal was using its hoof to help heal something in my chest, and in another reality, Dr. Blim was giving me paper dolls rather than using his true powers to help me. I was reliving all these experiences on a treatment table in an SER class in Florida.

Agnieszka was a brilliant facilitator and asked me where the giraffe, lion, and zebra would put their hooves and noses if they were with me now. In a low whisper, I described their respective positions, and the two therapists used their hands to simulate my animal friends. In the desert version, we chanted in a language I did not recognize and drank blessed water.

As I lay quietly on the table, I suddenly said aloud, "Oh, there is somebody else in this room who was there with us in the desert." With my eyes still closed, I pointed to the head of the table I was lying on. While I had been deeply immersed in this process, Chas had moved a chair to the head of the table. He did not speak or touch me, but I could feel him. The therapists held their positions as my body had a massive release. My back arched and my limbs flailed as I let go.

When the session was over, I was exhausted and emotional. Agnieszka and the other therapists surrounded me with love. I told them the scene in the doctor's office had really happened when I was four. I had gotten pneumonia while my parents were away, and my grandmother had taken me to Dr. Blim. The nurse brought in paper dolls in the shapes of jungle animals.

Now, decades later, remembering those silly paper dolls was the conduit to a profound awareness of another lifetime. Agnieszka pressing on my chest had simulated the sensation of my pneumonia, triggering the memory and deeper healing. My SomatoEmotional Release also showed me myself as a healer in another lifetime. I needed time to process all of this.

After the last day of class, I drove back to my hotel and sat on the balcony listening to the waves crashing on the beach below as the full moon lingered over the inland waterway. I slept well and awoke refreshed.

I made one last stop on my way to the airport. Every time I had crossed the drawbridge near MacArthur Park, I had seen what looked like a familiar marina. Back in 2006, my romantic partner and I had bought a sailboat in Fort Pierce, Florida. We wanted to have it retrofitted for offshore sailing, and while we waited for an appointment with the boatyard, we docked in a nearby marina. The day after the class ended, I drove to the marina I could see from the drawbridge and discovered it was now part of a private club. A security guard listened to my story and agreed to let me walk the dock.

As I walked, I smiled, remembering the evening we took our dinghy up the waterway to dinner at Seasons 52. I hadn't even heard of CranioSacral Therapy back then and could have never imagined becoming a practitioner. Here I was again expanding my capabilities, my identity and my sense of Self. I felt curiously giddy knowing there was still more to come.

CHAPTER 28
The Art and Paradox of Non-Striving

Looking to add to my wellness toolkit I enrolled in an eight-week course in *mindfulness-based stress reduction* (MBSR) at the Duke Center for Integrative Medicine (DCIM). I was eager to create wellness workshops, and mindfulness had become popular enough to make *TIME Magazine* and be included in corporate wellness programs. I discovered DCIM's program based on Jon Kabat-Zinn's approach to health enhancement and stress reduction was one of the top programs in the country. Our group met by phone for ninety-minute weekly calls. Most of the twenty participants were new to meditation and wrestling with *mind chatter* and all the typical resistance created by the ego. I saw students struggling with the same patterns I had wrestled with when I first started *Ascension* with Gomati and Vasistha. Listening to participants share their experiences reminded me how far I had come in fifteen years.

Duke's MBSR course concluded with an in-person "day of mindfulness." The day-long program required restraint because there was no speaking, reading, writing, or eye contact. I decided to travel to Durham for the experience. The night before the program, I cheered the Duke men's basketball team to victory, and the next morning, I drove to the day of mindfulness with my ears still ringing from the Cameron Crazies. Eighty MBSR students gathered in a middle school's multipurpose room. I brought a yoga mat and a pillow for the folding chair and floor.

Two instructors led guided meditations interspersed with long periods of silence. Another led mindful movement with very simple yoga poses and soft, flowing motions. It was a beautiful, sunny day, and we were allowed to walk outdoors briefly as long as we did not make eye contact or speak.

The woman next to me was fidgety during the first few hours, so I felt relieved when she quietly gathered her belongings and snuck out. I left the day-long program feeling cocooned in a deep, inner fullness and contentment. I planned to rush back to campus for another basketball game in Cameron, but I realized my central nervous system would likely stage a revolt if I were to go from seven hours of silence to the deafening roar of fans cheering. I decided to prolong my sense of serenity and practice mindfulness, so I ordered room service at the hotel, fluffed up a pile of pillows, and watched the basketball game on television with the sound muted.

When I returned to Atlanta, I was eager to create a program based on MBSR. Carrie, one of the physical therapists at the Center, coached competitive runners and triathletes and was one herself. Sports performance and the mental aspects of competition were the latest frontier in mindfulness, and Carrie agreed to let me pilot an introductory class with some of the runners she coached. I created a seventy-five-minute presentation customized for athletes, and Carrie recruited eight participants.

On the morning of my presentation, Atlanta had a snowstorm, and our program was cancelled. I was disappointed but trusted there must be a reason for the cancellation. I found the silver lining when someone I had just met offered the conference room in her office building for my class. The space had a more intimate feel and a screen for my PowerPoint, which showed professional athletes, coaches, and teams who used mindfulness to reach the top of their sports. I led the *awareness of breath* guided meditation and other traditional MBSR practices, infusing them with my own ingenuity. Instead of raisins for the exercise in eating with gratitude and attention to sensory detail, I used a carafe of colorful Jelly Bellies. The candy served the same purpose as raisins and also inspired a spirited debate over favorite flavors. I was subjected to playful scorn when I disclosed my favorite flavor was popcorn.

After this introduction, the participants said they would pay for a multi-week program. I went to work and created a six-week course emphasizing performance improvement through efficient recovery and managing performance anxiety. I also included ways to improve immune system function and regulate physiological systems like blood pressure and heart rate. I enjoyed melding the fundamentals of mindfulness with aspects of other modalities.

As Carrie promoted the course, we had so much interest we needed a bigger space. I was guided to an unoccupied office suite in the same complex as the Center for Love and Light. I sat in the space alone and quietly set the intentions that everyone would get something of value, and I would find the next steps on my path.

I was delighted to find many participants looking for more than shaving a few minutes off their race time. One participant who was trying to qualify for the Boston Marathon said he was looking for "positive results." When I asked him what that meant, he surprised me, saying, "A sense of wellbeing around family with more positive interactions."

Each week, our session started with the *awareness of breath* meditation followed by sharing the previous week's challenges and successes. I was always heartened by the self-realizations and the honesty. The group energy was terrific, like a relay team where each athlete encouraged the others to be their best.

One week my theme was "The Art and Paradox of Non-Striving." In sports competition, pushing through pain to finish a race is admirable. Non-striving was easily equated with laziness or giving up. I encouraged participants to listen to their bodies.

Hardcore endurance athletes knew over-training led to injury, and framing non-striving in that way helped them see it in a new light. I thought the *loving kindness meditation* might seem a little wimpy for hardcore endurance athletes, but they embraced it wholeheartedly. I asked the participants to complete sentences like, "The time I was kindest to myself was _____" and "The time I most appreciated my body most was _____."

Every week, our sessions became a journey into deeper sharing. The desire to improve athletic performance had become the conduit for something much richer and more intimate. Again, I marveled at honesty and vulnerability. The feedback was positive and reaffirming, so I offered the program to a second group of competitive athletes knowing this was another essential step on my journey.

I continued seeing clients at the Center and discovering more unconventional capabilities just waiting to be claimed. Sessions provided an opportunity for my intuition to come through and then a challenge to figure out how to translate it into something useful. One new client was a partner in a global consulting firm; we talked business while she was getting comfortable on the table. As she spoke about her background and family, one man in particular seemed to stand out and had a fatherly disposition. I felt a flow of deeply profound unconditional love and sensed this person had been part of her life but had died. She said her parents were alive, and when she spoke about her biological father, I did not sense a vibrational match to this love.

I gently asked if someone with whom she had shared deep love had died. She asked, "How do you know that?" I explained I could sense their deep love for one another. She cried as she spoke about an affair she'd had in her twenties with a man who was indeed a fatherly figure. They had kept their relationship secret. When he died, it had been difficult to process the grief because no one knew about the relationship. She got married in her thirties but had never experienced unconditional love the way she had with this man many years earlier. As she spoke tenderly about this relationship, I felt her release energy from her left hip, the area plagued by chronic pain that had brought her to our session.

My new normal was receiving intuitive insights and then watching where they led and how they benefited the client.

After nearly a year of subletting at the Center, I was told another group was moving into the massage room, so I would move down the hall. Then that plan changed, things got complicated, and I had no office. The timing was ultimately synchronistic because I was traveling for much of the following two months. I left thank you notes for all the people who had graciously welcomed me to the Center.

Just as a dream had originally led me there, I trusted something or someone would show up serendipitously to help guide my next steps.

CHAPTER 29
Big, Big Cats

In 2018, a few days after leaving the Center for the last time, I boarded a flight to Florida for my next adventure. It had snowed overnight in the Northeast, causing a ripple effect of delays and airline staffing issues in Atlanta. My flight was mostly empty, and everyone was talking about the weather. I had a window seat and noted the woman on the aisle looked familiar. She was friendly and good-natured but seemed exhausted.

Once the plane took off, I noticed her head bobbing as she tried to watch a movie. I needed to use the lavatory, and she politely let me out. When I came back, I told her she reminded me of a colleague I had not seen in years. I asked if she was related to Lynn Stone. She smiled and said, "I *am* Lynn Stone." We laughed, realizing we had met many times but always at conferences and in more formal settings. Now we were almost unrecognizable to one another in our casual clothes.

In 2010, shortly after my trip to Egypt and Jordan, I had hosted an industry association luncheon for 200 supply chain management professionals in Atlanta. The luncheon had featured a speech by Lynn Stone, one of the highest-ranking executives at The Home Depot.

I was still integrating Sekhmet, one of the most powerful spiritual experiences of my life, while experiencing my mainstream, day-to-day life in new ways.

I paused at the podium, looked out into the audience, and felt the room get still and silent. The dynamic of standing before a group and holding a field of energy was surreal and it was happening more frequently. I stood for a moment immersed in the sensation before I tookthe microphone and introduced Lynn Stone.

Eight years later, here we were, seated together on a flight to Florida. Lynn asked what I had been up to. I told her about my professional transition into wellness and mindfulness-based stress reduction. She admitted she was working too hard, stressed, and not good at meditating. She asked if MBSR would help with "mind chatter," and I assured her it would.

As we deplaned, she said she understood the serendipity of our paths crossing. She was only in Florida overnight for a friend's birthday and then flying to California to speak at a conference. She asked if I would email her information about my next MBSR class. I left the airport amazed at how my supply chain colleagues were serendipitously showing up and expressing interest in my new work.

I spent a long weekend on Sanibel before driving north up I-75. For the first time in twenty years, I was traveling to Sarasota for something other than supply chain consulting. Agnieszka, the teaching assistant who had facilitated my profound SomatoEmotional Release a few months earlier at the Upledger Institute, invited me to a program she organized for a small group of advanced practitioners. We would practice CranioSacral Therapy inside a sanctuary for rescued wild animals. I knew humans and animals were connected at levels beyond any logical understanding, so this program sounded exotic and intriguing.

The Big Cat Habitat and Sanctuary was on a sprawling piece of property where tigers, lions, buffalo, chimpanzee, peacocks, lemurs, and llamas lived and received care. I expected to see a few big cats, but the sanctuary housed more than thirty.

The first two days, the park was closed to the public, so we had the place to ourselves. We watched the staff do their daily chores and learned one big cat eats as much as twenty-five pounds of raw meat several times each week. Most cats had individual pens where they slept and large areas like playgrounds with trees, toys, and water features where they roamed for a few hours daily. I did a double-take when I saw a wolf and tiger living in the same pen. They had been raised in captivity and simply did not know they were supposed to be enemies.

I watched the two animals wrestle and play like children and laughed, thinking humans could learn a lot from these two mortal enemies living in harmony.

We entered the sanctuary early each morning and walked to our fenced outdoor platform, which was surrounded by two large pens with big cats roaming on the other side. Our treatment area was shaded by nearby trees and a tarp strung overhead, but it was open to wind and rain.

Sixteen of us started with a two-day retreat just for the therapists. Chas, the instructor from SER 2, led us in an experiential exercise where we were invited to pick an animal in the sanctuary and meld with it. Melding was a concept we had learned in CranioSacral Therapy that enabled us to be present with any client experiencing any situation.

I chose to meld with a tiger named *Bama*. As I sat quietly observing Bama, I closed my eyes and spontaneously melded with all the tigers in the sanctuary. Then I felt my energy field expand and I sensed all the big cats in North America. Then the field expanded as I remembered Egypt and my powerful experience with Sekhmet. I was tapping into a universal feline energy and something that extended multidimensionally. I basked in this profound expanse for several minutes before bringing my consciousness back to the chair where I sat beside Bama's enclosure.

I took a moment to catch my breath and collect myself. I smiled, thinking of my experience in SER 2 with Agnieszka and Chas when I revisited a lifetime where I did healing work with animals. Now, rather than wearing primitive sandals in a desert, I was here doing healing work alongside animals again, but safely separated by a double chain-link fence.

During the therapist retreat, we took turns receiving treatment from several therapists at once in multi-hands sessions. I loved experiencing the nuances and techniques of advanced practitioners and how their skills complemented one another. I also loved working outdoors in the cool of the early morning and listening to the animals.

On Days Three and Four of the program, the park was open and 1,800 visitors arrived to see the big cats and stare in wonder at the sixteen humans in a cage full of massage tables. We treated sanctuary donors, staff, and a group of local foster children. As we worked, a 700-pound cat would spontaneously show up and lie in the grass beside the fenced platform that held the massage tables.

My favorite big cat was a lion named Pharaoh. Sometimes, he would lie in the grass and look up at me. Other times, he would roll on his back with all four paws in the air. As if on cue, while a client was silently releasing emotions or transmuting pain, the big cats would grunt in unison. It sounded a bit like "breath of fire" in yoga, with quick-paced, rhythmic exhales. Thirty lions and tigers panting together made the therapists smile at one another and stifle giggles.

I saw the serendipity of the big cat sanctuary being just a few miles from the headquarters of my former client, HydraSolis. They were geographically close but worlds apart. I had traded business dresses for cargo pants and my laptop for a massage table. I was being nudged out of supply chain consulting, and this trip to Sarasota felt like another wink from the Universe.

At the end of the program, I thanked Agnieszka and said goodbye to my new friends before driving back down I-75 to a charitable event for Sanibel-Captiva Conservation Foundation (SCCF). The evening event, called "Beer in the Bushes," was held in a nature preserve and included tastings from some of Florida's best microbreweries and hundreds of people dancing to live music under the stars.

While on Sanibel, the plans for my next adventure began to take shape. Eugenia sent an email promoting an online summit called "Divine to Divine" where she was one of the featured speakers. The program description read, "This twenty-four-day journey supports you in creating a quantum shift in your consciousness into multidimensional and awake living as your Divine self."

It was 2018 and Danielle, the woman hosting the conversations, had been in my orbit for a decade. I had heard Danielle's name in 2008 while I was in Seattle, and I had read her book, *Temples of Light*, before traveling to Egypt. In these divine-to-divine conversations, I watched Danielle channel Thoth, one of the most powerful and well known ancient Egyptian deities. Something about *light language*, Thoth's sacred form of communication capable of bypassing the limitations of my linear mind, deeply touched me.

Danielle was living in the South of France and offered a program there that included light activations, a series of ceremonies to increase awareness of our ability to embody higher levels of consciousness. The first question in her online application was, "What vision do you carry for yourself, earth, and beyond?" I had been asked my career goals before, but this required a much wider perspective. I wrote a paragraph that included my desire to explore ways to bridge the mainstream and the mystical. After submitting my application, I received an email inviting me to a conversation with Danielle and Thoth and Divine Light Activation #1.

Our call was scheduled for 7 a.m. on the Monday after I left the big cat sanctuary. Our communication was in English, *light language*, and silence. I felt the immense potency of this exchange and was introduced to many multidimensional beings whose names I recognized as Danielle allowed them to speak through her. Thoth's invitation to partner with me directly was most intriguing. I felt the magnitude and accepted.

After the call, I went for a walk in the nature preserve and felt exhilarated. I smiled as dozens of ibises strolled the path with me. Thoth was often depicted as a man with the head of an ibis, so if this was a wink, I got it.

When I got back from my walk, I called Delta's Medallion line to book my flight, hoping to use frequent flier miles to get an upgrade. The best route was from Atlanta to Amsterdam to Marseille, but a basic coach ticket was $3,000. After trying several options, the agent put me on hold. Nineteen minutes later, the call disconnected, and I got a dial tone.

I was livid. All that time spent and no ticket. I called Delta and started over. The new agent took my frequent flier number as I vented my frustration. She came back with a ticket for the same dates and times along with the first-class upgrade for half the previous price, definitely the silver lining to the disconnected phone call. Two weeks later, I boarded the flight and started my next adventure.

CHAPTER 30
France: Luminous Light

I flew overnight to Amsterdam and then connected to Marseille. I had visited France many times before, including several trips to the Alsace region, Paris for Roland-Garros, and a leisurely week-long driving tour along the coast from Marseille to Nice. In France, I often knew the towns as if I had been there a century or two earlier. Particularly during a leisurely week-long drive along the coast in 2005, I would walk the streets of towns like Cassis, Frejus, and Antibes with an odd sense of having been there before.

I instantly recognized Danielle at the airport and met the two other program participants. We loaded our luggage into a rental car and headed east toward a bed-and-breakfast at a twelfth-century estate. The quaint inn was located close to a mountain called La Sainte Baume, one of the sacred sites where Mary Magdalene was thought to have spent the last years of her life. The estate had its own stone chapel, barn, horses, and 200 acres of land to roam.

When we were settled into our rooms, we had an opening ceremony in a lounge area at the back of the estate's boutique, which was filled with fragrant lavender and gifts. Danielle called in Thoth and other energy beings. They spoke through her about us as original architects creating blueprints for higher consciousness. The hugely intense energy during this transmission made me feel I might dissolve into a pile of molecules. And this was only Day One.

I spoke my intention to use this program to help me raise my current incarnation to its highest expression. Then I expanded my intention to include something more eternal—the highest expression possible in all lifetimes and all dimensions. Many ascended masters were energetically present, and one I had read about was Sanat Kumara, a multidimensional being whose consciousness was beyond that of any human master. Sanat connected me with energies from outside of our galaxy. I had an odd sense of energetic packages arriving like something I had mailed to myself long ago that were now finally showing up.

The following morning, after a delicious French breakfast with the traditional spread of croissants, cheese, prosciutto, muesli, yogurt, and café au lait, we drove up the steep, winding road to La Sainte Baume. We could see the mountain in the distance and walked through a grassy field toward a forest just as the sun was hitting the treetops. As we crossed a narrow footbridge over a small stream, I felt a sensation similar to passing between two pillars at Elephantine Island in Egypt. The footbridge represented more than just a way to keep your feet dry. It was a threshold into a magical forest.

We hiked through a picturesque, emerald-green forest at a leisurely pace, often in silence, pausing occasionally to gaze up at the tall trees and admire the glistening green moss covering boulders along the dirt path. Eventually, we came to a fork in the road. One path led to the top of the mountain where we would have to climb some steep, rocky terrain. The other led directly to Mary Magdalene's sacred grotto.

We made the challenging climb, and once atop the mountain, the view from 3,000 feet above sea level was spectacular. Looking south, we saw the Mediterranean, where shades of blue flowed endlessly until water and sky became one. We did another activation, enabling us to see beyond the human filters of body, mind, and emotion. Thoth used the metaphor of our panoramic view to illustrate how we each choose our focus. Looking in one direction, we saw the mountains, and in the other, the sea. No one moved; we simply refocused. I smiled, knowing I was applying that metaphor to many aspects of my life.

After the activation, we walked farther along the ridge to the tiny stone chapel of Saint-Pilon near the cliff's edge. Inside was a mural of Mary Magdalene appearing to rise between two columns and ascend through a starry night sky accompanied by two angels. The painting was so realistic it made Mary and the angels look like floating white statues.

On the hike back down to the grotto, we stopped briefly to photograph paragliders soaring gracefully along the sheer north face of the mountain with their colorful airfoil wings carrying them in the wind.

After the steep descent, we arrived at the grotto, a sacred site inside the mountain where Mary Magdalene was said to have lived the last years of her life. The dark cave was damp and cool and had been brightened with colorful stained-glass windows. We explored the shrines inside and did some sound toning in the lowest level where the acoustics were amazing.

I calculated that the little chapel of Saint-Pilon with the beautiful mural must have been 1,000 feet directly above us, thus symbolizing Mary Magdalene's path of ascension. I loved the alignment.

We continued descending down the trail and just before recrossing the footbridge leading out of the magical forest, I paused to savor the experience of La Sainte Baume with a moment of gratitude. In my mind's eye, I saw something that looked like a time capsule waiting to be opened and unpacked. I felt curious but a bit overwhelmed. I set an intention whatever this image symbolized would manifest with grace and ease.

That night, I had many more profound awarenesses and crazy dreams. It was still early in the trip and I was already drinking from a fire hose.

The next morning, we packed up and said goodbye to the lovely couple running the estate. We drove two hours west toward a coastal town, Saintes-Maries-de-la-Mer, home to an annual festival where statues of Saint Sarah, the Magdalene, and Mother Mary were carried out of the church and down to the sea in a ritual procession.

The beautiful Camargue region was a wetland and home to an ancient breed of horses and hundreds of species of birds. I had never seen so many pink flamingos in one place. We parked and walked out to the end of a jetty where we could hear the Mediterranean flowing under us. It was very windy, and occasionally, I felt the salt spray splashing up to where I sat in the sun on a long peninsula of huge rocks.

Danielle invited us to allow our consciousness to journey to a sacred, crystalline temple underwater off the coast and connect to the energy of another Egyptian deity, Isis. While my body remained in the sunshine on the rocks, I felt my consciousness travel to the underwater temple. I moved through the temple as though I had been there many times. I sensed I'd had responsibilities there. When we finished, I sat alone for a few moments knowing something extraordinary had just happened yet having no clue what it all meant.

After a lovely seaside lunch, we took a stroll through Saintes-Maries-de-la-Mer to visit the chapel and a few boutiques. Then we drove several hours north of Aix-en-Provence toward the Vaucluse Mountains. During the drive, my mind wandered to all the synchronicities that had aligned to bring me to the South of France. I thought back to stories Immanuel had told me during my trip to Abadiânia, and to books I had read, including *The Magdalene Manuscript*. As Danielle drove, I closed my eyes and felt a deep resonance with the land.

The last hour of our drive proceeded on narrow, winding roads through beautiful countryside in the area where Danielle and her husband lived. Danielle's neighbors owned a modern villa on a hillside with an infinity pool and sweeping views of the mountains in the distance. It was the owners' vacation home and became our basecamp for the next week. We looked out across the rolling acres featuring church steeples and tiny towns that dotted the hillside in the distance. I loved watching the morning sunshine light the big, open living area as we made espresso and enjoyed fresh *pain au chocolat*.

Our days were filled with hikes and light activations in picturesque spots. We visited a town called Roussillon and walked a beautiful trail called Le Sentier des Ocres where the soil was a deep-reddish orange with layers of yellowish gold. Another day, we hiked to the entrance of a cave in a remote area and descended a steep dirt path following Danielle's voice as the light from the entrance to the cave slowly faded and we walked down into total darkness. Eventually, we reached a flat, open space at what felt like the bottom of the cave. The acoustics in the cavernous space were ideal for toning, light language, and call and response. A hundred feet underground in the pitch black, we acknowledged ourselves as beings of luminous light with the ability to communicate between all the dimensions of ourselves. The transmission felt immensely powerful.

As we walked slowly back up the steep dirt path, I began to see a tiny speck of daylight from the cave entrance. Like birthing from the depths of darkness, we came into the light having activated more of our multidimensional capabilities. At the cave mouth, we discovered it had rained hard while we were underground. We were so deep we didn't hear it.

The following day, we drove up a narrow, winding road to the top of a ridge with spectacular views and an old, abandoned chapel. We stood in a square in the sunshine and tinkered with our positions until something clicked into place. Danielle called in a group of multidimensional beings. I counted more than three dozen, some with names I recognized from Egypt. *I felt the potency and magnitude.*

We did the activation within a hologram of group consciousness. Thoth invited us to imagine a six-pointed *star tetrahedron* and move into that shape vibrationally, connecting to other stargates with star tetrahedrons. It sounded like something from a science fiction novel, but as I imagined it, I felt a massive cosmic connection to a series of star tetrahedrons in several universes. Thoth spoke *light language*, and I felt as if a bunch of circuits had been connected creating a cosmic causeway bridging a vast space. Thoth suggested we imagine leaning into a large emerald in the center of our star tetrahedron, and I felt another octave of intensity.

Right when I thought I might faint, the transmission ended and the intensity dissipated. I stood looking out across miles of beautiful countryside, taking it all in.

Our activations were interspersed with delicious meals at delightful restaurants. One, Domaine les Andoiles, featured a huge, majestic tree with a spiral staircase encircling the trunk leading up to a deck built into the branches. We ate a leisurely lunch in the sunshine beside a koi pond before walking through an orchard to a vegetable garden and goat farm. Private villas and guest suites were nestled into the hillside. Sculptures and fountains flanked by thirty-foot palm trees led to a field of red poppies. I felt an earthy decadence as we strolled the grounds.

It rained the following day, so we did our activations in the villa. Danielle's sound bowls relaxed me and provided a conduit to my experience on the jetty at Saintes-Maries-de-la-Mer where I had entered an alternate reality. I was back inside the sacred, crystalline temple deep beneath the Mediterranean. I had somehow arrived at the temple from underwater. I walked up a few steps into a domed structure and through a room of prisms and crystals reflecting otherworldly light. An attendant helped me put on a special robe and then walked me to a throne where I sat and connected to a large group of multidimensional beings. The vision continued from there, deepening my awareness from the experience at the jetty.

When it stopped raining, we began our next activation in the villa courtyard at a long table outside in the warmth of the afternoon. The courtyard spanned the entire length of the house and was bordered by eight-foot stone walls, making it completely private. At the table, Danielle offered us a selection of art supplies. I did not consider myself an artist, but I picked up a box of chalk with an assortment of colors and started drawing scenes from the sacred underwater temple. I could not believe what flowed effortlessly through my hand and onto the blank pages. My artistic skills were poor, but my inspiration and connection to that space ran deep as I drew chalk sketches of each room, feeling like I had actually been there.

Rose bushes in large planters were situated near the table, and beyond those were topiaries arranged in a neat geometric pattern in the courtyard. Thoth, through Danielle's voice, suggested we move closer to the shrubs and then asked the other two women, "Would you be open to Ann directing you to move your bodies." I thought that meant calisthenics or yoga poses. We laughed as Thoth clarified that each of us is a unique piece of sacred geometry, and I was to position each piece in a way that optimized the whole. It seemed a bit like putting together a jigsaw puzzle and each human was a unique piece.

I started by orienting myself along the courtyard's south wall. Then I pointed to two positions about twenty feet from me. We stood in the shape of a giant triangle. Something about this felt right. I asked Thoth as embodied by Danielle, to stand directly behind me, and instantly, I felt as if I had been plugged into an electrical outlet. The energy surging through my body was profound. The activation ended with Thoth saying, "Ignite, ignite, ignite." I was already electrified!

After four activations in one day, we opted for a low-key dinner in the villa. I watched the sun set over the mountains before I fell asleep.

The next morning, we drove to a place called Lioux and hiked up the rocky terrain of a cliff with beautiful views. When we arrived at a flat spot, Danielle invited us to find a position we felt guided to. I found my place easily and watched as Danielle walked slowly backward from the group until we both sensed a click, like tumblers in a lock dropping into place.

In an unstructured, spontaneous flow, we verbalized our intentions to release anything no longer serving us or that held us back. The list of things we wished to release for ourselves and for humanity was long. From patriarchal overlays to doubt, confusion, fear, and disbelief, we said everything that came to mind. The cliff ran from southwest to northeast, and I sensed we had opened a portal at one end. Everything we said was being vacuumed into a huge, dark hole.

Once we had offloaded all we could think to release, there was a long silence. My feet felt cemented in place, but the others moved and changed the geometry. Our giant verbal purge had apparently freed up space the way cleaning out a closet would allow you to bring in fresh new outfits.

Over the next half hour, we spoke our intentions for what we wanted to embody. I verbalized my desire to use more of my unconventional gifts in my everyday life, to actualize more of my multidimensionality here on earth, and to openly receive all the divine support available to me. I had no idea how that might look, but it was what was in my heart.

When we closed the ceremony, I laughed and said whatever portal we had opened was so big I was happy no one had fallen into the abyss. I knew I had just claimed something bigger than I understood with my logical mind. I needed to rest in the shade of a small bush and just be alone for a few minutes before joining the others for our hike back down to the car. We came to refer to this as the "Grace Grid Portal at the Falaise," and it was one of the most expansive experiences of the trip.

Our activations in France culminated with a return to the cave where we met Thoth individually inside. I was the last of the group to enter the cave. Thoth started with an intense lightning round of *light language* with syllables, sentences, and sounds streaming through Danielle. I invited some of my favorite beings, including Sekhmet and Isis, to support me with their energetic presence. I received a potent transmission, and there in the cave, I was invited into the "Lineage of Thoth." One part of me had no clue what this meant but another part felt the significance with great reverence.

We had our final dinner at a lovely restaurant in a tiny town called Casseneuve. The picturesque backdrop and exquisite French food provided the perfect spot for celebrating all our adventures.

When we returned to the villa, I went to pack, feeling bittersweet. I was ready to get home to my own space and integrate all I had experienced, yet I knew I would miss France. I looked out the bedroom windows into the dark, starry night sky with gratitude for all that had happened.

Deep inside, I felt a stirring like I had felt in Egypt—like some memories or knowledge had been reawakened. The sense of expansiveness and potential felt infinite, and I wondered how these experiences would shape my life back in Atlanta.

CHAPTER 31
In the Roundabout

Back in Atlanta, I knew my priorities were changing. It was May of 2018, and with no office, no consulting projects, and no travel scheduled for the first time in decades, I felt a strange void. After nurturing Solertis for twenty-two years, I closed the legal entity and reduced the company to a splash page on a website with the logo and the words, "Founded in 1996. Forever evolving." I turned down meetings and events I would have normally moved metaphoric mountains to attend. The larger purpose of my life was unfolding, and I was grateful it was gradual and voluntary rather than caused by some tragedy or hardship.

One part of me got very still inside while another part was invigorated by physical activity. Carrie, who supported me in developing a mindfulness course for athletes, had just returned from Japan where she hiked Kumano Kodo, an ancient pilgrimage trail in the mountains south of Kyoto. She was an excellent partner for hiking, being both a triathlete and someone who understood my intuitive capabilities and shared my interest in metaphysics.

For several months, we hiked a new trail in the North Georgia mountains every week. One hike was twelve miles and was interrupted by a thirty-minute standoff with a four-foot rattlesnake sunbathing along the trail and blocking our descent. At the start of each hike, we used our intention to create an energetic structure like those I had experienced in Egypt, Morocco, France, and other places. We envisioned ourselves inside a big, translucent bubble and set intentions to interact with nature and creatures in the most respectful way. I am convinced this is one reason the rattlesnake did not engage and eventually slithered into the cool darkness of a large, rotten log. We meditated near lush waterfalls and on top of huge boulders in raging streams. North Georgia soil had the red ochre color I saw in France, so as we hiked in silence, I revisited experiences I had had there just weeks earlier.

Between hikes, I looked for office space, believing I would continue offering CranioSacral Therapy and hands-on treatment. I browsed websites and visited dozens of offices. Nothing fit. Several landlords said they wanted to book a session once I found a space, yet nothing materialized.

In the meantime, clients kept calling for appointments, and I resumed making house calls. A woman named Amy sent me an email after finding my profile on the Upledger website. She was a high profile businessperson, and she said she saw my picture, read my bio, and hoped I could help her with her headaches. Serendipitously, in a metropolitan area of six million people, she lived within a mile of me.

Working in a client's home provided interesting insights. Amy's husband carried my portable table up a long flight of stairs to their master bedroom. As I entered the beautiful room, I sensed the love between them and a nice, stable harmonic. However, the rest of the house felt more chaotic. Once Amy was lying comfortably on the table, she told me her story.

Her adult son had just moved back into the house and a much older relative was also living there but presumably moving out at some unspecified time. As Amy explained, I began to understand the disharmony I felt outside the bedroom. During the session, she became consciously aware of what she already knew. She and her husband needed to establish some boundaries. I predicted her

CHAPTER 31: IN THE ROUNDABOUT

headaches would leave with the houseguests and she would regain her usual good health and vitality.

Shanna was a referral who asked me to meet her in the underground parking lot of a new high-rise condominium complex in Midtown. I carried my portable table into the lobby and asked where we were going. Shanna said her boss was out of town, and she was taking care of the place.

We took the elevator to the thirtieth floor, where she opened the door to a spectacular corner unit with amazing views of Atlanta. Inside the main living area every flat surface was covered with clutter. The furnishings were exquisite but just barely visible under the debris. We cleared space for my table, and Shanna got comfortable.

Curiously, the session focused on her relationship with her boss. I found it remarkable that we were in the home of the person she was having an issue with. I also felt like we were being watched, so I whispered to Shanna, asking if there was a camera. She did not know, so I conducted the entire session as if it were being live-streamed. I kept asking, "What's the highest and best outcome for all involved?" Back in the parking deck after the session, I asked Shanna if her boss would be okay with a visitor in the condo. Shanna replied, "Well, I guess we will find out."

Matt was another client I'd had dozens of sessions with at the Center. He asked if I would treat him in his home. Matt had been a lawyer at the firm that represented my first company. We had known one another for decades, and he was now CEO of a multinational company. He had chronic back pain and had already endured several surgeries. Our sessions gave him some relief, and I agreed to a house call.

As he had done many times before, Matt slipped into a totally relaxed state and appeared to nap on the table. His body signaled it had spontaneously dropped into its own healing wisdom in what Dr. Upledger called "still point." After thirty minutes, Matt awoke and asked about the flow of energy he sensed between my hands. I encouraged him to trust his experience and be open to more.

Matt continued to request sessions regularly. Once when he returned from two weeks in South Africa, he asked for a "wellness visit." I was delighted to learn he was not reacting to pain but proactively addressing his wellbeing.

When I arrived at his home, I was surprised to find it bustling with a small army of workers preparing for a charitable event with 200 guests. The caterer was setting up, the florist was placing large arrangements, and the cleaning team was in overdrive. Matt said his family thought he was nuts to schedule the session, but he was adamant about prioritizing his wellness. He relaxed into inner stillness despite the dog barking, the doorbell ringing, vendors yelling instructions about chafing dishes, and the cleaning people running the vacuum cleaner into the door just a few feet from the massage table. I chuckled at Matt's ability to tune it all out and drop into that beautiful state of healing.

Many things seemed to be coming to their natural completion. I kept seeing the number 999 everywhere. I smiled knowing when one thing ended, something new could flourish. Over time, my curiosity had led me to many different practitioners offering different perspectives and techniques. I started a list and discovered I had studied with more than seventy practitioners and programs over twenty years. I also owned 500 books about various self-improvement topics, both practical and esoteric.

I wanted to draw on my quantum soup of experience and create something original. I had observed dozens of gifted practitioners creating energy structures and transmissions for a particular purpose. Intentional creation through consciousness was the foundation of most of the programs and methods I had studied. I knew I had the ability to use intention to create a safe space while hiking, and I had fostered some kind of group harmonic resonance while standing at a podium in the Federal Reserve Bank.

CHAPTER 31: IN THE ROUNDABOUT

No one had given me an instruction manual on how to create geometric energy structures, but I felt a natural instinct along with an impulse to test my capabilities. I looked through my list of clients and picked twelve of the most open-minded. I wrote an email titled, "Invitation to the 9-9-9 Transformation Hologram." I wrote about completion and letting go, then offered remote support during an energetic transmission to amplify resolution and closure for anything no longer serving them. I invited them to privately set their intentions for anything they wanted to release and sent a link to sign up.

On the eve of my "9-9-9 Transformation Hologram," I sat in deeply relaxed meditation. Like dropping a pebble into a tranquil pond, I released my intentions to the ethers. I waited and watched as a giant, shimmering geometric structure slowly began to form in my mind's eye. I watched a beautiful dance of shapes, color, and form moving fluidly within a multidimensional opalescent structure. It was breathtaking. I felt a sense of deep compassion. I gave gratitude to all who were supporting me and witnessed an incredible light show.

I came out of meditation and journaled about everything I had just observed. Then, at midnight, I used my intention to float this beautiful stellar creation out to the participants who had signed up. At sunrise, I meditated and looked at what was happening in the energy field of each client. I let my mind become a blank movie screen and silently invited each client to project information or imagery onto the screen. Each had used the holographic pattern in their own way. I observed until I sensed we were done and then did a completion ceremony to thank the unseen forces supporting me, the hologram, and the clients.

I had been doing sessions with Isabelle consistently for ten years, so she saw the big picture of my life. When I mentioned my "9-9-9 Transformation Hologram," Isabelle likened my program to exiting a roundabout and trying a new road. She said I had been going around and around looking at options and congratulated me for getting myself into the roundabout rather than sticking to a more conventional path.

I laughed at the synchronicity of her analogy. The previous week, Gomati and Vasistha had visited me, and we had taken separate cars to dinner. We came to a roundabout in a residential neighborhood, and as a joke, I went around the entire roundabout twice before exiting. In the rearview mirror, I could see them howling with laughter. Isabelle's analogy just days after my prank felt like yet another wink from the Universe.

CHAPTER 32
Surrender

I had moved out of Industrious in late 2017, but during the three years I'd had an office there, I had teamed up with several groups of entrepreneurs on consulting projects. One person I frequently worked with was William, whom I had gotten to know after I intuited his hip pain days before he had surgery. William had climbed the corporate ladder to the upper echelons of a $50 billion communications company before being passed over for the chief technology officer job. He left the company shortly after and picked up consulting gigs while looking for his next big role.

We worked together on several projects, including one involving months of work with a large food retailer. When we were almost done, we were asked to brief a member of the board of directors. In a crazy bit of serendipity, the director was the woman who had been promoted into the CTO job William wanted. The three of us met in a conference room at the client's headquarters, and despite having won the coveted CTO position, she must have felt threatened or insecure. She made several demeaning comments to William and subtly belittled him. I held compassion for both within whatever dynamics were playing out. If this was the environment she thrived on as a leader, I was happy William had moved on.

Just as I moved out of Industrious, William took an executive position at a startup, which included working in Dallas, so we no longer saw one another regularly. When I returned from France, I got a text from William saying, "I miss you. Where art thou?" He had finished his last week of work in Dallas, and we made plans to meet for lunch.

William was working on a number of business ideas and had read dozens of books on leadership and business. I was intrigued when he cited statistics about loneliness and depression in men in their fifties. He was squarely in that demographic himself and spoke of a men's group he was forming through his church because he found intimacy challenging.

I always felt a certain ease and honesty in our conversations, and as we walked to our cars after lunch, I asked if he remembered our first conversation at Industrious. We had been in a conference room talking about a colleague's idea for a medical concierge-type service when I had intuited the pain in his right hip. William remembered and said he had told his wife the story when he got home that day. He chalked up my intuitive capabilities to *mirror neurons*, a term he had read in a business book by Simon Sinek.

As my career moved in new, unconventional directions, I wanted to be prepared to talk with skeptics about metaphysics or multidimensional reality. William provided me an opportunity to become more confident in my responses and the way I explained myself to a mainstream audience. William had served as a mentor to several of his former colleagues and offered to help me. We met to whiteboard a framework for developing my wellness business and discuss some of his ideas.

William was physically fit and zealous about his CrossFit workouts. He got great satisfaction from really pushing his physical limits. Sometimes I sensed he was in excruciating pain. One day, William was in so much pain he had to lie on the floor of his home office. He said, "Physical limits and pain are tangible. Other things are more complicated." I understood his vigorous workouts were his primary outlet for emotions, but the hardcore physical nature

CHAPTER 32: SURRENDER

was also the cause of injuries and pain. He admitted he "tortured himself" in the gym to assert his dominance over all the aspects of himself he could not risk letting out of his control.

I knew William had long been on a path of self-inquiry. He had been questioning many of the principles and beliefs instilled in him at a young age. He had told me twice that people get to an age where they realize they have been "living a lie." Not necessarily a lie they created but one they bought into. I agreed. For years, I had chased what I thought success should be and what those around me valued. Questioning my beliefs and thoughts started the bend in my trajectory.

Now in his fifties, William was weighing the aspects of himself he had kept tightly suppressed or had discounted as unimportant. I noted William's latest business ideas were based on seeing and honoring humanness in the workplace. He used the term "human-centric" and advocated for compassion and decency. I hoped he might start with himself.

In the context of helping with marketing for my wellness business, William agreed to act as if he were a new client, including an "inventory and assessment" where I brought my massage table and did diagnostic work on his musculoskeletal system. He completed a brief questionnaire in advance, and I learned this healthy, physically fit man was averaging one surgery every eighteen months, with twelve surgeries requiring hospitalization and significant recovery time. William had never experienced any alternative or holistic care, but he agreed to a pilot session, presumably in the interest of helping me with marketing.

I set up my portable table in William's home office and encouraged him to relax and say whatever came to mind. I listened to the words while my other senses picked up the more subtle energy and unspoken information he transmitted. In the middle of the session, I asked William, "If your right hip could talk, what would it say?" William paused and said his right hip would say, "I am back in business." He had undergone a second surgery on his right hip followed by a long recovery and was now back to his intense workouts. I asked about his left hip, and it said, "I am in so much fear of the future." William knew his left hip would likely need surgery, and on several levels, his left hip knew the pain the right one had already endured.

Next, I asked him how he felt about the word "surrender." He said it had a negative connotation, with a loser surrendering to a winner.

In the pilot session, we explored a lot of his inner terrain, perhaps venturing further into raw, unfiltered honesty than anticipated. I knew William had really surrendered to the experience, and as soon as the session ended, he quickly returned to his more comfortable position at the whiteboard where he could rationalize the experience and depersonalize it as an experiment. I silently speculated his desire to reestablish control was triggered by the vulnerability of lying on a massage table with someone reading his energy while touching him.

We spoke again days after the pilot session. William said he thought the pilot session had gone beyond diagnostic, and that I had been "giving" as well as getting information. He said I had a unique way of sensing things. I smiled inwardly and agreed.

He read scripture daily and had been thinking about the term "surrender." The biblical interpretation meant faith and trust in God, not defeat. I agreed and offered that surrender could also be a conscious choice to let go of something to reach a deeper level of inner harmony.

My ears perked up when William used the term "dimensions" related to the holistic nature of life. He said, "We are comprised of many convergent dimensions, and if you don't see that, all you do is treat symptoms. You are going to help people become aware of the multiple dimensions of their being and develop their skills in understanding ways they can affect those states."

CHAPTER 32: SURRENDER

Although William continued speaking, I could no longer track his words because the galaxy had opened up. The room dissolved as if I had been swallowed by a dark void. I tried to hold on to my desk even as it seemed to disappear. I had no spatial reference in the three-dimensional world. I thought I might have to lie on the floor, but as William finished, I felt myself coming back into my chair.

William said he trusted me and his time on the table had felt calming. He told me, "I talked about a lot of things I don't talk about…and certainly not in that totality." William expressed his gratitude and said he always got so much from talking with me. I felt the authenticity of his sentiment and was grateful he could express it. As we hung up, I was aware something important had just happened, even if I could not put words to it.

The following week, William was offered an interim executive position he had been pursuing at a small company. He had joked he could finally declare himself Chief Technology Officer. He had to travel to Wisconsin every week, which meant the end of our work together.

I understood his priorities, but I felt abandoned. I knew we had both gained something meaningful from the interactions despite the abrupt ending. No longer orienting my marketing plans around William and the whiteboard, I was eager to keep the momentum going. As I tried to galvanize my new direction, I found myself thinking, *How did I get here?*

In my next session with Isabelle, she observed I had created my own PhD program. She viewed my time in corporate wellness as the bridge that helped me move from supply chain and Solertis into the roundabout of CranioSacral Therapy and mindfulness. I knew my work was becoming more of an expression of my true essence. I was accustomed to having a plan and executing it, but I was learning to surrender and allow crazy synchronicities to lead me.

CHAPTER 33
The Full Litany

Clients continued to ask for sessions, and I continued to make house calls. I was heartened when Matt asked for another "wellness visit." As we were finishing, he asked if I had ever considered synthesizing all my capabilities into a program rather than offering single sessions. He observed I had an unusual range that included business experience, CranioSacral Therapy, yoga, mindfulness, and coaching. He knew my work with private equity firms and called me a "strategic thinker." He offered the term, "Holistic Executive Leadership Coaching" and said CEO-types would pay a lot of money for "the full litany of skills."

Then he said, "Speaking as one, we don't want too many people in our ear because that gets confusing." I appreciated him sharing his vision and asked if I could get a half hour on his calendar so we could discuss it.

A week later, I waited in the modern, minimalist lobby of a two million-square-foot landmark that Matt and his team had purchased and transformed with a big vision and a $250 million investment. I thought back to the mid-1990s when I was leaving corporate America to start my consulting company. I needed legal advice because I intended to solicit some of my employer's biggest clients, and I did not want to get sued. Matt was an attorney and someone I had known for years, so I called him for advice.

Now I sat in his office lobby thinking I had come full circle. Again, I was asking for his perspective, and thankfully, this time it was for an entirely new expansion of my career and not threats of a lawsuit.

Matt greeted me, and we walked to his private conference room—the paintings were done by the same artist as those that hung in his home. We began talking about his vision for "Holistic Executive Leadership Coaching," and he said he had hired a coach who worked with many of his senior staff but she was a psychotherapist with no business background. My consulting business had given me perspective on corporate culture, operations, and leadership, and Matt was a big fan of using outside expertise.

One of my unique advantages was having run a successful consulting company while also utilizing my less-conventional skills and capabilities. I walked my talk and invested proactively in self-care and personal growth.

In our conversation, I discovered Matt had paid for a mindfulness program for his employees but had no experience with it himself and little patience for meditation. We settled on the components for a thirteen-week program and agreed to a mix of phone and in-person sessions. He loved our CranioSacral Therapy sessions, so we agreed to those along with one session targeting physical flexibility. Our fifteen-minute phone sessions would center around mindfulness-based stress-reduction techniques. For a CEO with his schedule, this was a significant time commitment. I emailed him a proposal, and we started the following week.

Around this same time, I was communicating with my mom's doctor in Kansas City, a close friend from high school named Eric. Mom was having difficulty sleeping, and my sister and I were concerned about her ongoing use of prescription sleeping pills. I tried to teach Mom some breathing techniques and ways to self-soothe, but she still relied on pills and was experiencing side effects. I emailed Eric with my concerns. I mentioned I had been pharma-free for ten years and disliked long-term use of insomnia medications. I also wrote I had offered Mom some mindfulness techniques.

Within minutes, I received a reply that read, "I am interested in your mindfulness experience. I am starting a new company providing comprehensive physicals and health resources to executives and part of our program is an introduction to mindfulness. Can we talk about this?"

When we spoke, I learned Eric was weeks away from starting his program. He had recruited a dozen doctors and healthcare providers who would provide services at a one-day event, but he still needed someone to teach mindfulness. In addition to his private practice, Eric was one of the team doctors for a professional sports franchise in Kansas City and had access to their training facilities. He planned to bring his executive clients to this new, state-of-the-art facility during the off season for a day-long program he called "Premier Physicals." Part of the program's allure was an exclusive use of resources enjoyed by elite professional athletes like cryotherapy chambers, advanced training equipment, a private dining room, and other amenities.

Eric had recruited providers of services from echocardiograms to skin cancer screening to the Gallup Strengths Based Leadership evaluation, all to be performed in this beautiful facility. The one thing he had not yet found was someone professional enough to present mindfulness to executives. I was already planning to travel to Kansas City to visit family, so I offered to do a demo presentation for Eric and his team.

A week later, I flew to Kansas City from Atlanta, knowing I was taking a bit of a risk flying in on the morning of the presentation. When I arrived at Hartsfield airport, I was surprised to find long lines for security snaking back and forth through the terminal. Tamara, the benevolent TSA employee who had occasionally saved me from long lines, was not working, so I headed for another area called the T-Gates. That line was also long, and the man in front of me said it was not moving. While waiting, I called the Delta Platinum hotline, and they confirmed my flight was already boarding and offered to rebook me on the next flight to Kansas City.

I wasn't ready to give up just yet. Seconds later, I smiled as I heard a walkie-talkie and turned to see a man carrying a clipboard. I had been flying out of Hartsfield for two decades and knew the man with the clipboard would open another lane for screening. Several passengers let me jump ahead in the newly opened line, and I got through security quickly.

Next, I did something I had never done in twenty-five years of flying. I ran for my gate in a dress and bare feet. I arrived and saw the boarding door was already closed. I sighed and approached the agent at the desk, out of breath from running with my luggage. She looked at me and my bare feet and said, "I bet you're Ms. Elliott."

Apparently, while I had been waiting in the long security line, there was a sudden thunderstorm and a lightning strike on the tarmac. All of the passengers waiting on the jet bridge had been brought back inside the concourse until the storm passed. Half the passengers were on the plane, and the remaining thirty were waiting for the boarding door to reopen. I could not believe the serendipity. Three hours later, Eric picked me up at the Kansas City airport, and we drove to the sports facility.

In the team's media room, I did a shortened version of the introduction to mindfulness presentation I had created for athletes a year earlier. Eric and several people from Premier Physicals watched and participated in my *awareness of breath* meditation. For most, this was their first guided meditation, and they seemed to enjoy it. After mindfulness, I wanted to do a short demonstration of one-on-one sessions and CranioSacral Therapy, so we set up the table, and I gave short demo sessions. I was delighted when Eric was so relaxed after ten minutes that he did not want to get off the table.

Eric and the team concurred I was a good fit for the mindfulness presentation, and he agreed to let me provide the same mini, one-on-one sessions to the participants while pitching my executive wellness program. Mindfulness would be a group presentation, and then each of the ten executives would rotate through my station just as they did with echocardiogram, skin cancer screening, and all of the other services. My goal was to introduce myself and my services and sell executive wellness programs. Eric agreed.

CHAPTER 34
Going Solo

While plans moved forward in Kansas City, I continued to look for an office in Atlanta. I spotted one on Craigslist I had looked at twelve years earlier while pursuing my vision to expand the Center for Holistic Health. I thought back to that time working to grow someone else's wellness business—it felt like another lifetime. The space was too big for what I needed as a solo practitioner, but I noted the name of the property management company, Elmhurst Realty, and went online to see what else they had.

Elmhurst had an office in Decatur that caught my eye. The brochure showed a photo of the front of a cool, retro Class B building. One of the offices was a simple room on the third floor with a one-year lease available. While it was far from the trendy luxury of Industrious, it was entirely affordable. I called Elmhurst Realty and they agreed to show it the following day.

After navigating a narrow alley to the parking lot, I found a door at the loading dock. The only elevator was at the opposite end of the building, and it was out of order, so I walked up three flights of stairs. I noted the worn carpet and outdated light fixtures, but I also felt an odd sense of welcoming.

The agent was already there, and she opened the door to a bright, open space with two big windows, sunlight streaming in, and beautiful trees just outside. I basked in the beauty for a moment before noticing the paint color was an atrocious pea green, the drywall was badly chipped, the ceiling tiles had yellowed, and worst of all, the carpet had nasty stains. The agent said they wouldn't do any improvements without a three-year lease.

The small kitchen on the second floor had a full-size fridge and a coffee maker, but it was barely big enough for two people. It was nothing like the deluxe coffee bar at Industrious. The bathrooms were tiny and looked like something from my 1970s elementary school. The marketing materials said Wi-Fi was included, but it was not working. The agent said the previous tenant wanted out of his lease, so the space was available immediately. I suggested the tenant might be willing to cover some of the costs to repaint to get out of the lease early, but the agent said no.

I decided to move forward despite multiple issues. The space just *felt* right. I talked to Alston, the managing partner at Elmhurst Realty, and made arrangements to see the space again. I drove back to the building, walked down the narrow alley, and climbed three flights of stairs. As ugly as the space was, I felt a sense of inevitability. I knew I could create my own sanctuary inside Suite 303. I measured the walls and drew the space to scale on a piece of graph paper. I overlaid the feng shui bagua and planned how I would fit everything into 120 square feet.

That night, I dreamed about Renee, a client I had not seen in a year. Renee had been a painter at one point, so I sent her a text. She met me at Suite 303 the next day, took a peek inside, and agreed to spackle and paint.

Alston said the paint color would have to be approved by the landlord and specified in my lease. He again refused to ask the current tenant about sharing any of the costs to repair the walls, chafed at my suggestion, and emailed a thirty-three-page lease agreement containing ridiculous provisions, including a $2 million liability insurance policy. Alston said the landlord required it and he again seemed annoyed by my questions.

Later that day, Alston called and barked about whether he wanted me as a tenant at all. He was tired of answering my questions and said he would think about it overnight. I hung up and laughed. I had worked with a lot of high-strung CEOs but was surprised at how little it took to irritate Alston. He called next morning and said he had added a page of "special stipulations" enabling him to terminate my lease for any reason on thirty-days' notice. When I asked if that stipulation was mutual, I thought Alston would explode. I could not get a word in edgewise while he yelled, eventually ending his rant with something about how he did not like me "up in his kitchen."

When we were about to hang up, I asked if this meant I would not be permitted to use the little kitchen on the second floor. He asked what had given me that idea, and I reminded him he had said he didn't want me "up in his kitchen." Alston laughed. Apparently, "up in my kitchen" was synonymous with getting too far into somebody else's business. My ignorance softened his fury.

Despite the "special stipulations," sub-standard aesthetics, and poor design, my sense of inevitability never faltered. With all its flaws and imperfections, I knew Suite 303 was it. I surrendered and signed the lease. When I went to pay the deposit and first month's rent, I serendipitously discovered Alston himself was the majority owner of the building, and everything he had said about "the landlord" not wanting to pay for improvements was really him not wanting to pay. This also explained some of his fury at me getting "up in his kitchen." He did not want to take responsibility for refusing to compromise, so he hid behind the anonymous landlord. I felt like I was in another version of *The Wizard of Oz*.

I purchased two gallons of "Agreeable Gray" and met Renee on Saturday to paint Suite 303. While she painted, I sat in the hall and assembled a pneumatic stool. I also silently worked on the energetics of the space. Renee patched and painted as I released residual energy from the room. Meanwhile, a few tenants, mostly therapists and lawyers, stopped by to say hello.

The carpet cleaner came on Monday with a shampooer the size of a riding lawn mower. He had to push it all the way up the alley to the front door where, thankfully, the elevator was back in service. When the cleaning was finally done, the carpet looked perfect.

Tuesday morning, I opened the door to Suite 303 and nearly fainted. The carpet had dried, and the stains were much worse than before. I called the carpet cleaning company, and around 5:30 p.m., another cleaner arrived and tried dry vacuuming rather than using the wet vac. When he started up the machine, it sounded like a small child was being tortured. Tenants came running from every office—apparently, many therapists had evening appointments. After I apologized profusely, they agreed to allow the cleaner ten minutes to finish the job.

With the paint dry and the carpet in a state I could tolerate, I brought in a beautiful wood chest I had originally purchased for my Industrious office, a deep navy chair in a stylish design, a six-foot-tall plant in a woven basket, and a cool lamp. I hung a beautiful, clear, spherical crystal unobtrusively from the ceiling in the wealth corner designated by the feng shui bagua and placed a gorgeous amethyst crystal on a pedestal in another corner. The windowsills had flat granite ledges perfect for glass vases filled with tall stalks of bamboo. I was really pleased with how it had come together and how much I had enjoyed the process.

I passed a man on a ladder in the hall and discovered he was in charge of maintaining the internet connection. He rebooted the Wi-Fi router so I had internet access. I met Jerry, the janitor, who laughed and knew exactly who had damaged the walls and stained the carpet in 303. A guy named Zeke installed my nameplate on the door. Everything had finally come together for my first solo wellness office.

Clients began to come for sessions, but I still felt something was missing. The wall between the two windows screamed for artwork. In my mind's eye, I saw what I wanted. Six years earlier, I had been at

CHAPTER 34: GOING SOLO

a business meeting in downtown Chicago on a September morning and took a walk along Michigan Avenue. I had been to Chicago dozens of times, and nostalgically recalled childhood experiences at Oak Street Beach and Water Tower Place. As I walked, my attention was drawn to a banner with images of blue spheres and the word *Cosmologies*. I felt my pulse quicken with curiosity as I discovered *Cosmologies* was an exhibition at the Loyola University Museum of Modern Art, just steps from where I stood.

I went back to my hotel, changed my flight, and at 10 a.m., I entered the exhibit and was instantly mesmerized. Every piece had a multidimensional quality. I was captivated by a huge floor exhibit called *Pemarom* with hundreds of overlapping compact discs arranged in a spiraling circle, twenty-five feet in diameter. A spotlight above created a shimmering rainbow of color as it reflected off the CDs' metallic surface. An audio recording of the mantra "Om Mani Padme Hum" played softly. I was awed by the creative genius that had taken an ordinary pile of CDs and turned them into something so truly sacred and magnificent.

Another piece, called *Buddhapada*, was made from everyday pushpins like those used on a bulletin board. The pins were pressed into a wall-sized, navy-blue cloth in the shape of a foot, complete with all of its chakras. Each painting had a breathtakingly cosmic quality. I lingered for over an hour, hypnotized and delighted to be alone in the exhibition.

I purchased a catalog with color photos from the exhibit and an essay titled "Infinity and the Palm of a Hand." *Cosmologies* had been a truly transcendent experience.

Now, wanting something to spice up the agreeable gray in my new office, I pulled out the *Cosmologies* catalog and googled the artist, Andra Samelson. Within days, I had purchased one of my favorite paintings—*Unannounced*—and had it mounted to look as if it floated in front of the wall between the windows. I hung it with the intention it would be a portal into a realm of healing and divinity. I wanted every client to have their own version of the transcendent experience I had in *Cosmologies*.

Suite 303 continued to be a sanctuary inside an otherwise quirky building. One evening, I was getting ready to leave when I heard a group of angry men shouting in the hallway. The words and tones were so confrontational and abrasive that I was afraid to open my door. When there was a break in the noise, I peeked out and saw no one in the hall, so I decided to make a run for the parking lot, hoping the altercation had not moved down there. As I passed the conference room, I could hear a therapist giving instructions. The yelling was a role-playing exercise and part of a Wednesday evening men's therapy group. I was relieved and happy I had not called the police.

CHAPTER 35
Premiering

As I was getting settled in Suite 303, Premier Physicals confirmed the date for the program in Kansas City. On pre-event calls, I learned the practitioners included an orthopedist, audiologist, nutritionist, bone density analyst, exercise physiologist, chiropractor, vascular specialist, and strengths-based leadership consultant. Each client would rotate through stations over eight hours. I noted my group mindfulness presentation followed lunch, as did my one-on-one sessions.

I also received a file with short patient profiles. One patient was CEO of a Midwestern biotech company and on the board of a small venture capital firm. Another was president of a small manufacturing company based in Oklahoma. The most intriguing was Manny, an entrepreneur turned podcaster. I listened to excerpts from several of his podcasts and found them brash and aggressive with an unwavering commitment to winning at any cost. Manny tended to promote avoiding emotion to succeed in "crushing the competition." I also learned Manny had lost his father at seven, and his grandfather had groomed him for the relentless pursuit of success.

I noted the intuitive information I received as I studied each client's name and photo. With the biotech CEO, I felt tightness across my eyes and forehead. With the executive from Oklahoma,

I sensed reluctance. With Manny, I got the image of dozens of spinning plates and a persona of gritty invincibility thinly masking something much different just below the surface.

As I drove to the sports facility the morning of the program, a beautiful rainbow spanned the entire sky parallel to the car. I smiled, realizing the rainbow seemed to meet the horizon at the highway exit for the facility.

Eric and Tom welcomed me with warm hugs. I was one of the few practitioners without a starched white lab coat. Many of the others, whom I'd met during pre-event calls, said hello and asked about mindfulness. Eric told us a camera crew would be filming intermittently during the day for marketing purposes. I privately wondered if the clients had consented to be filmed.

Once everyone arrived, we gathered in a large circle and introduced ourselves. I noted the practitioners and staff outnumbered the clients by at least four-to-one. Each client got a swag bag with the Premier logo and gifts along with a concierge assigned to lead them through the huge facility to the correct station and attend to their needs.

The room for mindfulness was in the farthest corner of the building. It was dark and freezing cold, so I quickly had to figure out how to use the sophisticated controls to turn on the lights and program the thermostat.

Fortunately, I had followed an intuitive impulse to pack twenty-five feet of HDMI cable because when I went to connect my laptop to the massive screen, the wireless system was not working. Once connected, I ran through my PowerPoint slides, meditated, and set intentions.

Lunchtime finally came, and people trickled into the dining area. A buffet with salads, sandwiches, chips, fresh fruit plates, yogurt, and granola parfaits along with a selection of desserts was set up. As the group finished eating, Eric warmly introduced me and directed everyone to the media room where I had my presentation ready to go.

Apparently, most of the group was interested in mindfulness, and we ran out of chairs, so a contingent of men in white coats stood along the back wall. I started with a brief version of my personal story and how I had worked in supply chain, started my own company, and done a stint in corporate wellness before finding my way to practicing holistic health modalities and mindfulness. I said I invested proactively in self-care, so I only needed to see the men in white coats at events where I was teaching mindfulness. They laughed.

Because we were in a sports facility, I gave examples of professional teams using mindfulness to keep athletes centered and focused, mitigate performance anxiety, and regulate breathing. Hoping to plant seeds with some of the executives, I also gave examples of corporations offering mindfulness to employees.

Next, I invited the group to participate in a basic *awareness of breath* meditation. I encouraged them to get comfortable and close their eyes. I told them we would stay with it for five minutes, with the only exception being a fire alarm. I felt everyone settle in as I began guiding them through the meditation.

When I closed my eyes, I immediately sensed something moving. When I opened my eyes, I was surprised to find the video team had moved quietly to the front and was filming from behind me, over my left shoulder, over my right shoulder, and from directly in front of me. It was more distracting than anything I had previously experienced while trying to lead a guided meditation. I thought it would make things worse to wave them off or ask them to leave, so I just kept my focus internal, which was the purpose of mindfulness anyway.

The video people eventually stopped filming and joined the meditation. The room became blissfully still and harmonic. After five-and-a-half minutes, I used my chimes to signal the end of the exercise. The group clapped enthusiastically and thanked me before leaving the room. I was privately delighted that everyone, even the guys in white coats, had been open minded enough to try something new and had benefitted from the experience.

I set up my massage table in the room where we had done the mindfulness program. My first twenty-minute session was with Buck, the biotech CEO. I began by reading his rhythms, starting at his feet and moving up. I held my fingertips lightly under the base of his skull and asked what he was experiencing. He said he was aware of a "tension band" around his eyes. He said this was often a marker of stress, so I suggested he close his eyes and feel them relaxing in their sockets. Then I suggested he allow his eyeballs to float and gently look down toward his feet. This technique relaxed the nerves in his cranium, and Buck felt it instantly.

When I asked about stress at work, he said his company was either going to make an acquisition or be acquired. He was hoping to find venture investors or a private equity firm that could keep up with the company's growth. I laughed and said it was usually the other way around. The private equity firms I had worked with were always striving for faster growth.

As I held his head, putting light pressure on his occiput, I felt him relax. Even as we discussed business, he continued to relax in response to light touch. Buck said he was very competitive and wanted "two more shots on goal" before he retired. I loved the metaphor given we were in a sports facility. I gave him some suggestions for ways to relax the tension he felt around his head just as the concierge came in to whisk him to the next station.

Next was Alan, the president of a small manufacturing company based in Oklahoma. He apologized because he was sneezing and coughing, having caught a cold a few days earlier. He relaxed on the table, and I asked how he had found Premier if he lived in Oklahoma. He had been Eric's fraternity brother, and just as I had sensed upon seeing his name and photo, he had not been particularly

CHAPTER 35: PREMIERING

eager to drive four hours to attend this program, but he wanted to be supportive.

Alan's only experience with alternative modalities was acupuncture for "tennis elbow," and he was quite surprised it had worked. I held light contacts on his temporomandibular joints (TMJ), and he agreed he was prone to clenching his teeth. I stopped talking and watched as Alan fell deeply asleep. As I worked in silence, in my mind's eye, I saw a highlight reel of the events and injuries Alan had experienced.

After ten minutes of quiet, we were both startled by the concierge's soft knock on the door. As Alan was putting his shoes on, I asked if he had ever injured his right shoulder. He smiled and said he had "wiped his shoulder out" playing football in seventh grade and could not play anymore. Alan had unknowingly released a lot of energy from the shoulder during his nap. I suggested he drink plenty of water and rest.

Next was Manny, the participant whose bio and background intrigued me. I smiled when he tried to psychoanalyze me as I started the traditional CranioSacral Therapy protocols. I asked if he could relax his neck, and he said it *was* relaxed. He talked fast and told me he was launching two more businesses. It was his crew that was filming all activities at Premier in a swap of services and as I suspected, Manny confirmed no one had signed a release form.

I held contacts over and under his heart, feeling a lot of tension. I felt like I had my hands around a plate of armor, not a human torso. I softly asked, "What's going on here? Why do I feel tension?" He paused and said there were "too many things to choose from." I knew the aggressive, competitive part of him from his podcast, so I asked, "Who gets to see the soft underbelly?" He paused again, then said, "Yeah…no one. Even when it seems I'm going deep, I don't go very deep. I just don't let people go very deep."

I sensed he could have a huge release if I kept my palms = around his heart, but at that moment, the concierge knocked. Manny sat up and said he might like a full session sometime. As soon as we had exchanged phone numbers, the concierge whisked him to the next station.

My last session was with Joey, a military veteran who knew CranioSacral Therapy helped with PTSD. When he had returned from Iraq, he had tried to kill himself. He had a traumatic brain injury that put pressure on his optical nerve, and he had constant headaches. My attention went to his left leg. He had dislocated it in an accident, had nine surgeries, and become addicted to fentanyl and oxycodone. He had weaned himself off the drugs because he knew they were killing him, and he had found alternative therapies to be far more effective.

I thought back to the Upledger Institute and the room where Chas and Dr. Upledger had helped hundreds of veterans. I silently prayed to reconnect with the healing energy that had been created in that room in West Palm Beach. Joey's system dropped into a spontaneous *still point*, a glorious place of natural healing. When we finished, Joey was euphoric. He asked if he could give me a hug, and he said he wished CST was available to all veterans.

A week after the event, I participated in a conference call where the practitioners shared their insights. I was fascinated to hear what each had discovered using medical equipment and their own diagnostic skills. I saw the benefit in collaborating and synthesizing diverse perspectives, but as a business, I thought the odds of Premier's success were low.

As with the Center for Holistic Health, I noted areas that could have been improved and saw opportunities, but Premier was not my enterprise, and I was learning to engage where my input was valued and rewarded. I had really enjoyed delivering my mindfulness presentation, working with the clients and practitioners, and reconnecting with Eric. I also knew it was time to find a place for my next premiere.

CHAPTER 36
Turning Toward the Light

Back in my new office in Atlanta, people I had never expected scheduled sessions. I got a text from William saying he had taken a week off from his gig in Wisconsin. Our whiteboard sessions had ended abruptly four months earlier when he had started the weekly commute. I had not seen him since the pilot session when he had experienced hands-on treatment in preparation for helping me write marketing materials. I was surprised when he suggested visiting my new office and having another session.

Suite 303 was a long way from Industrious in pretty much every sense. We chatted a bit before he relaxed on the table. His physical body felt incredibly tight, and he said he had just done heavy squats. When I again observed that his outlet was hardcore physical activity, he said, "If I didn't do that, I might be lost."

I sat at his head with my fingertips under his occiput, gently adding a bit of traction, and my awareness traveled all the way down his spine to his toes. He said he had no sensation in his right big toe and arthritis in the left one. His head slowly began to roll in the direction of the windows. He thought I was turning it intentionally, but I was following his body as he began a SomatoEmotional Release. When he figured out it was happening spontaneously, he joked he must be "turning toward the light." I agreed and smiled silently at the metaphor.

I held one palm under his sacrum and another under his neck. I felt his central nervous system relax while I listened to him talk about his Wisconsin gig. He noticed his own impatience and need for control. He knew he was cycling through some of the same behaviors from his previous corporate job. I thought back to the beautiful ideas for *human-centric business* he had outlined on his whiteboard and asked if the Universe might be providing him with a place to test some of his ideas. The whiteboard had captured theory, but this Wisconsin gig provided a living laboratory. I saw the synchronicity of the executive role offering the opportunity to demonstrate his human-centric brilliance while serving as a CTO.

When I suggested this idea, his whole body responded. He felt it too and asked what had just happened. His entire physiology relaxed as we discussed Wisconsin as a chance to develop and demonstrate his new inner leadership while leading a team rather than repeating the same old patterns. I invited him to surrender to gravity while lying on the table and feel the possibilities deep within himself.

As he was leaving, William commented on how different this office was from Industrious. I agreed and laughed. Now, instead of Industrious colleagues sitting in my guest chair telling stories and leaving when they felt better, I had formalized the exchange and was being paid for my intuitive insights and metaphysical awareness.

I hugged William goodbye and watched him walk down the hall toward the stairwell to the parking lot.

The next morning, William sent a text:

So good to see you yesterday! I feel better today than I have in weeks! Not sure if it was just restorative to have seen you or if the treatment and talk hit the spot. Whatever the case...
THANK YOU!

I texted back that I was happy he felt better and I looked forward to seeing him again sometime. Privately, I hoped I had planted some seeds about inner leadership, metaphysics, and how our ever-

CHAPTER 36: TURNING TOWARD THE LIGHT

evolving truth, beliefs, stories, thoughts, and emotions influence our physical bodies.

A few weeks later, I got an email from Ralph, a colleague I had not heard from in several years. I originally met Ralph at a conference, saw he had a head cold, and intuited some causes. Months later, he hired me to evaluate a business opportunity and his relationship with the company owner. Ralph wrote he was coming to Atlanta for a conference, and invited me to a networking event. When I told him I was working in wellness full time now, he requested a session. He also wrote that in the six years since we had last talked, he had started a software company, lost control of it, and watched as "all the stock got washed." He was still bitter over the experience and was writing a book titled, *Smoke, Mirrors, and Silicon Valley Puppeteers*. I liked the catchy title and sensed the residual pain.

Ralph came to Suite 303, reclined on the massage table, and started to talk about the previous six years. In addition to working too much, he had health issues and difficulty sleeping. He seemed high strung and admitted he consumed a lot of coffee just to keep going. I sat on my stool and held my fingertips along his spine as I listened. Since losing his software company, his finances had suffered, and he was paying down debt.

Ralph shared personal pain and vulnerability beyond anything he had spoken about previously. As I gently pressed my thumbs into the arches of his feet, he said he felt a wave of energy running up his legs. His rate of speech slowed, and he had a hard time finding words. By the time we finished the session, he had released a lot and admitted he was having a hard time forming a coherent train of thought.

Ralph was catching a flight to the West Coast. I encouraged him to drink water and rest. He asked about continuing to work together, and a few days later, we began regular sessions by phone. He found value in the combination of my business expertise and intuition.

We worked together for a year after his first visit. In that time, I discovered Ralph had been deceived and betrayed in most of his significant relationships. He had been in the process of a divorce when I had first met him. After he married again, his second wife had an affair with one of her colleagues. He was betrayed when someone he had hired took his software. The list was long. If his outer world was a reflection of his inner world, Ralph was healing from self-deception and self-betrayal and had attracted some painful lessons.

In our sessions, I saw Ralph's tendency to weave illusions into a story until the truth finally caught up and dissolved the illusion, and he had to come to terms with reality. Just as he was becoming aware of these dynamics within himself, he decided to move to another country. On the surface, it was a business decision, but I sensed there was more to it. Ralph said he needed some time to get situated in his new home and wanted to take a break from our sessions. I understood and wished him well.

Around this time, I emailed Dee, a friend and colleague, to wish her a happy birthday. Dee worked in international supply chain for an apparel retailer. We'd been friends for more than a decade and played a number of roles in one another's lives. We were originally introduced by a colleague when Dee moved to Atlanta to take a new job.

Over coffee and brunch at the Flying Biscuit, we had found we had many shared interests beyond work. Dee was openly curious about subtle energies and deeper meanings. She celebrated synchronicities and believed the Universe often orchestrated serendipitous meetings for our benefit. Dee trusted my work in supply chain and hired my company for multiple projects.

Dee also knew my personal commitment to wellness and my interest in holistic health and alternative modalities. She heard I had trained in CranioSacral Therapy and had scheduled a session with me when I was first starting to practice. Dee went on to have intermittent sessions over many years. From the conference room and warehouse to the treatment table, our work offered a unique opportunity to observe Dee in her professional capacity as a vice president of a Fortune 500 company and then to work with her at a very personal level on everything from health and wellness to personal empowerment.

During corporate meetings, I observed her body language, vocal tone, energy field, mannerisms, and interactions with colleagues. Seeing her in action proved valuable in our private sessions. Dee was excellent at building teams and had won her staff's loyalty. She was friendly, personable, and willing to get into the trenches. From a corporate career advancement perspective, Dee's challenge was to be seen as an executive by those at the top. She had the capabilities and depth of experience. The next frontier was changing the perceptions of those in positions to which she aspired.

When I watched Dee interact with top executives, I saw her tendency to occasionally revert to subtle, subconscious, nervous habits. Her voice would go up an octave, making her seem flighty. Her energetic center of gravity would rise, making her seem less grounded. These subtle tendencies did not engender confidence. All she really needed to do was become aware of her patterns, watch for them, and self-correct. We practiced keeping her center of gravity low in her hips while remaining in her authentic inner authority and sovereignty. These small modifications made a huge difference. Dee got a significant promotion and took her place among the top twenty highest-ranked women in multi-billion-dollar corporations.

Dee came to Suite 303, and after one session, she enrolled in my Executive Wellness Program and committed to weekly sessions. I knew consistency and continuity were important, and I began to understand how I could deliver that value to my own clients.

CHAPTER 37
AWE & Co, LLC

After several months of sessions in Suite 303, I wasn't sure I really wanted a full-time private practice, but I had come this far, so I decided to create a website. I had no design skills and thought myself a pretty average marketer, so I started by emailing people I knew in design and marketing. I thought back to when I had branded my consulting company back in the 1990s by hiring a woman to do focus groups with our clients. I ultimately chose a name I discovered, "Solertis," a derivative of the Latin word for "clever." A small herd of creative folks had designed our logo and marketing materials. I thought back to one of the copywriters I really liked, Geri, and tracked her down.

I quickly discovered Geri's interest in the mystical world and her capabilities in the mainstream one. She proposed using astrology, numerology, and other insight tools to align my narrative, expertise, and intentions to create a "strategic brand manifesto." This sounded perfect.

I found Geri had two modes. One day, she was on point and tracking. The next, she could not spell my name correctly. Geri came up with some good ideas, but it seemed like she was better as a catalyst for my own thoughts than translating concepts into words. While her input was valuable, I was not yet on the right path.

When I realized a "strategic brand manifesto" was more than I needed, I looked for resources to simply build a website. Friends graciously offered suggestions. I found a wide range of possibilities from college kids to a highly professional firm with a unique eight-week process for developing a brand, positioning it, and then building a website.

I had coffee with several marketing experts. One wrote a proposal and suggested having a session at my office so she could experience what I offered. After I told her I sensed her grandmother's passing and mentioned her Zoloft prescription, she disappeared. Later, she sent an email apologizing for "ghosting" me, reneged on the session, and sent me an invoice for our coffee meeting.

Next, I went to a website where I could post a description of my business and have graphic designers from across the world submit ideas. I had already incorporated a business in the State of Georgia and named my new company AWE & Co, LLC based on my initials and my love of the awe in every synchronicity. At the website, I filled out a form, wrote a design brief, and submitted my application. I chuckled when the company suspended my application because it had a problem verifying my identity. I knew this hiccup was a reflection of my own inner transformation and uncertainty about who I was becoming.

Once my application was approved, I was flooded with ideas and hundreds of logo designs created for AWE & Co, LLC. The designers' riffs on AWE were so creative. Their work showed me I needed to clarify my purpose and what I stood for more than I needed a logo. I was aware of my desire and capacity to bridge the mainstream and the metaphysical. The challenge was to capture that on a website. Meetings with experts confirmed I was a good enough writer, but this was more than a simple branding exercise. It was about publicly claiming a new identity.

I floundered, waffled, and sought reassurance from Isabelle in one of our sessions. She applauded my persistence and then helped me to energetically deepen into a sense of safety in my new work. I made a lot of false starts, and weeks flew by, along with thousands of dollars. I was grateful the Universe repeatedly interceded and prevented me from making a five-figure investment in something that would not produce a website I felt good about.

I downloaded free online resources. One company, GoLive, offered a "branding formula" and hosted a webinar with how-tos for building a website. They pitched their services and a range of options from a simple template to a full-blown "design sprint" to get a site launched in one week. This seemed amazing given I had already tried for four months and had nothing to show for it.

I emailed a salesperson at the company, Deb, and she expedited our preliminary call because she was going on vacation. We talked two days before Thanksgiving. Deb was very excited—her vacation was for her destination wedding. When I asked about this magical destination, she said it was a small island off the coast of southwest Florida no one had heard of, but the resort was beautiful and could accommodate 150 friends and family.

When I asked the island's name, she replied, "Captiva." I laughed out loud. I had just been there three weeks earlier. My family had been vacationing on Sanibel and Captiva for several decades. I knew the exact spot where she was getting married. This seemed like a wink from the Universe.

GoLive normally had a seven-week wait for one of its coveted design sprints, but Deb said they had a cancellation for the week before Christmas. I had been stumbling around for months, so I decided to take a leap of faith and grab the spot. In their promotional materials, GoLive looked like a group of cute, young gals with perfect curls under stylish fedoras posting on Instagram every time they got a cappuccino. But they produced results. Deb thoroughly explained what they had done for each client whose work I sampled. This felt different than anything I had tried so far. I paid the deposit and signed their contract.

GoLive had a witty online questionnaire that asked about aesthetic preferences, brand personality, site navigation, and other basics. I purchased a domain and set up a hosting account at Squarespace. GoLive had clearly honed its methods and gave me step-by-step instructions. Its recipe required me to assemble all the ingredients before the design sprint.

The most challenging part was explaining what I did and defining my skills. Every session was slightly different. I was a CranioSacral Therapist, an executive coach, and a psychic. One client had joked, "With Ann, you get three gurus in one." I offered a unique range, but it was difficult to describe what I did.

I decided to add GoLive's copywriting package to my contract. The copywriter assigned to me had phenomenal credentials. Her bio and resume were outstanding, but my intuitive read of her was much different. I did not get a good vibe, but no other copywriter was available. We had our first call the week before the design sprint. The writing she sent back the next morning was atrocious. I was disheartened and reluctantly decided I was better off writing it myself. Design week was starting, so I was forced to do the best I could with only a few hours to write the copy and comb through thousands of stock photos to find images.

Morgan, the designer, was the silver lining. She made the website a true collaboration. She sent me screenshots of what she was doing. I would comment and she would adjust, I saw the divine synchronicity in how the project unfolded. I was deeply involved in the details, and that was helpful in producing a site I felt good about.

Morgan scheduled a Zoom call to do the site walk through and hand off on the Friday before Christmas 2019. I flew to Kansas City on Thursday to visit family. My mom had moved into an independent living community, and I had reserved a private dining room and arranged to use their Wi-Fi so I could be alone and uninterrupted for the hand-off call. I slipped away for two hours so I could work without making a big deal about the website. In the dining room, I set up two laptops. I wanted one for Zoom and a second for notes. I planned to learn as much about Squarespace from Morgan as I possibly could in ninety minutes. When the call ended, I was going to be on my own. Morgan had years of experience with Squarespace and explained some of its quirks.

Morgan was patient and thorough. She covered everything. I thanked her and said I would like to hire her for more design work. As we were about to sign off, she said, "One last thing...I need to show you how to make the site live." She used her mouse to hover over a button marked "Publish." The site was not perfect, but I knew it was time. I felt relief and closure as Morgan clicked on the button. My first website was live.

With Morgan still on Zoom, I sat with my hands over my heart and expressed my deepest gratitude. I had fumbled around for six months, and finally, my site had come together in one week-long sprint.

I said goodbye to Morgan and signed off. I sat in the dining room alone and cried. I was finally claiming my work as a coach, CranioSacral Therapist, and intuitive. With the winter solstice arriving in just hours, I felt the significance of the moment and sat for a bit longer before packing up my laptops. Surprisingly, my family did not ask what I was doing for two hours on the Friday before Christmas. I continued to quietly check my phone and smile at my new website, but I did not tell anyone it was live. I wanted a day to celebrate the milestone privately.

Going live with my website was the perfect culmination to an extraordinary year of expansion. I now occupied my first solo office where my name was on the door. I had created and delivered my first executive wellness programs. I led a mindfulness program and offered a series of one-on-one sessions to the group at Premier. And I ended the year by announcing myself on the worldwide web.

I had wrestled with internal resistance to claiming my mystical side and integrating it with my mainstream capabilities. Now I was passionately committing to being a new kind of innovator, risk taker, and visionary.

CHAPTER 38
The Fixer

Days after launching the website and claiming my new professional identity, I had another referral. The new client was an executive named Rory who had led Fortune 500 companies and was now in the early stages of a startup in Atlanta while also running a company headquartered in France. Even with his crazy schedule, he agreed to three sessions in three weeks.

Rory's first session was on a Sunday evening, and I drove to his beautiful home in Buckhead. The front lawn was well manicured and two luxury cars were in the driveway. He greeted me at the door and introduced me to his wife before ushering me down to the basement, which was clearly his domain. I had seen dozens of home gyms, but Rory's took it to another level. He had every machine imaginable.

Beyond the gym was the entertainment room with a massive, wall-sized video screen and huge leather sofas. Recessed into the far wall was a fish tank spanning at least ten feet. I had never seen such a large home aquarium.

Rory excused himself to use the bathroom while I stood mesmerized in front of the lighted, 1,200-gallon tank watching colorful fish of all sizes, shapes, and varieties swim in and out of undulating marine plants. Rory himself was small in stature but everything he did and owned had a certain grandeur.

Rory had a massage table already set up. When he dimmed the overhead lights, the fish tank glowed prominently. He got on the table and immediately began describing an extensive list of business challenges. He called himself "The Fixer." Cash flow at his current startup was tight and had elevated his stress to a new level. Rory had initially taken money from a group of angel investors, and when those angels wanted out, he bought their stake with capital from a group in Asia.

As I listened, I quickly surmised the Asian investment was contingent on him fixing one of the other companies in their portfolio. That's why he was commuting to France. He called my observation "astute" and hinted their investment in this other company was nearly one billion dollars. They needed someone to fix it, and their investment in his startup gave them leverage over Rory. I could feel the tension in his physiology.

Rory said he was jet lagged at least 50 percent of his life and working fifteen-hour days. He planned to prove himself for three years. Then his investors would buy him out, allowing him to run a $4 billion enterprise. He said that was the level at which "things got interesting." He admitted he had not slept well in years and had to use either melatonin or pharmaceuticals to fall asleep. He rarely got more than four consecutive hours of sleep before his mind was awake and running full tilt again.

When I put my fingertips under his occiput, he asked, "What exactly are you doing?" I gave him a technical description of how I assessed sub-occipital tissue and the rhythmic movement of cerebrospinal fluid. He said it felt relaxing and acknowledged the tension he carried in his neck and shoulders.

I repositioned my fingertips to the sides of his face at his jaw and felt a sudden jolt. Rory said he had broken his jaw as a teenager. In my mind's eye, I saw a flood of imagery I could hardly believe. I saw a fight break out among hundreds of people during a sporting event in a high school gymnasium. Rory said a group of people had nearly

CHAPTER 38: THE FIXER

beaten him to death when he was a teenager. They had fractured his skull and ribs along with his jaw. He didn't really remember what had happened, presumably because he had been unconscious. He said he felt lucky to be alive. Rory's jaw had been wired shut to heal. I rested my fingers on each side of his jaw as he released the trauma held there for thirty years.

Rory had also experienced several concussions while playing high school sports. I watched a highlight reel of injuries in my mind's eye while Rory's central nervous system released excess charges like little invisible sparks.

I moved to Rory's side and held my palms under his neck and sacrum with the silent intention of releasing any trauma held in the nerves in his spinal column.

At that moment, we both heard a muffled boom followed by a zapping noise, and then the electricity flickered. Rory wondered aloud if a storm had suddenly whipped up or perhaps a car had hit a power pole. It never would have occurred to him that he was emitting this kind of energy as he released trauma. The room was quiet for a few moments, and then there was another big, unexplained zapping sound. I could feel static in the air.

The power went out and the room got completely dark except for the fish tank. Rory said he had auxiliary power for the tank because of all the sophisticated systems it required. I silently prayed the fish would not be harmed. The power flickered back on, and we heard whining as the family dog came bounding down the stairs, barked, and then lay down under the table. Rory said this dog never came down to the basement. I welcomed the dog, figuring it wanted to offer support.

Moments later, my cell phone rang. I was certain I had put it on vibrate. I quickly fished it out of my purse. Strangely, the caller ID said it was the managing partner of one of the private equity firms I had worked with years earlier. I turned the phone off, slipped it back into my purse, and smiled at the synchronicity. The temperaments of these two men were remarkably similar. Both were super-achiever, Type A personalities accustomed to powering through just about any adverse conditions with little regard for the toll on their bodies or relationships.

When I sensed we were nearing the end of the session, Rory's system added a metaphoric exclamation point with a spontaneous *still point*. Neither of us spoke, and time stood still. I enjoyed the depth and fullness of a few precious moments of stillness. I finished by standing at Rory's feet with the intention that our session benefit all sentient beings. Rory asked what he should expect after our session. I paused, smiled, and said, "A good night's sleep." I knew he had released enough energy to disrupt the power grid, and I suggested he drink water and relax. We agreed to meet the following Sunday.

At the next session, Rory said he'd had his best night of sleep in years after our session. He had been so excited, but subsequent nights had not been as good. I appreciated his honesty. I knew session consistency would bring results, and results were cumulative. Rory assumed one session had corrected decades of overriding his body's needs.

Rory exercised daily, so I suggested he add a few minutes of self-care to his routine. I offered to send him one of the guided meditations I had recorded for mindfulness classes and a link to Hemi-Sync audios from the Monroe Institute. I doubted he would use either, but I wanted to plant some seeds.

After talking for a few minutes, Rory got on the massage table while I marveled at the beautiful fish gliding around their huge, crystal-clear aquarium. I stood at his feet and slowly moved my hands to his shins and then his quadriceps. His quads were in full spasm. He said he had gone for a run earlier and had probably overdone it. I was amazed he could lie still on the table.

Rory eventually relaxed and dozed for a full ten minutes. The serenity of the aquarium, the gentle hum of the pump, and the effortless motion of the fish was a calming effect in a sea of stress. During our sessions, I observed how Rory attributed most of his physical discomfort to old sports injuries. His truth did not leave any space for metaphysical reasons for his pain, and I accepted that because it had once been my own truth.

In our third session, Rory said he had a head cold for several weeks and had been coughing up "sticky stuff." I had not observed this during our time together, and Rory confessed he had taken a lot of cough suppressant so our sessions would not be interrupted. While I appreciated his polite sensitivity, I also observed the synchronicity. After just two sessions, Rory was coughing up phlegm. I understood the metaphysics and marveled at his physical body's release as he discounted any connection.

After our third session, I drove away from Rory's lovely home admiring him for trying something new and celebrating his many markers of progress, which brought me joy as a practitioner. I knew I could help Rory further, but he had to want help and see value in what I offered. I also knew deeply personal transformation could not be forced or rushed, and I respected Rory right where he was.

I had long gravitated to super-achievers, business leaders, and those society deemed successful. Peeking behind the veil of success into humanness fascinated me. My professional evolution into this more personal work was reshaping my ideas about power and success. As I moved beyond mainstream definitions, I wanted to attract clients who knew all forms of effective leadership started with a commitment to good inner leadership.

My experience with Rory was an inflection point. I did not aspire to be a "Fixer." I knew I had more to offer than pain relief. I wanted to contribute to a new paradigm of leadership.

CHAPTER 39
Business as an Expression of Consciousness

In 2012, I had joined the advisory board at Duke University's Center for Entrepreneurship and Innovation (CEI) in the Fuqua School of Business. At the time, I had been among a small but growing number of alumnae working in supply chain. During the years I served on the board, my professional focus had shifted, the board had expanded, and Duke had hired Jamie, a new executive director who had many accomplishments, including founding a business accelerator with the mission to link financial returns to positive social and environmental outcomes.

Jamie expressed interest in my wellness work with executives, and in preparation for our February 2020 meeting, she asked if I would lead a short mindfulness meditation. I was thrilled and viewed the invitation as both a sign of global interest in incorporating wellness practices in business and another wink from the Universe in support of my professional path.

On the same day as our CEI board meeting, Duke kicked off Women's Weekend, a gathering of alumnae from across the world. I flew to Durham just in time for the steering committee meeting and the afternoon keynote address given by Renee, a Duke graduate and former adjunct professor at Fuqua. Renee was also vice president at a multi-billion-dollar financial services company and an author.

We all received a copy of her recently published book in which she shared her views on what being successful looked like.

Renee was a petite, well-dressed woman who carried herself with authority. I sat in the first row, and as she crossed the stage, all my attention curiously went to her abdomen and the area below her navel. She introduced Peter, a colleague who would serve as moderator. Renee explained she had recently had surgery, so rather than stand at a podium, she and Peter sat onstage in comfortable club chairs.

Renee spoke about living in several foreign countries, lessons learned throughout her life, and reframing her definition of success. After her presentation, I spoke with her and discovered we lived just two blocks apart in Midtown Atlanta. She told me privately she'd had a significant gynecological procedure a few weeks earlier, explaining my intuitive focus on her lower abdomen. We agreed to meet for coffee back in Atlanta.

I rushed back to the hotel to meet the CEI group for dinner. I took a seat at our long table in the dining room and smiled, thinking how much the group had changed in the eight years since I had joined. In addition to our new executive director, we had many more women, more ethnic diversity, and more diversity of professional experience. Marty, Reid, and others who had provided meaningful conversations in my early days were no longer attending regularly.

More significantly, my ambitions and priorities had also shifted. I had initially been attracted to the prestige conferred by membership and the opportunity to interact with successful entrepreneurs. Now I was more intrigued by observing the humanness in my fellow board members and demonstrating some of my less conventional capabilities.

Overnight, Durham was blanketed by beautiful, pristine snow, and the start of the CEI meeting was delayed. Eventually, the roads were cleared, and the hotel shuttle dropped us at Fuqua. Rather than the usual stately, wood-paneled conference room, Jamie chose

CHAPTER 39: BUSINESS AS AN EXPRESSION OF CONSCIOUSNESS

a classroom for the board meeting. The location change, along with fifty pages of pre-meeting reading material, signaled a new level of expectations.

Once we were seated, we went around the room introducing ourselves. I talked about the merger of my professional passions, business, entrepreneurship, wellness, holistic health, and how my clients benefitted from my executive wellness program. Since I was the last to introduce myself, this was a perfect segue to Jamie's invitation to start the meeting with a five-minute *awareness of breath* meditation.

Serendipitously, I had learned mindfulness just a half mile across campus at the Duke Center for Integrative Medicine. Now I had come full circle and was leading a guided meditation in a meeting at the Fuqua School of Business.

I began the meditation by dropping my vocal tone and slowing my speech. I encouraged everyone to close their eyes and felt the group settle in. I spotted one executive holding mudras under the table and I winked at another who peeked every few seconds to see if others had really closed their eyes. After five minutes of guided breathing and silence, I used my chimes to signal the end of the exercise. We had a few minutes of discussion, followed by a bit of polite applause before we continued with the agenda.

The CEI meeting adjourned after lunch. We said our goodbyes, expecting to see one another again a few months later. The snow had melted, and I quickly walked across campus and back to the Women's Weekend program. I wanted to see a presentation titled "The Joy of Missing Out: Creating Space for Your True Self." The presenter was an alumna who sought success climbing the traditional corporate ladder before circumstances caused her to question her priorities. She had used a life coach, and then she became one. I resonated with her path of self-discovery, leading to a huge personal and professional shift that better expressed her authentic self, leading to deeper satisfaction.

On Saturday, I chose to attend an event called "Reaching New Heights." The organizers were a group called Business Oriented Women (BOW), which was formed long after I graduated. I arrived late and found the room packed with several hundred attendees seated at round tables. BOW had recruited impressive speakers, and it was standing room only.

The first speaker was already on stage. I nodded hello to a young woman who turned out to be the student president of BOW. She insisted on walking me to the front of the room where the only remaining seats were at the speakers' table. I sat among female executives from Delta Airlines, Fidelity Investments, Burt's Bees, and a New York City branding agency. Each woman presented her own story of self-empowerment and authenticity. I smiled, thinking I would love to give a presentation as inspiring as those I heard, and I wondered if I might sit at the speakers' table again one day.

Duke had afforded me amazing opportunities over many years. As we were adjourning at the end of one of my first CEI meetings, a Duke staff member encouraged us to stay and attend a special event, but he would not tell us what it was. A few of us elected to stay, and we were ushered into a small auditorium where we watched Tim Cook, CEO of Apple and a Fuqua graduate, being interviewed by the dean of the business school.

Cook's remarks were heartfelt and uplifting. He talked about keeping his eye on his own "North Star" no matter what noise was going on around him. He put his hand over his solar plexus and said after graduation he had no plan and no job, but he trusted something inside himself and a voice that told him to "Go West." He spoke about his career at Apple and used the term "joy" five times in thirty minutes. With childlike exuberance, he reminisced about the delight he had felt when Apple had first created a way to take your entire music collection with you on one handheld device, the iPod.

Cook's definition of ethics was leaving things better than you found them, and he said this devotion encompassed your whole persona, not just your work. I was deeply inspired by his humility, humanity, and humor.

As the audience filed out, I decided to walk down to the stage. Cook was posing for photos with a few students, and when it was my turn, I told him I had bought my first MacBook and Apple stock on the same day. Without missing a beat, he smiled and asked which had performed better. I laughed and said I was equally thrilled with both. I drove to the airport feeling grateful for the serendipitous opportunity to hear Cook's stories and experience his humanness and authenticity in person.

On the flight home, I thought about how coaching, wellness, and intuitive work were crystalizing into my full-time profession. I wanted to work with clients who embodied joy and vitality and knew money was only one form of compensation. I wanted to attract those eager to consciously create their own beautiful evolutionary path and authentic self-expression while being good stewards of personal and planetary resources. I loved business and ambition, but not at the expense of consciousness—more as an expression of it.

CHAPTER 40
This or Better

Shortly after my trip to Duke, the world came to a screeching halt with the spread of a virus called COVID-19. By late March 2020, only David was still coming to Suite 303 for sessions. David had averaged three sessions each month for many months. He came for his first session while nursing a shoulder injury. He was a former college and professional football player, had lived in several countries, and owned his own physical therapy business serving executive clients.

David exuded love and was certain his guardian angels had saved his life during a bad car accident on a rainy highway. In addition to being an entrepreneur, he worked a 3 a.m. shift at a company offering great benefits, which allowed him to provide health insurance for his four teenage children. A few weeks before David's first session, he had lifted a large piece of equipment at work and badly injured his right shoulder. The accident qualified him for worker's compensation and care from company-sanctioned medical practitioners. David was required to have periodic evaluations to see if he could return to work.

After several months, David's employer gave him an ultimatum—return to work or have surgery on his shoulder. Just talking about these possibilities caused discomfort in his right shoulder. I suggested David reassure his shoulder there would be no surgery, and I felt his entire body relax when we gave his shoulder permission to function at 100 percent while he sorted out his options. Within weeks, the company offered David a cash settlement. His right shoulder felt great, and he went back to working out.

My lease was expiring and I knew I did not want to renew it. Serendipitously, David was my last client in Suite 303, and after our session, he offered to help carry my beautiful wood cabinet down to the street so we could load it into the back of my SUV. With his shoulder back to full strength, I saw the divinity in him being the one to help me carry the heavy piece of furniture.

On the first weekend in April, I went to the office one last time. I looked around Suite 303 and remembered all the love I had poured into the space and celebrated all that had happened in the past eleven months. I laughed about the quirkiness of the place and took a moment to silently offer gratitude for all those who had shown up to support me. I placed "goodbye and thank you" notes in the mail slots of my neighbors and hid the key where it had been left for me almost a year earlier. I walked down the three flights of stairs for the last time.

Within days of closing Suite 303, Richard, a supply chain colleague, reached out to me. I had known him for fifteen years. His message read, "I know we've had this conversation before. I am thinking about a career change." He asked if he could get my thoughts. Richard was a leader at a publicly traded corporation and had referred consulting opportunities to me over the years.

When we spoke, I mentioned I was working with executives in a coaching capacity, and the call turned into his first session. He updated me on the past few years of his life. He had loved the company he worked for until it had been acquired by a multi-billion-dollar behemoth, XPD. As part of this huge enterprise, his division was about to deliver a project they had worked on for two grueling years.

Richard had traveled for weeks at a time and lamented missing his wife's birthday and a friend's funeral. He described a "cutthroat

CHAPTER 40: THIS OR BETTER

environment" where people were expected to "kiss asses" and "play the game." Despite his making great money, I sensed he was leaning into the new paradigm of leadership where money was only one form of compensation. Our first Zoom session led him to my executive program.

Richard had a non-compete agreement with XPD and was considering starting his own consulting firm much like my situation when I started Solertis twenty years earlier. I loved this dynamic because I could use my full range of skills. I had negotiated with huge corporations and understood business, and I could track energy and use my intuition. Richard was ready to leave the toxicity of XPD and start pursuing consulting gigs, but I suggested he wait a week before submitting his resignation.

I had no reason for my suggestion, only an intuitive impulse. Monday morning, I got an email from Richard that said, "Holy Crap! Read below." Prior to the pandemic, the top fifty employees at XPD had been promised substantial bonuses based on a strategic review process. With everyone working from home, the company decided to scrap the review itself and pay the bonus. Instead of waiting another three months, Richard would receive his bonus in two weeks. If he had resigned the previous Friday, he would not have been eligible. The bonus was six-figures.

The project Richard and his team had led for two long years launched successfully, and he was given many accolades on a company-wide Zoom. This praise along with the early bonus felt like closure. When his first consulting gig was briefly delayed, I encouraged Richard to be patient and keep stating his preferred scenario. I encouraged him to envision it in detail, speak out loud to affirm it, feel the resonance in his body, and then say the words, "*This or better.*" His alignment with his own truth and values demonstrated by his willingness to walk away from a toxic environment sent a message to the Universe and opened an entirely new world of possibilities.

He emailed me with an update, writing, "On a side note, if things couldn't get more strange...the X on my keyboard stopped working today. I took it as some sign I am done at XPD!" I laughed.

I sensed the right time was approaching for Richard to resign. Rather than doing it on a Friday afternoon, I suggested he wait until early the following week. Again, I did not have any logical explanation, just intuition. Despite the pandemic, Richard planned to fly to the company headquarters and resign in person rather than by phone. He felt that was the honorable way to leave. Before he went to the airport, his boss, the division president, abruptly scheduled a team Zoom. Shockingly, his boss announced he was leaving XPD to take a position elsewhere as CEO of a billion-dollar company in the portfolio of a private equity firm. The company grapevine buzzed about a possible violation of his non-compete agreement.

The following day, Richard resigned by phone with little fanfare because his boss's departure was getting all the attention. The Universe had definitely optimized Richard's timing. On Richard's last day at XPD, his farewell video call was emotional, with colleagues telling stories and saying how much they would miss him. I felt how deeply this touched him.

Richard would be taking a well-deserved week of vacation with his family before starting his first consulting gig. As we hung up, he said, "I couldn't have done this without you."

As the pandemic continued and Zoom became more widely accepted, I found I liked working remotely and wanted to promote myself to a bigger audience. I wrote an email titled "Uplevel Your Wellness" and sent it to businesspeople I had met through various organizations. I offered a complimentary, twenty-minute session by Zoom. I wrote that during the pandemic "I accessed new tools and technologies that enabled me to uplevel my ability to work remotely." This was a subtle nod to my intuitive capabilities and energy work.

CHAPTER 40: THIS OR BETTER

The first person to schedule a session was Sheryl, a successful entrepreneur I saw every six months or so in business meetings. Sheryl said the pandemic had been hard on her and acknowledged more emotional ups and downs than usual. She was very busy but admitted not one thing on her schedule the previous day really held her interest or had any meaning. I appreciated her honesty. She also said she had received hands-on energy work and described it as critical to her recovery from a bad accident.

She went on to say she felt a personal connection every time we were together at board meetings and would look at my website in more detail. She confessed when she had signed up for this complimentary call, she had just thought the offer sounded interesting. Later, she realized she knew me. Something in my email had attracted her, and that felt like a nudge for me to cast a wider net to reach more clients.

My "Uplevel Your Wellness" email also reached Renee, the keynote speaker at Duke Women's Weekend just before the pandemic. In our call, I learned Renee's life had been changed dramatically by traumatic events. Where my life lessons came from gentle bends in the arc of my trajectory, hers came from seemingly horrifying incidents. Renee wanted to set a new baseline for internal stability. She signed up for a package of sessions, and we began practicing the energetics of staying grounded and creating an internal safe space regardless of what was happening externally.

After the response to my "Uplevel Your Wellness" email and experiences with clients, I knew I wanted to work with those who were metaphysically curious, eager to prioritize personal growth, and ready to embrace a new paradigm of leadership. Each conversation gave me deeper clarity about which clients I could best serve. I just had to figure out how to reach them.

CHAPTER 41
The Hero's Journey

The pandemic lockdown dragged on for months, and the loss of most of my external activities created a lot of space in my inner world. On the morning of my birthday, July 2, I sat on my balcony at my condo enjoying coffee and a delightful breeze. I jotted a list of all the past birthday celebrations I could recall and savored the memories. After adventures on sailboats and visiting friends in different cities, I knew this birthday would likely be the most uneventful, yet I also felt great contentment.

I opened birthday cards from my friends and family and read dozens of celebratory text messages. I watched as a hummingbird came to check out my Lantana plants' orange and pink blooms. The hummingbird had a beautiful, iridescent, blue-green body and a long beak perfectly designed to gather nectar. I smiled at nature's wisdom as it darted around and then disappeared.

While gazing at the clouds, I got the idea to read my old intuition journals. Years earlier, I had intentionally cultivated my intuition using exercises I read and some I had made up. I had chronicled my intuitive hits in entries neatly handwritten in a dozen Crayola sketchbooks intended for children's artwork. I don't remember why I started using unlined, square, spiral booklets with cartoon animals on the cover, but I loved them. I laughed as I read remarkable stories I had completely forgotten.

Sitting with the pile of spiral notebooks in my lap, something caught my eye. When I looked up, the hummingbird was hovering directly in front of me, just twelve inches from my face. I had a moment of sheer terror looking at its long beak aimed straight at my forehead. It hovered for two seconds before cocking its head and darting off. The whole incident happened so fast I was dumbfounded. In years of watching hummingbirds, I had never seen one come so close and definitely not with its intimidating pointy beak aimed at my face.

I felt the preciousness of my interaction with this delicate creature. I knew the totem of the hummingbird was joy, and I sat in wonderment for a moment just feeling the connection.

I looked down at the pile of journals, and suddenly knew what I was going to do next. I was going to teach a class on intuition. I was energized, and within a day, I had written the course outline for "Intuition Masterclass." Whatever the hummingbird had transmitted landed deep within me.

As I prepared the course, I got an email with the subject line "Unusual Proposal" sent by a woman I knew from spiritual circles named Jo Ann. She was a published author working on another book. This one was an anthology, and her unusual proposal was for me to write one of the ten chapters. I was delighted by the possibility and asked if she could send me an outline. She had no idea I was working on an intuition course. I looked at the topics and thought intuition would fit in nicely. Jo Ann agreed.

By the following week, I had advertised "Intuition Masterclass" to clients, posted notice on social media, and signed up the first group. I was swept up in a flow where things were easy and fun. I taught the course via Zoom and started each weekly session with a short *awareness of breath* practice to get the group centered and gathered in a coherent field. I included photos and stories of my experiences with intuition and presented my list of *conducive conditions* for receiving intuitive insights.

While fun and sometimes mystical, I also found intuitive information to be practical and valuable. I spoke on using intuition for buying and selling stocks and to select airline flights. I created exercises I called "Target Practice." One target was a photograph of a horse that had just won a race in Saratoga Springs. Another target was a series of alphanumeric characters. I asked participants simply to note their impressions before I disclosed any information. I had found this type of practice helpful when I was cultivating my own intuition, and it was amazing what the participants intuited.

I spoke about the neurophysiology of intuition and used Albert Einstein's brain as an example of the role of the glial cells (a type of cell that provides support to neurons and myelin, increasing the speed of conduction of electrical impulses). I also encouraged participants to be okay saying "I'm not getting anything" if no information showed up. Embracing uncertainty was often so liberating it actually enabled answers to come through.

I ended class with my cautionary tale from the US Open, when I incorrectly interpreted an image and offered my interpretation to my friend before she played one of her last professional tennis matches. My story highlighted the importance of neutrality and objectivity, the need to avoid leaping to conclusions without considering timelines or our inherent bias toward seeing what we want to believe. This regrettable incident had taught me to share intuitive insights wisely, delicately, and with reverence.

As I taught the class, I came to see intuition as part of our journey along an evolutionary spiral into higher states of consciousness. I saw a continuum with empathy, serendipity, synchronicity, extrasensory perception, and guidance from one's higher self as tools to support our evolution.

I offered the course to multiple groups of clients, and the Universe orchestrated the mix of each group with skeptics and believers, men and women, business executives, lawyers, spiritual seekers, authors, an actor, and a documentary film producer. We learned from one another by sharing our unique observations. From "Spidey Sense" to clairvoyance to the quantum field, everyone used different terms for tapping into a larger, cosmic database of information.

I recalled presentations I had made to business school students promoting my ideas about balancing intellect with intuition and allowing space for unexpected synchronicities. Those presentations had deepened my commitment to advocate for intentionally developing a softer set of skills alongside more traditional ones.

With the deadline approaching for my chapter for Jo Ann's anthology, we picked one of the examples from the intuition masterclass for the book. I put my story into a thousand-word essay and found writing very enjoyable. In addition to the Crayola notebooks I used as intuition journals, I had also been keeping a file on my computer with dozens of instances of intuitive knowing compiled over several decades. I had been telling these stories to friends and clients, but this was the first time I turned them into prose.

My solitary birthday kicked off a series of events unobserved by most but potent in evolutionary value. I had been working with Isabelle consistently for twelve years and had traveled with her groups to Egypt, Jordan, Morocco, and the Canary Islands. She could see the bigger picture of my life and had been gently nudging me into my own truth and authenticity. Every day I was getting more information intuitively and spontaneously.

Perhaps as a result of weeks at home with no travel and very little external activity, I picked up subtle energetic imprints before my intellect could override them. To satisfy my curious mind, I spent hours on unnecessary validation and fact checking rather than trusting myself. I recounted several specific instances to Isabelle in a session. She encouraged me to shift away from my overactive detective skills and toward using *internal technology* and the wiser parts of myself to find information and make decisions. She also suggested trusting grace; if I needed to know something, I would get the information or find it was not important and let it go.

CHAPTER 41: THE HERO'S JOURNEY

I hated this idea! I was trained to check facts, follow up, and corroborate details. I was a pretty good internet sleuth. For the first time in 12 years of working with Isabelle, I was mad and felt completely deflated. Apparently, the idea of trusting my natural abilities and *internal technology* triggered my "pain body," which wanted me to remain reliant on external technology. This trigger set off an epic emotional response inside me. Part of me was aware a big shift was happening in that moment, but I was also angry.

Isabelle handled this masterfully. I could feel her working in my energy field and helping me stabilize. I had just bumped into some old, deeply ingrained patterns, and my internal structure was recalibrating. I felt lost, and my ego was going berserk. Deep inside, I knew I was going through a profoundly transformative moment. Isabelle called me "brave," but I was mad. The session ended, and for two weeks, all I wanted to do was pout and wallow in despair, anger, and bitterness. I did very little physical exercise and only left home for groceries. I hid from the outside world and was utterly miserable.

Two weeks later, we had another session. I had processed the emotion and was done wallowing in negativity. I was eager to discuss what had happened and learn from it. Isabelle called this *The Hero's Journey* and again commended me for my bravery. I acknowledged feeling her energetic support in the days after our session and thanked her. She had pointed me toward a distortion pattern lurking in my aura and some part of me chose to plunge right into it. The decision to plunge was orchestrated by higher powers, but it felt awful, like a total assault on my identity and everything I had relied on for much of my life.

I thought back to my intense experience in Egypt where I stood before Sekhmet, surrendered my need for control, and fell to the ground. As difficult as it was, I was ready to evolve. My "need to know" was a type of trauma woven into my superpower. Now I was learning to embrace *not knowing* while trusting I would always have the information I needed. I was taking a new stance and learning to rely on a new kind of technology. Despite being uncomfortable, it felt oddly inevitable and ultimately beneficial.

During this period of unsettledness, I received a copy of Jo Ann's book. Seeing my chapter in print energized me and served as a welcome contrast to feeling so deflated. I had already been writing short vignettes based on intuitive experiences but I sensed there was a better way to weave these into something deeper and more powerful.

I decided to write about my own personal evolution and events that had led me to some of my deepest truths; the things I had come to realize and hold dear, even if they were unconventional and often inexplicable. This idea of publishing my private thoughts felt terrifying. My physical body seemed to shudder at the thought, but as I sat with my fear, some part of me felt the desire to reveal more of myself in an honest, authentic way.

I was a mainstream business woman and I dreaded being judged just because I am also spiritual, intuitive and perhaps psychic. I was still finding the courage to embrace hidden parts of myself. Did I really want to write about them in a book?

When I began to see the publishing of my stories as a way to inspire others to find their path, I felt emboldened to take the risk. I knew the transformative potential available to those who could embrace and utilize their most quirky and nonsensical capabilities. I had observed the power and grace afforded to those who dared to create enough wiggle room to question logic, expectations and conventional reality in order to step into the unknown.

From this perspective of encouraging others along their journey from mainstream to mystical, I saw myself as a new kind of visionary, risk taker, and leader. As I held onto this vision and stepped more deeply into it, I gained just enough fortitude to nudge me beyond my fears.

CHAPTER 42
Quantum Alignment

As I integrated more aspects of the epic session with Isabelle and felt more resolve to write a book, more synchronicities and guidance showed up. I was on a Zoom call with a group of Duke alumni when Len, an old friend, sent me a private message asking if we could catch up sometime. I had served on boards with Len for almost ten years and always found our conversations meaningful. We set a time to talk the following Saturday afternoon.

Len was curious about my working in coaching and wellness full time and asked how I engage with clients. I talked about my remote work, teaching the Intuition Masterclass, and writing a chapter for an anthology.

About ten minutes into the conversation, Len said he wanted to ask me a highly personal question. He paused and said, "To the extent you are willing to share, what one thing has been most revealing about yourself for yourself in the things you have seen with other people?" I took a breath and asked if he could repeat the question, wondering if he was reading a new self-help book.

He asked his question again, curious how my work was revealing things to me about myself.

I laughed nervously as I quickly formulated my answer. I said if I had to summarize, it was that I had found another part of myself I was not using in supply chain consulting. I had access to intuitive knowingness and skills not widely valued in business or taught in academic institutions. I explained I was learning how to receive and use information to benefit my clients while treating it with extreme reverence, since it was often very sensitive. I mentioned a specific instance when I sensed something about him, and then hours later, it was confirmed privately in a hotel elevator. He chuckled, remembering the incident from five years earlier.

We went on to talk about Len's new law practice advising small and mid-sized companies on business and legal strategy. He was invigorated by using his skills in new ways. I could relate.

After we hung up, I sat in silence for a few moments. I knew I had just given Len a safe answer to his question. And I knew stepping outside this safe zone was both a necessity and a reason for writing my book.

The 2020 winter solstice was just two weeks away, and I had read about the astrological phenomenon with the grand alignment of the two largest planets in our solar system. Even mainstream publications like *Forbes* reported this once-in-a-lifetime event. The last time Jupiter and Saturn had orbited this closely to Earth was in late May, 2000. That time had been the start of something spectacular and expansive in my supply chain consulting work, catapulting me into the most lucrative years of the business.

As I thought back to my excitement, I was invigorated by the potential of replicating that prosperity and growth in every dimension of my life. I sensed this planetary alignment carried an opportunity to anchor a bigger vision into reality for myself and for humanity. I wrote a blog about my personal experience after the last Saturn-Jupiter alignment and offered an energetic hologram to amplify the energies. Like my "9-9-9 Transformation Hologram," I used a similar process to create a holographic blueprint and maximize the support available by pairing the expansive possibility of Jupiter with the practical reality of Saturn in a quantum alignment.

I encouraged participants to ask themselves the same two questions I was pondering:

1. If I could attract anything into my immediate orbit and align with it, what would it be?
2. What could I actually expand by using more discipline and structure?

A small group signed up for the *Quantum Alignment Hologram*, and on the solstice, I was guided to meditate, sense the energies of Jupiter and Saturn, and feel them merge. I set an intention for each participant to use these energies for their highest good without any expectation of how that might look.

In my mind's eye, I brought up a holographic image of each human. As with the "9-9-9 Transformation Hologram" each participant engaged with the energies differently as I watched. When the processes felt complete, I offered my deepest gratitude for all the support I sensed. Spontaneously, a holographic image of the earth flashed with a huge crystalline matrix surrounding it. I expressed gratitude to whomever or whatever was anchoring that universal energy, as it felt imperative to sustaining abundant life on the planet.

The days between the solstice and the end of the year were solitary and introspective. The pandemic was still causing uncertainty, disrupting plans, and limiting holiday festivities, so I chose to stay home. With more hours of darkness than daylight, I meditated and explored inner planes. I reflected on my involvement with some groups.

With the Center for Entrepreneurship and Innovation, I loved the new executive director, but the shifts in my direction, focus, and interests meant my service on the board was no longer as beneficial as it had been when I joined. In a phone conversation with Jamie on the last day of the year, I spoke my truth and shared my perspective. She understood and supported my new direction. With a few words of connection and levity, I resigned from the board while leaving the door open to contributing in new ways.

After achieving much closure at the end of the year, I awoke on January 1 inwardly committed to writing a book. I had been dancing around the idea and knew it was time. With no travel and plenty of space on my calendar, the conditions were perfect. I had learned so much about myself by journaling and taking notes from my sessions with healers over two decades.

I started reviewing these journal entries and notes and discovered I had already chronicled the most significant events of the last twenty years, not knowing they would become the basis of a book. It was then a matter of choosing stories and putting them into narrative form.

I loved the topic of intuition, so I began writing vignettes from my intuition journals. I had tons of material and chose to write about what I thought would be most valuable in helping readers become more aware of synchronicities and their own capabilities for intuitive awareness.

Serendipitously, the week I started writing, I got a thick, manila envelope in the mail from a high school boyfriend whom I had followed to Duke. Inside was something titled *The Most God-Awful Long Holiday Letter You Will Ever Receive*. Other than his familiar handwriting on the envelope, nothing was personalized, so I surmised this ninety-page, professionally bound collection of stories with color photos was sent to his many friends.

The writing was excellent and included stories about meeting celebrities and traveling to exotic lands presented in an entertaining flow. As I turned to the last page, I saw a photo of him standing alone on the Giza plateau with the pyramids in the background. I smiled, sensing this particular photo was both a wink and a nudge, as I recalled my profound experience inside the King's Chamber.

While our paths through life had started out similarly and we had been leaders in our respective pursuits, I had allowed synchronicity

CHAPTER 42: QUANTUM ALIGNMENT

and higher guidance to influence my choices in surprising ways, bending my life's trajectory from mainstream to mystical. I had visited many of the same cities and countries he wrote about, but my experiences in each included a multidimensional, transformative quality and often unearthed deep self-awareness. My interactions with celebrities and leaders were about finding the humanness behind the public persona and what I learned from them. I wanted my storytelling to have a message and reveal the essence behind image.

The uncanny timing of receiving his booklet solidified my desire to write about my journey. I found myself waking before sunrise eager to write. I felt the framework forming as I looked back through notes, journals, travel itineraries, receipts, and photos. I reminisced while sorting through stacks of business cards I had gathered over two decades. I reread email written fifteen years earlier.

Traveling back through my life enabled me to see how my path had been guided by unconventional twists and turns, requiring me to be receptive and vulnerable. I had a unique story to share, but I had no idea the depths to which writing it would take me.

CHAPTER 43
Intuition and Multiplying Money with Ma'at

I continued to work with clients by phone and was fascinated by several who showed up unexpectedly. In one instance, Mark, someone I had spoken with for ten minutes at a charitable event in early 2019, purchased a package of three sessions on my website. I had originally met Mark at a long-time client's home. My client was CEO of a prominent company in Atlanta, a community leader, and host of an event for big donors to a local non-profit. As I parked my car and walked to the front door, I silently set the intention if I could serve someone at the event, please let the Universe connect us.

After wine and hors d'oeuvres, my client gathered the group and made the first formal remarks of the evening. I serendipitously ended up standing directly opposite him across a huge room filled with guests. He introduced the evening's speaker, and then stepped aside. For the next few minutes, I felt a beautiful flow of subtle energy moving fifty feet across the room between the two of us. Occasionally, my client would make eye contact and nod subtly as we listened to the speaker's remarks. I consciously expanded the field between us to include the speaker and everyone present.

Later that evening, my client introduced me to guests and gave a glowing report of how I had helped him. Several asked what it was I did exactly and I felt my fears creep in as I bumbled to give an acceptable answer that wouldn't have me look crazy. One man seemed to understand and took me aside. Mark lowered his voice, and quietly said, "I am an empath."

I smiled and replied, "Great! What does that mean to you?"

He whispered, "I feel everything."

Then he asked, "Are you familiar with Judith Orloff?"

I smiled again and said, "Yes, I have studied with her."

He said, "I'm one of those."

We exchanged business cards, and I laughed thinking "Judith Orloff" was code for a secret society of highly sensitive intuitives.

Now, more than two years later and during a pandemic, Mark tracked me down and purchased a block of sessions. He was CEO of a non-profit and his board of directors had recommended he hire an executive coach. He had thought of me from our brief meeting two years earlier, found my website, and purchased sessions online.

Weeks later, he scheduled his first Zoom, and we laughed recalling the evening's events two years earlier. He said his board was paying for him to get coaching, and he saw it as an opportunity to work with me. I asked him what he wanted to get out of our sessions. He said he needed time to think about it.

I quickly discovered he was not personally or financially invested in our work. He had been instructed to hire a coach, and he had checked the box. I always observed a subtle dynamic with clients who scheduled sessions to appease a friend or family member. When the initiative did not come from within, I felt a different quality of interaction. Mark's package also included my program, *Intuition 101*, and he was genuinely enthused and engaged in that topic.

By this time, I had one client, Dee, who was two years into weekly sessions. Dee worked in international logistics and had intermittent CranioSacral Therapy sessions interspersed with supply chain consulting projects over many years before making a commitment to my executive wellness program. I watched as her dedication to personal growth was translated into her everyday life. She received promotions at work and was recognized for her excellence in team building. She was selected for a coveted position on her company's sustainability task force, giving her an opportunity to help the environment. Dee was also chosen for a high-visibility assignment requiring brief relocation to the West Coast where she managed a strategically important project for her company.

While Dee excelled and expanded professionally, she also quietly renegotiated some of her friendships to improve the balance of giving and receiving. She learned to say "no, thank you" when an invitation did not serve her or she needed rest.

As an empath, she became more astute about what was hers and what she was picking up from others. She trusted herself rather than listening to those telling her what she should feel or do. She came to regard discomfort in her physical body as an opportunity to dig for metaphysical causes. A mild rash on her arm sent her inward to identify the circumstance or situation creating the underlying irritation while she honored her physical body with homeopathic remedies to relieve the itch.

As she listened to inner wisdom and prioritized self-care, she experienced fewer physical maladies because she was increasingly proactive and expansive in her approach to wellness. Her body became her barometer of inner peace and energetic alignment.

Like all humans, Dee had tough days, but she also had a solid emotional foundation and tools to handle challenges. She took responsibility for her circumstances and the reality she created.

In the midst of the pandemic, she was tested. After finally getting accustomed to working from home and not being in physical proximity to her colleagues, she was notified she was being laid off along with her boss and dozens of others.

Dee was loyal and would have never left to explore new opportunities, so the layoff forced a change and presented an opportunity. A month later, she received a generous severance package and felt new freedom. Dee was highly sought after, contacted by executive search firms and recruited by dozens of companies. Often her criteria for accepting interviews included the company's contribution to the planet, her alignment with their products or services, the quality of leadership at the highest levels, and the opportunity to build a team and contribute. Financial compensation was never at the top of her list.

Between interviews and while considering options, she supported a friend's entrepreneurial startup, evaluated franchise opportunities, worked at her favorite grocery retailer, and traveled to visit old friends. Dee lived with a new sense of spaciousness and curiosity. I was constantly in awe of the paths she chose to explore.

We continued our weekly sessions and stumbled into another silver lining. Dee's severance package included stock in her soon-to-be former company. I asked if this form of compensation was taxable, and that got us talking about finances. I discovered Dee had turned over management of her multi-million-dollar portfolio to a well-known financial services firm. She had never executed a stock trade and did not know how her money was invested.

I was shocked. My parents had taught me their financial philosophies and practices before the training wheels were off my first bicycle. I assumed every kid came to the dinner table knowing the interest rate they were getting on their babysitting money. I bought shares of mutual funds before I could (legally) drink beer.

Dee had interest in learning, so I quickly wrote a proposal and a syllabus for sixty days of financial mentorship in a program I called "Multiplying Money with Ma'at."

Ma'at was a concept I had read about and experienced in Egypt. It refers to the ancient Egyptian principles of truth, balance, order, harmony, law, morality, and justice. Ma'at was also the Goddess personifying these concepts. I used the term to invoke the energy of aligning money and investments with the highest truth possible, bringing benefit and harmony to all.

CHAPTER 43: INTUITION AND MULTIPLYING MONEY WITH MA'AT

The mentorship program was a blend of practical tips, spiritual exercises, intuitive insights, and decades of my personal experience. Our first session was called "Excel-fest." After a gratitude practice and celebration of abundance, I showed Dee the Excel spreadsheets I used to track and manage my own holdings. The second session was titled "Asset Assessment" in which we looked at how Dee's holdings were allocated and uncovered hidden fees buried in 14-page monthly statements. We also cleared some ancestral imprints and scarcity patterns and revved up the spin of her second chakra.

In our third session, Dee learned the value of mindfully aligning her investments with her values by pouring money into companies she loved. She learned how to buy and sell stocks online in her portfolio and began detaching from a patriarchal system which often gave investment advisors a disproportionate amount of influence and power. Her first online stock trade was a six-figure investment in a company whose products she used and admired. She was energized and invigorated as she overcame her fears and reclaimed another aspect of her strength and sovereignty.

We observed the propensity for those enticing credit card offers with 0% APR to suddenly become expensive if not paid off and the freedom that comes with living debt free. We explored beliefs around creating wealth and Dee began to use the metaphor of a sandbox to symbolize her financial portfolio. This playful image sparked a sense of fun and amplified an amazing flow of abundance. The more sand in the sandbox, the bigger the castles she could build.

As Dee continued to reassert her authority over her money, more showed up. I watched her manifest unexpected financial windfalls, expand her sandbox and build beautiful, metaphoric castles through smart investing. We giggled at the huge pile of sand as Dee's investments continued to grow along with her confidence in her ability to make choices and execute stock trades. I had long used the financial markets to fund my investment in self-care and personal growth. Multiple synchronicities guided me to invest in a company whose share price quintupled in two years. I bought several thousand shares, and as the company's stock price increased, I sold shares to fund my trip to France and opportunities for self-exploration as I pivoted professionally to embrace my uniqueness and life purpose. I used multidimensional awareness in the three-dimensional system. When I aligned my purest personal ambitions with respect for money and the principles of Ma'at, I delighted in the results.

Dee was still celebrating her strength, adding to her portfolio, and expanding her profits a year later. Her success reaffirmed the power of integrating ancient Egyptian wisdom into very mainstream systems and decisions. I knew I would offer the program again one day so others could conquer their uncertainties and gain self-confidence through aligned investing and Ma'at.

CHAPTER 44
Seeding a New Paradigm of Leadership

Funding my existence through supply chain consulting, corporate wellness, and the stock market had served me well, but I was also curious about other possibilities. I had added value to consulting projects beyond subject-matter expertise using my intuitive awareness and by modeling effective inner leadership along with a collaborative style. I had been hired for work in corporate wellness partly because I embodied the lifestyle we hoped to get employees to adopt. I held energy fields in places like the Atlanta Federal Reserve building, supply chain conferences, a charitable event, and other meetings.

I kept asking myself how I could bridge the conventional and the unconventional, the gross and the subtle, the quantum and material worlds using the full array of my capabilities while receiving compensation in the form of dollars as well as fulfillment, satisfaction, and a sense of purpose.

A 2004 movie called *What the Bleep Do We Know?* explored the idea that consciousness could affect the material world. One of the people interviewed was Dr. Amit Goswami, a theoretical physicist and university professor. In the years following the movie, I read several of Dr. Goswami's books including, *Quantum Economics: Unlocking the Power of an Economics of Consciousness*. I was so captivated I read the entire book in a weekend.

I went online and found an interview with Goswami from when the book was first published. I was astounded when he told the story of one of his students taking him to the university bookstore to buy *Tao of Physics*, the book he said started his journey from science back into spiritual traditions.

I could not believe the synchronicity. It was the same book my aunt had recommended two decades earlier that had led me to begin contemplating the convergence of mainstream and mystical. In the interview, Goswami said he had been invited to write a chapter for someone else's book, and while not his usual topic, he decided to write about healing and the role of creativity. His chapter served as a seedling for his next book just as my chapter on intuition in Jo Ann's anthology had led me to write my own book.

Quantum Economics espoused a worldview that legitimized not only sensory experience and material needs but also our higher needs. Humans desire to live lives with greater meaning, purpose, and fulfillment, but our culture ignores the role of the non-material and vital energy. I was most interested in Dr. Goswami's ideas about how subtle energies might be turned into money-making endeavors, so I enrolled in his online course "Journey to Quantum Enlightenment."

I entered questions about quantum economics in the class portal and admittedly, they were outside the course content. Several days later, I received a polite message from Dr. Goswami's assistant saying he was busy and giving me a list of stops on his latest book tour. I loved Dr. Goswami's engaging videos and found value in his course. Outside the book, I found few details about this subtle energy economy and knew I wanted more.

I continued to attract clients who celebrated the grace and synchronicities in their everyday existence. From Richard, with his serendipitously timed exit from one company into a more fulfilling experience as an entrepreneur, to Dee, who recast her layoff into a few months of self-exploration, these clients were eager to redefine success rather than perpetuate outdated definitions and systems.

Dee was well into her third year of regular sessions when she received an intriguing job offer. A company in Texas had recruited her previously, but the position was not quite aligned with her skillset, so someone else got the job. Dee had acknowledged her own hesitations over the title, salary, and relocation requirement. A year later, things had changed and the company was back with a new offer. While still not the compensation package she would have liked and with relocation still required, we both sensed a higher purpose.

Early in Dee's decision-making process, I had a spontaneous vision I shared with her. I saw what appeared to be a typical corporate organizational chart flattened so Dee stood with a huge group of people fanning out behind her. The image felt significant and the configuration instructive because there was no hierarchy. While Dee would not be leading a group of thousands of employees in this role, I interpreted the vision to mean her leadership was needed in Texas and would ripple out globally. Something about this offer felt inevitable, formative, and progressive.

Dee's compensation and relocation packages were negotiated until she felt comfortable accepting the offer. A week of negotiations had exposed the temperament of her new boss in a way that seemed to signal the potential for future disharmony. As a result, Dee decided to keep her home in Atlanta and rent an apartment in Texas.

Despite assurances of "flexible Fridays," which would have enabled Dee to fly back to Atlanta for long weekends, her boss, Ilesha, seemed to have expectations that employees would be at their desks during business hours regardless of company policy. Ilesha subscribed to an archaic idea that her staff was not working unless she could see them.

By the end of the first month, it was clear Ilesha relied on Dee's technical expertise but was threatened by Dee's ability to quickly garner her colleagues' admiration. Dee invested time mentoring each team member and was genuinely congenial while Ilesha was task-oriented to the point of being dismissive, rude, and inconsiderate. Ilesha explicitly told Dee to shorten meetings and stop being so nice because it was inefficient.

Ilesha's admonishment brought me back to my job in the Hallmark Humor Department where I had delighted in playing practical jokes on colleagues while being paid to oversee a process to manufacture greeting cards. We produced much funnier material when we were in a zone of playfulness and while that got us kicked out of the headquarters and into a satellite office down the street, it was exactly what we needed to thrive. Endless pranks fueled our exceptional creativity and that creativity served as both a cause and an effect of our inefficiency. As a business person, I understood how insufferable this inefficiency might seem to executives, but from the inside, I saw the undeniable impact on camaraderie and teamwork.

Dee embodied an inclusive style that honored the uniqueness of each individual contributing to the greater whole. The company also prided itself on diversity and inclusiveness, but it supported the more quantifiable kinds like age, gender, race, and ethnicity that provided attractive statistics for the annual report.

Dee led with compassion and heart. I often called her a lighthouse because she could show up and radiate her beautiful light, making people eager to support her mission. Whether mopping the floors or leading a strategic corporate initiative, Dee was highly effective at team building and engendering support. She texted me a picture of the tag on her tea bag with the message, *"Spread the Light—be a Lighthouse."* I loved it when synchronicities showed up and clients celebrated them.

Dee was given the results of the company's employee engagement survey. Nearly a year earlier, an outside vendor had polled employees anonymously and tabulated numeric ratings. Not surprisingly, the department scores had dropped significantly the year after Ilesha was hired as vice president. Dee was living the survey results firsthand. Just when I thought things could not become any more paradoxical, Ilesha told Dee to "Fix it" by creating an action plan for improving the next survey's scores.

CHAPTER 44: SEEDING A NEW PARADIGM OF LEADERSHIP

Dee also found herself in a values conflict when she was instructed to book reservations for dinner with a vendor and was chastised for not picking a fancy enough restaurant since the vendor was paying. At Dee's previous employer, such arrangements were not allowed, and Dee's personal code of ethics did not align with intentionally taking advantage of a vendor's generosity.

An hour before the dinner meeting, an unexplained power outage occurred in the city block where the restaurant was located. Traffic was snarled for miles and dinner was canceled. The Universe had magically handled the situation, perhaps in better alignment with the highest, most beneficial outcome for all. We marveled at the amazing support available to people consciously working toward elevating consciousness.

By the end of her fourth month, Dee was nearly ready to quit. I sensed how the disharmonic was affecting her energy field, and she confirmed the impact on her physiology, sleep, and normal self-care regimen. Some days were unbearable, but we agreed it did not yet seem like time to resign. On dark days, someone always showed up with a smile or words of encouragement that affirmed her decision to stay.

Unlike colleagues relying on a paycheck, Dee had consciously created freedom and abundance and was not beholden to anyone. I encouraged her to play full out and embody her own brand of leadership. I suggested she use her lighthouse to radiate a harmonic frequency others would sense.

Dee was pulling long hours, so our sessions often took place while she was still in her office. Occasionally, our call was interrupted by the appearance of a colleague who sought her counsel. I loved overhearing these interactions while sensing the emanation of radiance from the lighthouse.

When Dee told me our sessions were "uplifting at a soul level," I smiled and said I was simply reflecting and amplifying her highest and best self so she was more consciously aware of her brilliance and ability to serve. I smiled inwardly, knowing others had done the same for me over the years.

Persevering through Ilesha's challenging demeanor, Dee created occasional moments of rapport while deepening her ability to stand in her truth. I could sense the effects seeping out into the entire organization, and I was reminded of the spontaneous vision of Dee standing as if leading an army of supporters. Dee's work was about so much more than the duties and responsibilities outlined in her job description. She was a skilled empath, using her compassion to understand Ilesha's insecurities, acknowledging how these vulnerabilities fueled unkind behavior.

Despite subtle belittlement and daily criticism, Dee refused to stoop to the same level or retaliate. Taking the high road garnered even more admiration from her peers and colleagues who looked to align and support her. She may not have always been the designated leader in the room, but heart rather than hierarchy caused people to look to her for direction. Dee was seeding a new paradigm of leadership in a job that had become a spiritual boot camp.

CHAPTER 45
Maximizing the Human Spirit at Work

While watching Dee bring her style of leadership to a job that had become a test of fortitude, I came across others who were doing the same. A year earlier, two people in two days mentioned to me the microbiome and the name, Zach Bush, while recommending a liquid supplement called Restore, now rebranded as Ion Biome. I went online and listened to a podcast interview titled "Eat Dirt: The Secret to a Healthy Microbiome."

Zach was a cancer researcher with an impressive resume and three medical degrees. Like Dr. Upledger, Zach spoke about inherent intelligence in every part of the body and a profound ability for cells to communicate among themselves and with those capable of listening. Zach was looking to crack the code of chronic disease. With conviction, he said this purpose was why he had been born, done a "ridiculous journey in academia," and become an entrepreneur.

He spoke of quantum physics, the miraculous nature of life, and how he kept himself encircled in a sense of awe. With humility, he said the science behind his discoveries and not his product would change the world. Zach finished the interview with three pieces of advice and wisdom:

- You are enough.
- We are connected to the entirety of Mother Nature.
- Love yourself because it is a healing vibration.

As the podcast ended, I was heartened by what I had just heard from a classically trained Western medicine doctor who had worked successfully in a very mainstream system. He had clearly stepped way outside conventional norms with this perspective. I smiled and set an intention to match Zach's passion and leverage all my past experiences and education just as he had done with his.

I looked for other new paradigm leaders like Zach and Dr. Goswami, and I thought about the past thirty or forty years of corporate initiatives like workplace wellness and diversity, equity, and inclusion. As I researched the origins of these programs, I found mention of Lewis Griggs, a pioneer in corporate diversity training.

In a strange twist of serendipity, my online search took me to an interview Griggs did with the woman who founded the Center for Love and Light where I had sublet an office for CranioSacral Therapy. In the interview, Griggs recounted two Near-Death Experiences (NDEs) that had shaped his work and life.

In the first, he was called to the Light and asked, "What keeps you from being all you can be?" Griggs felt he did not know how to "bridge the gap," and his life mission was born from awareness of his own blind ethnocentricity, leading him to create a national diversity conference and massive impact through training programs for more than 5,000 corporations.

I was further intrigued by Griggs' perspective that companies and the teams within them had to find and embrace a common goal to truly value uniqueness and differences as gifts toward achieving that goal. If the group could not agree on a goal, it simply needed to widen its focus until it did.

Griggs believed legal and behavioral compliance did little to maximize human potential and went on to say the consciousness of noticing energy was the most important aspect of how we relate to one another. In the first ten seconds of meeting someone, you instantly feel either enhanced or depleted. Enhanced energy leads to

CHAPTER 45: MAXIMIZING THE HUMAN SPIRIT AT WORK

connection, trust, productivity, and the potential to be your fullest self."

Griggs said everything originated with energy, but in Corporate America, he could not call it "energy work." Executives required language that meant something to them so he called his program "Maximizing the Human Spirit at Work."

When I thought about Griggs' clandestine use of "energy work," I was flooded with memories of when I had held harmonic energy fields, allowing others to step into their own best selves, maximizing both individual and collective potentials. I thought of Maidenform, where Nigel and I had created trust and brought management and the labor union to agreement on productivity standards while planting seeds for a collaborative style of leadership. I recalled a two-day meeting with a CEO and his executive team in a hotel conference room where I created an energy field enabling the group to work harmoniously toward a common goal. I thought of the chamber of commerce event where I knew we would change the world if we could get more people vibrating together in a coherent energy field.

I marveled at what would happen if every business meeting started with a short *awareness of breath* meditation as we had done in a board meeting for the Center for Entrepreneurship and Innovation. I felt euphoric as I thought of all the possibilities for "energy work" to raise consciousness in corporations while also maximizing health, wealth, abundance, and Ma'at.

I flashed back to businesses I knew were using spiritual energy in very practical application. I had enjoyed delicious meals at Café Gratitude restaurants in three cities. Their owners had built a spiritual community inside the workplace. They saw their business as an opportunity to make a lasting positive impact on customers and employees with financial success and spiritual fulfillment, and I felt that in the food and the service. In the founders' book, *Sacred Commerce: Business as a Path of Awakening*, their managers were deemed stewards of consciousness who were expected to lead inspiring meetings and be responsible for the company's quadruple bottom line of profitability, awakening, social justice, and sustainability.

In another instance, I stumbled on the less-overt, spiritual underpinnings of a small company selling my favorite organic, gluten-free, vegan protein bars. I found Pure Bliss at the Saturday farmers market in the park nearest my home. Something about its booth had attracted me, and after months of buying its "Naughty but Nice" bars by the case and using them as my go-to portable snack food during business trips and long airplane flights, the company owners took me up on my offer for a few hours of free consulting on distribution and logistics.

I drove to their office in suburban Atlanta where they had prepared a delicious vegetarian lunch we shared in the conference room. I kept repeating there was something special about their products beyond the high-quality ingredients, great taste, and clever packaging. One of the owners looked up from her plate of food and said, "Oh, just show her." I watched as they moved a cloth obscuring part of a bookshelf to show me a shrine built to honor Lord Krishna. All of their products were offered with gratitude and devotion as part of a spiritual tradition to bless everything they manufactured. I was astounded because I had definitely sensed the energetics before knowing anything about their spiritual practices.

I met several women in various phases of startups related to personal and professional development. Chris was a Silicon Valley exec I met through a colleague from CEI. She had raised several million dollars of angel money to pursue her dream of building a positivity platform to gamify personal growth through online learning quests and challenges participants could complete in five to ten minutes. The prototype did indeed look like a game you would play through an app on your phone or tablet.

Chris confided her real goal was to "raise the vibrational state of the planet," and the platform was one means. With fundraising, her

CHAPTER 45: MAXIMIZING THE HUMAN SPIRIT AT WORK

investment criteria involved much more than money. Her investors' values, attitudes, and perspective were every bit as important as their financial capabilities.

Twelve years earlier, during my time working in corporate wellness, one of my clients had saved millions converting several thousand employees to a consumer-directed health plan with a higher deductible and rewards for wellness activities. I wondered how much more money and time could be saved with preventative approaches using what the CEO had labeled as my "goofy" modalities.

My business mindset kicked in as I imagined how cool it would be to study a group within a corporation and measure the return on investment produced through expansive, unconventional wellness strategies. I began to visualize ways to set up this experiment, quantify results, and capture the qualitative, subjective feedback from participants as well as any resulting sense of loyalty to the company.

I also revisited websites of conferences I had attended ten years earlier and found the definition of workplace wellness had expanded greatly. Conference session topics went far beyond biometric screening and smoking cessation. Now, the sessions had titles like, "Moving from Health to Well-Being," "Workplace Spirituality," and "It Starts Within."

I spotted a LinkedIn post written by Seth Goldman who I had met once at a conference at Emory University. Seth founded Honest Tea and years later, sold it Coca Cola. Upon learning Coke was discontinuing the brand, he decided to get back into the bottled tea business quickly. Launching in just three months, Just Ice Tea replaced Honest Tea as a certified organic, kosher and fair-trade tea line.

The post detailed Seth's five keys to accelerate the launch. I smiled reading the fifth key, "Karma." Seth wrote that his vendor partners were super-responsive because he and his team had treated them well. Seth credited balanced relationships, seamless communication and strong relationships among attributes that gave vendors an extra boost of motivation to support the launch. I loved the nod to karma and I commented that the post should be required reading and a case study in MBA programs!

The more I looked, the more I found dozens of instances of open-minded leaders openly embracing spirituality and energy in the workplace. These leaders were well accustomed to producing results so the imperative for profitability was never relegated in priority. Instead, financial prosperity was synergistic with tools and technology to deepen self-awareness and help people consistently embody a higher quality of consciousness.

Self-mastery generated positivity and wellbeing, producing results that resonated out into the company and the collective. I felt the excitement and acceleration of a global paradigm shift and knew others were picking up on it just as I had.

This intention generated so much goodwill that people expressed gratitude for her heartfelt support and her humanness.

Many of my clients used LinkedIn for professional networking and to keep up with their respective industries. I found myself wondering how resumes and LinkedIn profiles would change if it became popular to include credentials demonstrating one's ability to hold harmonic frequencies, utilize intuition, and engineer higher states of consciousness.

I pondered how the world might change if a candidate's "Professional Objective," the paragraph often at the top of the resume, included the intention for an emotionally satisfying, spiritually lucrative position contributing to wholeness and the planet's evolutionary trajectory.

I chuckled wondering what if interviewers asked candidates to name a specific synchronicity that occurred as a result of being in an optimal state of receptivity and how that synchronicity had led to something unexpectedly wonderful?

I had a moment of glee thinking how business and commerce could be expanded exponentially if instead of separating spirituality and mindfulness from our professional pursuits, we used them as fuel.

My ambitious vision extended to roles in the C-suite. What if the traditional role of CIO (Chief Information Officer) became the Chief Intuition Officer, with that executive responsible for adding intuitive expertise to decision-making while inspiring and training other employees to do the same? I chuckled thinking maybe one day the CTO might really be the Chief Telepathy Officer, representing an expanded kind of technology. Many corporations had created the position of Chief Diversity Officer to address diversity, equity, and inclusion, and I wondered when we would consider neurodiversity.

I noted companies were hiring their first-ever Chief Wellness Officers, particularly after the pandemic. The job descriptions and responsibilities varied widely. I smiled at one description with the term "human-centric," the same term William had written on his whiteboard years earlier.

As corporations realized a desirable environment meant more than casual Fridays, foosball tables, and free kombucha, hybrid work models and attention to more facets of wellness became perks to attract top talent. I wondered if corporate culture would ever progress so far as to create a position for Chief Spirituality Officer. I smiled imagining the job description and how many *lifetimes* of experience might be required.

I envisioned a time when corporations hired candidates who demonstrated skillful use of the subtle and vital energies that Dr. Goswami and Lewis Griggs wrote about. I knew from personal experience that the energy work I received over the years, along with my commitment to effective inner-leadership, had mitigated any health insurance claims. I knew firsthand how a coherent energy field could enhance creativity, increase productivity, and influence outcomes, all valuable conditions in business. I wondered when the rest of the world might catch on.

I read an article listing the top twenty most popular LinkedIn Learning Courses. More than half of the descriptions included softer skills like communication, collaboration, curiosity, and mindset. I watched a morning news interview with a LinkedIn career expert who confirmed the growing importance of soft skills and candidates selling themselves through their own unique collection of experiences. I noted LinkedIn offered several certifications for technical skills and giggled wondering if it would ever offer a certification for intuition or patience

I knew the importance of both of these and recalled being chastised for not having enough of the latter when I was trying to get revenue flowing into my first company. Our office was in a three-story residential townhouse. I was driven by my tremendous bias for action and needed to know my employees were working, thinking and making daily progress. One morning I came in and found a sheet of paper taped to the wall above the folding table that served as my desk. In bold black letters, it simply read "PATIENCE."

It took years for me to learn the patience to wait for nudges and synchronicities to lead me to the most effective and aligned actions and the optimal timing but it was certainly an ability I found valuable. We were already delegating decisions to artificial intelligence and popular books were written about the benefits of emotional intelligence. Was it a stretch to think other forms of intelligence might become coveted skills?

During my days in supply chain consulting, I had seen warehouse workers being encouraged, if not required, to warm up with calisthenics before a shift. Corporations could quantify the reduction in workers' compensation claims. I wondered what might happen if it became standard practice for meetings in conference rooms to start with a simple two-minute practice to boost the immune system or a ninety-second guided meditation to decrease stress. I speculated CEOs might support a few minutes of guided breathing if it improved employee productivity or reduced the cost of health benefits by a generous multiple of the investment required to train staff to properly lead these practices.

Companies continue to invest in myriad leadership training programs focused on developing the skills needed to lead a team. Countless times, I have observed that effective inner leadership is the bedrock for every other kind of leadership. Only recently have we begun to offer training on how to bring your whole and best self to work. Leading others is most effective when done from a place of wellbeing and wholeness. As a humorous reminder of proactive self-care first and foremost, I often repeat the decades-old announcement made by airline flight attendants, "Put the oxygen mask on yourself before attempting to help other passengers."

Perhaps as a result of the pandemic facilitating months of stillness and self-reflection, thousands of employees left their jobs in

CHAPTER 46: MAINSTREAM MEETS MYSTICAL

what was termed the Great Resignation. Across all levels of the org chart, leaders felt a potent calling to seek meaning and purpose as well as a paycheck. Rather than chasing a prestigious job title at a big corporation, they went in search of something more.

I watched my clients and colleagues aligning their passions with their professions while leveraging all the skills and experience gained throughout their careers. The term "pivot," once reserved for lean start-ups and business ideas not gaining traction, was now being used by leaders who were personally changing course to honor and incorporate more of their wholeness far beyond what was previously acceptable at work.

Some were reacting to a workforce reduction or layoff, but many proactively chose to explore a new, more liberating path. I watched as those who had outgrown a persona built in conformity with an old system and were no longer able to squeeze into a limiting paradigm. They were breaking free to encompass more aspects of themselves as they broadened and personalized their ideas of success.

As the Universe nudged many of us toward more soul-aligned roles, work and business became an expression of our expansion in consciousness and that meant honoring our humanness as well as the full range of capabilities from mainstream to mystical.

CHAPTER 47
Full Circle

More than 20 years ago, my desire to improve conference presentations followed by the impulse to reach out to a woman I saw profiled in a newspaper article, triggered an unbelievable cascade of events. I could have never fathomed how business presentation coaching would become a conduit to me understanding myself and the more mystical nature of life.

I had spent my early years proudly powering through any challenge, denying emotions and ignoring my wellbeing. My drive for perfectionism and my need for success went so far as to cause me to miss out on the small joys of life. As I slowly accepted more of my imperfections and humanness, I gradually softened into compassion and discovered a new kind of preciousness.

Life is a journey and wading through its messiness has always led me to discover a better, truer version of myself. Often the mess was unpleasant or deeply painful but I preferred to define myself by wisdom gained rather than trauma endured. Inevitably, I found silver linings embedded in difficult challenges and came to see the events of my life as reflections of my progress as well reminders of the places I still have work to do.

Behind roles I played and labels I tacitly accepted, some part of me has always been curious to know myself at the deepest levels and the Universe has provided a steady stream of revelations. I have found great freedom in the ability to reinvent myself over and over again outside conventional norms and expectations. My personal truth has evolved with my experiences and my consciousness. What I believed in and strived for in my 20s and 30s has certainly evolved and that's where the magic is; the continual rediscovery of the essence of my Self.

One truth that has never wavered is my belief that anything is possible. We live in a quantum soup of possibilities and the Universe conspires to support us by choreographing incredible synchronicities in alignment with our intentions and opportunities for growth. Once I adopted the stance that I am the architect of my reality in divine collaboration with the Universe, I was empowered to decide how I wanted my reality to look.

From this perspective, I view my professional pivots as responses to upgrades in consciousness and a deeper drive for more soul-aligned work. Thankfully, my pivots were largely driven by choice rather than hardship and if something didn't quite turn out as planned or had a short shelf life, I trusted something better was coming next.

My physical body has become my most reliable barometer of harmony, truth and alignment. If I am experiencing discomfort or some part of me needs attention, I go looking for a cause that both includes and transcends the physical. When I am ready to release old beliefs or toxic thoughts, my body might spike a fever to support the upgrade and burn off whatever needs to go. Often, I sense the release coming and can navigate the timing so I'm in a comfortable, supportive environment with everything needed to make the process as easy as possible.

Because I embrace *metaphysics*, it's easier to be patient with my body and never make it wrong or bad. I trust it as a marker of inner peace and energetic alignment beyond anything my ego may want me to believe.

CHAPTER 47: FULL CIRCLE

The foods I eat and the quality of water I drink constantly evolve with my consciousness and not as a result of the latest fad diet or scientific research. Each trip to the grocery store or meal in a restaurant is an affirmation of trusting my inner knowing of what is right for me. My needs are dynamic so what worked well in the past may not be the best recipe for today.

I give myself permission for stillness, rest and sleep as well as physical movement. I place a premium on living in a peaceful environment with serenity, silence, solitude and time in Nature. The balance and nuances are forever evolving, requiring regular recalibration.

Human existence requires material resources and I find that when I am aligned with a purpose, a soulful mission or an opportunity for deeper learning, resources abound. Support often comes when I let go of logic and allow synchronicity or intuitive guidance to become apparent. From a taxi at LaGuardia just before a downpour to a publicly-traded company whose stock price quintupled funding months of exploration, support comes in many forms.

I have also learned to accept the opposite dynamic; when I am no longer aligned, resources dry up or something shifts forcing me to move on. Once I sense the change occurring, resistance quickly becomes futile.

Life exists on a continuum from patience to assertiveness, effort to allowing, being versus doing. And mastery comes from choosing the most appropriate spot on the continuum. Effective inner leadership precedes all other types and my ongoing commitment to self-actualization helps me to serve from a place of fullness. Those pre-flight instructions to put the oxygen mask on yourself first are aptly applied here. I am better at serving others when I prioritize my own wellbeing.

I have been fortunate that dozens of practitioners, teachers, and healers have shown up to nudge me along and show me new ways of perceiving myself and the world. Often, their ability to see the best in me – a kind of soulful greatness and wholeness – was something I aspired to but I was not capable of fully embodying at the time. It's a journey and I appreciate the love they showed me as they held the mirror up and waited for me to see myself.

Continually softening into more vulnerability and humanness requires humility. For me, that softening is not easy and has meant enduring discomfort but it has helped me shift beyond the limitations of my ego and explore new parts of myself. As I have compassionately embraced my own humanness, it has helped me to accept the humanness in others. The ability to see people at their potential best, and then accept them right where they are, is a talent I witnessed in dozens of my teachers.

I believe the Universe is always trying to communicate and at any moment, it's possible to feel a spark of inner knowing and instantly gain a deeper truth of reality. When I allow a little wiggle room, synchronicities and flashes of intuition pop in and awaken me to some magnificent new perspective or opportunity. This is the same spark I hope to ignite in others.

As I move through life, I keep redefining my ideas of success and ideas for a new paradigm of leadership. And I attract others who are doing the same, even if they label it as something else. We seek depth, meaning, purpose and fulfillment and we want to utilize the expertise and skills we've already developed to achieve this while leading others. Because I have navigated many of the same challenges and found answers to questions, there's a resonance that binds us together. That resonance brings courage to explore and enables us to contribute to humanity in unique and meaningful ways.

Writing another edition enabled me to memorialize and let go of even more of my old identities so I have space to explore new ones. With this last chapter, I come full circle and start anew.

EPILOGUE

The process of writing the first edition of this book, which began in earnest January 1, 2021 and ended in early 2023, was punctuated by a steady stream of synchronicities and seemingly coincidental reunions. Before writing each chapter, I revisited my notes, photographs, and journals. As I wrote about my adventures, particularly in Egypt and Morocco, I unexplainedly experienced many of the same physical symptoms I was writing about. Thankfully, few were as intense as the original versions.

With each chapter, as I wrote about old friends, acquaintances, and teachers, I looked online to see where life's journey had taken them. I found several had written their own books. I purchased and read them to see what had transpired and who they had become. Often, the people I was writing about in a chapter showed up unexpectedly again either in person or through email, text, or social media. From teachers to colleagues, people I had not seen in years serendipitously reconnected. Their timing was always uncanny and seemed like a wink to the interconnectedness of all life.

After two years of writing, I had far too many stories to put all in one book and reluctantly chose some to leave out. One I omitted was about Grant Hill, a Duke alumnus and NBA legend whose path I had crossed many times. Beyond basketball, I admired Grant for his philanthropy and for introducing me and others to the work of Romare Bearden, an artist who brought attention to African-American rights. I also admired Grant for producing and promoting a documentary film about Duke's history-making track coach, Al Buehler. I spoke with Grant on several occasions, and I was always touched by his humility and his funny, self-deprecating stories. He had soared to the pinnacle of his sport and received incredible accolades, yet I was always most fascinated by the human behind the trophies.

The morning I deleted several stories I had written about the humanness I observed in Grant, I watched him being interviewed on a national news program and discovered he had just published his own memoir. I listened to him speak about how revelatory it had been to go back and unpack life events in a way he had not made time for as they had happened. He said, "To go back at this point in life and look at what lessons I've learned, to live in those moments again, it was exciting and a little scary." Tears rolled down my cheeks as I related deeply to his journey to write a book.

Weeks later, I serendipitously ended up in a hotel elevator with Grant. In another full circle moment, I mentioned how inspiring that interview had been. The elevator stopped for my floor before I could tell him about my book.

In March 2022, on the exact week I was writing about my time in France, one of the women I had traveled with in 2018 sent me a text message. She knew from friends that I was writing, and she asked what my book was about. I replied, "The book chronicles my journey from mainstream to mystical and how it has unfolded over the past twenty years." She wrote back, "Wow, that sounds amazing—from mainstream to mystical." As more friends and colleagues asked about the book, the title organically took root.

In the fall of 2022, as I neared completion of my first draft, I reconnected with Dean, a friend I had not seen since 2015 when he left the board of Center for Entrepreneurship and Innovation. Dean had published a dozen books and was working with startup companies after founding and selling his own. Our paths crossed at a reunion of board members in Durham.

After the meeting, we ended up in the same Adirondack chairs near the putting green at Washington Duke Inn where we had sat on many previous occasions. We caught up and traded stories in the beautiful fall sunshine. When I mentioned this book, Dean offered to read the manuscript. A few hours later and just before my flight back to Atlanta, I emailed forty-five chapters from the Sky Club at Raleigh-Durham airport.

Five weeks passed without communication, and then at 10 a.m. on a Sunday, I got a text from Dean that simply said "Finished." His next text said he had three hours of time while driving on the New Jersey turnpike. I called his cell phone and listened as he provided meaningful feedback and valuable advice.

Dean encouraged me to envision what I wanted to have happen on the biggest scale I could possibly imagine, saying, "You owe it to your journey to declare your intentions and who you are in the strongest of terms." I felt the magnitude of his words.

At the same time that Dean was encouraging me to embrace my identity and claim more of my mystical gifts, I found myself in the biggest online identity hack I had ever experienced. A few days before my call with Dean, I discovered two emails from Hilton congratulating me on redeeming my Hilton Honors points on Amazon. Someone had hacked my account and transferred 85,000 points. I contacted Hilton and reported fraud.

I assumed this was an isolated incident, but two days later, I received an odd text from Uber asking me to verify my account. The next morning, my inbox was flooded with messages from Microsoft, Amazon, Netflix, Facebook, and others asking me to verify my identity. I was also getting emails from companies I did not recognize. Apparently, the culprit was using my email address to set up new accounts.

I mentioned to one of my neighbors I was playing an online game of Whack-a-Mole trying to reset passwords before another breach. My neighbor worked in digital security and encouraged me to immediately change the passwords on all my email accounts and the password for the provider of my cell phone service. Losing control of those would enable the hacker to take over my two primary forms of communication. I dashed home to my computer.

A day later, I went to check in for a previously-scheduled Delta flight and found my password would not work. I called Delta and the agent put me on hold while she contacted security. When she came back on the line, she said a link had been sent to the recovery email address on file. It took another ten minutes to figure out someone had already changed the recovery address so the link was likely going straight to the culprit.

After a week of fearfully opening my inbox every morning, wondering if I would find another account compromised, the deluge began to subside. I had finally restored more than thirty different online accounts. I felt like I had run the gauntlet and survived.

Just as I was starting to breathe a sigh of relief, I opened the inbox of a Gmail account I rarely use. Inside were two emails from names I did not recognize. The hair on my arms stood up as I opened the first one and began to read. The email was a forwarded copy of a long exchange I'd had with Alan, a fellow author.

After reading the first twenty chapters of my book, Alan had emailed me with specific questions related to my beliefs, my view of multidimensional consciousness, and my definition of the new paradigm of leadership. I had replied and explained in detail many of my spiritual and metaphysical truths that were strengthened as I wrote this book. The exchange with Alan had crystalized ideas and truths I did not often have occasion to explain.

Our entire string of emails had been poached from the original account that was hacked and now forwarded to me at a little-used Gmail address. The culprit also embedded a link, purportedly to files containing the manuscript of my book. I stared at my computer screen in shock and disbelief.

I took a deep breath and opened the second email. It was equally shocking, containing an exchange I'd had a month earlier with friends who worked in the book industry. I again resisted temptation to click on any of the embedded links. If someone did have my files, I reassured myself it was unlikely they would publish my manuscript. The thought of someone trying to pass this story off as their own was just ridiculous enough to ease my sense of terror.

In decades of using the internet, I had never had any kind of hack whatsoever. I knew this breach both reflected and exposed deeply-buried, unconscious fears about claiming more of who I really am beyond the conventional, mainstream definitions. This was not just about hackers extorting ransom money; it was about me overcoming deep-seated fear of visibility and the truth of who I am.

I also saw the beautiful synchronicity of the timing. The Universe provided an opportunity for me to experience my fears in a private way before I published a book exposing more of my unconventional, mystical capabilities.

I was deeply grateful for the grace and smiled at the symmetry; Dean encouraged me to boldly claim my identity, Alan questioned the foundation on which it was built, and a hacker caused me to have to rebuild the online version.

Two weeks later, I boarded a flight to Kansas City for a holiday visit to my parents and extended family. Despite my Delta Medallion status, I was stuck in a center seat in coach. I lamented the lost days of automatic upgrades while sensing some odd purpose to this less-than-ideal seating arrangement. I stowed my luggage, took my seat between two passengers and made a quick call to my sister. My dad was having debilitating, intermittent back pain, and I hoped I could get him a doctor appointment as soon as I arrived.

The passenger in the aisle seat, Mike, overheard my phone conversations and said he was sorry about my dad. We got to talking about Kansas City, and I learned he was traveling there on short notice to provide chiropractic care to a client.

As I listened to him speak, I suddenly realized I knew his voice and understood why the Universe and Delta had stuffed me into a middle seat. Twenty years had passed since I had last seen Mike, but this was the *renowned chiropractor* I had written about in Chapter 1. I might not have recognized him behind his beard and glasses, but I definitely knew his voice.

For the next two hours, we caught up on the past twenty years. I told him the story of this book and how a coach had led me to a medical intuitive and to a deeper understanding of the mental, emotional, and spiritual aspects of my physical pain.

Mike was surprised to learn I had closed my consulting company, trained in CranioSacral Therapy, and was now working in holistic health and coaching. We laughed, reminisced, and marveled that we were serendipitously meeting again after two decades.

When I asked Mike why he was flying all the way to the Midwest for a client, he said he was still working with elite NFL players as he had done in the early 2000s. As he talked about his client, I began getting intuitive information. I could track this player's personal challenges and how those were manifesting in his right hip and knee. Mike agreed with my assessment and knew intuitive capabilities like mine were a very real thing. Years earlier, he had been introduced to someone who had similar gifts. Although Mike said he could not understand how intuition worked, he found the information accurate.

We deplaned together and walked out into the terminal. Mike had a black SUV waiting curbside. We exchanged a warm hug, and he asked me to let him know when the book was available. Forty-six chapters were complete, and I had returned to the point where my story started. My beliefs and perspectives had expanded greatly in the years since I had last seen Mike, and I sensed his had too.

I smiled in awe at the astonishing synchronicity and magic of another full circle moment.

AFTERWORD
Full of Grace

As I wrote this book, I remembered serendipitous events that foreshadowed I would write a book well before I started. One occurred in the spring of 2007 when I went to Key Biscayne to watch a tennis tournament. After tennis, I ended up in the hotel bar at the Ritz-Carlton late one evening and met a couple from North Carolina, Stewart and Susan. They were not tennis fans, but we connected over a college basketball rivalry with the game being shown on the big screen behind the bar. Stewart worked for a private equity firm and had been at the hotel for his company's board meeting. He and Susan were winding down with basketball and a nightcap.

I was always looking for opportunities in supply chain consulting, and executives at private equity firms were squarely in the sweet spot of potential clients. Stewart introduced me to another couple in their group, Peter and Dottie. Peter was Chairman of the Board of two of the operating companies owned by the private equity firm where Stewart worked. I tried to strike up a conversation so I could talk about Solertis and work we had done, but Peter had little interest.

Peter's wife, Dottie, had the presence of a movie star and a Southern drawl that belied her residence in New Jersey. I pegged her as a socialite who lunched at The Club, played bridge like high stakes poker, and could spend an hour describing the table settings at her last dinner party. Dottie might have been all of these, but I also discovered she was Dorothea Benton Frank, a *New York Times* best-selling author of more than a half-dozen novels set in coastal South Carolina.

Stewart, Susan, and Peter eventually retired to their hotel rooms, but Dot was just getting warmed up. She was telling stories, and eventually, she and I and the bartender were the only ones left in the bar. I had sailed in the coastal Carolinas and was happy to listen to stories of the quaint communities around Charleston and her childhood home on Sullivan's Island. The Lowcountry provided the backdrop for her books, the first of which had debuted on the *New York Times* bestseller list at #9 and went on to sell more than one million copies.

Dot was jovial and loud and seemed happy to have an attentive listener, me, who was entertained by her storytelling. I also loved hearing about her journey into writing and about what it was like to be a best-selling author. She hinted at the discipline it required. Writing seemed like a pretty solitary pursuit for someone so gregarious and extroverted.

By the time the bar closed, Dot was slurring her Southern drawl. When I realized she had gotten off the hotel elevator on the wrong floor, I helped her find her room. As we stood in the hotel hallway, she spoke emphatically about the challenges of writing. Under the influence of alcohol and talking to someone she presumed she would never see again, she spoke with intensity approaching anger about the pressure to produce one new best-selling novel every year.

She screeched, "*You have no eye-deeee-uh how hawwwwd it is to write a book!*" I winced at the decibel level and assured her I did not have a clue what it took to write a book. Then I quickly excused myself, hoping she would actually use the electronic card key in her hand and enter her hotel room before someone called security.

The next morning, I exchanged emails with Stewart related to potential business with his company, but I did not see Dot again before leaving Key Biscayne.

In a crazy bit of serendipity, a week later, I discovered Dot was coming to Atlanta to promote her latest novel, *The Land of Mango Sunsets*. The venue her publisher chose, the Margaret Mitchell House, was just six blocks from my condominium in Midtown. Arriving late from a business trip, I stood at the back and watched as Dot entertained devoted readers with some of the same stories I had heard in the Ritz-Carlton bar. She was colorful and witty and knew how to captivate an audience.

After Q&A with her adoring fans, I waited in line to get an autograph. I did not purchase the hardback book she was promoting during her tour. Instead, I had brought along a paperback I picked up at an airport gift shop. During the three weeks since meeting Dot on Key Biscayne, I had been carrying this book around everywhere, but I had not read one word of it.

Dot seemed to recognize me, but she clearly had no recollection of our late-night exchange. The intensity and fury I had observed in the hallway outside her hotel room were gone and she was back in character.

Fourteen years after those two serendipitous meetings with Dot, I began writing my own book. As I persevered through long hours at the keyboard, I thought back to her loud admonishment in the hotel hallway, "*You have no eye-deeee-uh how hawwwwd it is to write a book!*"

Looking for inspiration, I dug out the paperback she had autographed for me in 2007. I smiled as I discovered the book was titled *Full of Grace*. Dot's other books had titles like *Sullivan's Island*, *All Summer Long*, and *Plantation*. I giggled because I did indeed consider my life to be full of grace and that was the book she had autographed.

After savoring the inscription she wrote in her bold and loopy penmanship, just as flamboyant as she herself was, I opened to the prologue and laughed aloud. I doubt many of Dot's novels start with mention of quantum mechanics and metaphysics, but this one does. Dot introduced the main characters as two hard-core cynics. One of these cynics, Michael, a research physician, had observed a lab experiment by quantum physicists who used meditation to change the pH of water. Michael pondered that if you could apply human intent and bring about physical change, it had monumental implications and it might just *"explain a lot of the inexplicable."*

Full of Grace is certainly not Dot's typical summer beach read. She questions the nature of faith and prayer and explores conflicts between the modern world and religious beliefs. The short version of the story is that Michael, a cynical scientist and atheist, ends up on a spiritual pilgrimage to Mexico City with a group of Catholics. While touring the Basilica of Our Lady of Guadalupe, where the Virgin Mary is believed to have appeared, Michael has a supernatural, spontaneous healing of brain cancer and his life is changed forever. Dot also added a grandmotherly character who receives communication from deceased loved ones, information corroborated by other disbelieving characters in the story.

One reviewer simply wrote: "Not your usual Dorothea Frank, but surely compelling enough. It feels like a very personal book."

I looked to see how many more books Dot had published since we met in 2007, and just as she had predicted outside the door to her hotel room that night, she had completed one book every year. I figured I would send her a copy of my book along with a note about her prescience in the hotel hallway. I hoped to learn what led Dot to write *Full of Grace* since it was so different from her other books.

Sadly, I discovered that Dot had passed away in 2019 from a rare form of leukemia. Unlike Michael, her character who had a spontaneous healing of brain cancer, her obituary says she went from diagnosis to death in two months. Dot was sixty-seven.

Fourteen years ago in Key Biscayne, I would never have guessed Dot was foreshadowing what I would come to realize myself; I had no idea how hard it is to write a book. I also had no idea how magical, cathartic, and revelatory it would be to write about my experiences of intuition, divine guidance, and synchronicity.

Writing necessitated me revisiting events and timelines. It brought me deeper levels of self-awareness, helping me to reap more benefit and see how some of the most challenging times were ultimately *Full of Grace*.

Along with embracing the unknown, I've learned to pay attention to winks and nudges from the Universe. When my logical mind cannot seem to find a clear purpose for an event or interaction, I inherently trust I gained value even if I don't know exactly how the experience served me or what it means. Trust keeps me in the flow of life and, often, eventually leads to a big reveal of the greater purpose.

Life has many chapters. I celebrate the learning within each of them, and I look forward to writing my next while contributing to the one we are writing together.

ABOUT THE AUTHOR

Ann W. Elliott is an entrepreneur, author, coach, and trusted guide to hundreds of dedicated leaders, executives, and high-achievers. She is a traditionally educated graduate of Duke University and a trained practitioner of alternative healing modalities.

She founded a supply chain and logistics consulting firm in 1996, a wellness company in 2010, and a hands-on healing practice in 2019. Ann currently offers her unique blend of capabilities through leadership programs and 1:1 coaching.

She has lectured in business schools on "Lessons Learned" from two decades as an entrepreneur, sharing her perspectives on the role of curiosity, intuition and synchronicity in a new paradigm of leadership.

Ann is a recipient of distinguished service awards for volunteer leadership at multiple organizations including Metro Atlanta Chamber of Commerce, Council of Supply Chain Management, and Duke University. Ann is a longtime Yogi and began her daily meditation practice in 2003.

For more info, go to www.annelliottllc.com

Printed in the USA
CPSIA information can be obtained
at www.ICGtesting.com
JSHW010149061124
73057JS00001B/5